# CHAIN OF
# EVIDENCE

# CHAIN OF EVIDENCE

## A TRUE STORY OF LAW ENFORCEMENT AND ONE WOMAN'S BRAVERY

# Michael Detroit

A DUTTON BOOK

DUTTON
Published by the Penguin Group
Penguin Books USA Inc., 375 Hudson Street,
New York, New York 10014, U.S.A.
Penguin Books Ltd, 27 Wrights Lane,
London W8 5TZ, England
Penguin Books Australia Ltd, Ringwood,
Victoria, Australia
Penguin Books Canada Ltd, 10 Alcorn Avenue,
Toronto, Ontario, Canada M4V 3B2
Penguin Books (N.Z.) Ltd, 182–190 Wairau Road,
Auckland 10, New Zealand

Penguin Books Ltd, Registered Offices:
Harmondsworth, Middlesex, England

First published by Dutton, an imprint of Dutton Signet, a division of Penguin Books USA
Inc.
Distributed in Canada by McClelland & Stewart Inc.

ISBN 0-525-93671-8

Printed in the United States of America
Set in New Baskerville
Designed by Leonard Telesca

*To Dorothy, my wife,*
*who is, and always will be, my motivation.*

# ACKNOWLEDGMENTS

The story of *Chain of Evidence* is told through the eyes and minds of its three principal participants: Victoria Seele, Sergeant Wayne Carlander of the Orange County Sheriff's Office, and civilian Clifford Mowery. Sheriff Brad Gates, portrayed in the following pages, had the insight and courage to approve and guide the program in the first place and monitored it as it developed, virtually on a day-to-day basis. Important contributions were also made by Lieutenant Sim Middleton, Sergeant Skip Mitchell, and Investigators (now Lieutenants) Randy Blair and Steve Carroll. Deputy District Attorney Tony Rackauckas, Jr., now Judge Rackauckas, did extraordinary work as the key prosecutor of an important homicide case brought against members of the Hell's Angels, as well as on other cases.

Orange County Deputy District Attorney Ron Kreber, now Judge Kreber, deserves special recognition here.

If I knew words special enough to describe editor John Paine's contribution to this book, I would use them here. He's the best.

# FOREWORD

Although the undercover operation described in these pages occurred in 1976 and 1977, its effects reverberate to this very day. It was a singular undertaking, one that will not likely be duplicated because of the unique circumstances that made it possible. The program began modestly as an attempt to probe the inside workings of an outlaw motorcycle gang, then grew in scope daily as it took advantage of its own success. It ultimately altered the balance of crime that was beginning to tip in favor of certain motorcycle gangs in southern California, and culminated in a major blow against organized biker crime from which the gangs even now have not recovered.

In writing this book I studied hundreds of documents that are a matter of public record and some that are consigned to official repositories. I even examined private diaries of police who wrote in a kind of code lest the records of their activities be lost and fall into "wrong" hands. I examined crime reports, arrest records, grand jury subpoenas, wire and telephone tap transcriptions. I interviewed dozens of police, district attorneys, judges, undercover operators, and other uniformed personnel.

I also spoke with biker gang members, some still active, who were intimately familiar with persons written about on the following pages. I made no promises about who would be portrayed in a particular light, only that anonymity would be respected in all cases.

Dialogue is used in the book not to fictionalize but to dramatically enhance the reader's interest. Quoted material appears only when at least one of the participants was interviewed or distinctly recalled what had been told them later.

Some of the undercover officers involved have since left police work and have been removed from their original locations for their own protection. Others continue anti-gang activities in different venues. When the arrests were carried out, even before trials took place and convictions were returned, "wanted" posters of three of those involved were placed by Hell's Angels in biker bars throughout southern California. The posters offered bounties of $25,000 cash for the death of each.

Thus, because of the dangerous instability of some of the people connected with what was, at the time, the largest number of arrests from a single operation ever made in the history of California, certain identities have been changed. Certain events that would be easily recognizable have been altered in order to protect those involved.

The decision to press the investigation forward to its extraordinary conclusion has by law enforcement standards led to overwhelmingly good results. To this day the Hell's Angels have not established a chapter in Orange County. As a direct consequence of this operation, many key members of Los Angeles County's Hell's Angels chapter moved farther north to escape the heat. The Angels remain a major criminal enterprise and a highly significant drug manufacturer and supplier throughout California. But not in Orange County.

Finally, if the reader is offended by ethnic or racial slurs in the remembered dialogue, that discomfort is shared by this writer and his publishers. It is a fact, however, that the Hell's Angels and their associate biker "clubs" are racial extremists. It is therefore not honest to recount any story about them without quoting such remarks.

# CHAIN OF
# EVIDENCE

# PROLOGUE

Back in 1979 I heard pieces of a story that sounded like fiction. A police undercover operation that went bad, one source said. There was a female cop involved. She was supposed to have ridden with the Hell's Angels. Rumor had it that she had fallen in love with the outlaw whose bike she shared. It was a department-shaking embarrassment, the rumor said. There were many arrests. There was a bloodbath.

I contacted Doug, a person in law enforcement who had been a long-time source of reliable information, and asked him if he had heard anything about the case. He said that he had, but knew few details. He offered to make some calls, see what he could find out. Although we had a good relationship, I was a professional writer and he always kept silent when I neared certain areas that he could not discuss.

When Doug called back days later, he said that some of what I had heard was true but that he could not reveal much of it with certainty. Was the case unfinished? I asked. His answer was yes. I asked if there was any part of it he could talk about. He said he would rather I got it from another source. I lightly replied that he was my other source. No laughter. Doug clearly was not comfortable.

During the next few weeks I brought the subject up with other contacts, but no one seemed to know anything. I had other projects to keep me occupied, so I put the fragments I had gathered into the back of my mind. As months went by I would attempt to learn more about the case, only to encounter the same wall of silence that had existed from the beginning.

Several years later I met an Orange County deputy sheriff assigned to extremely hazardous duty: bomb disposal. In casual conversation she confirmed that such a case had occurred. She knew one of the persons involved, but she believed that the cocoon of silence was serving as needed protection. Protection for whom? She smiled, apologized for not knowing more, and changed the subject.

There had to be records of the case, I reasoned. People had to have been involved, and those people had names. Knowing the case had graced the dockets of Orange County Superior Court, I began looking for anyone connected with the arrests of Hell's Angels in 1977. It seemed to be an easy task. After all, the Hell's Angels were admittedly a rowdy bunch, but in the end, weren't they just a group of guys who liked to hoist a few beers and ride motorcycles? Society is full of divergent lifestyles. Marlon Brando in *The Wild One* provided me, as a youngster, with my prism of distortion through which I viewed all motorcycle gangs.

So the police had caught some of the Angels breaking laws. Why the secrecy about that? I found out when I got to the people part of the equation. The story of *Chain of Evidence* closely involves three people who came from entirely different backgrounds. They were forced together by circumstances none of them liked or wanted. They formed a critical mass that exploded into the largest series of arrests ever made in the history of California, involving a year of court trials resulting in an astounding near 100 percent conviction rate and prison sentences meted out to every felon, save one. The crimes included drugs, extortion, assault, theft, and ultimately murder.

After the first day of arrests, gang members who caused the bikers harm were murdered by execution teams. Non-bikers were targeted as well. The Hell's Angels were revealed as a criminal enterprise while registered as a legal corporation in California.

I learned the name of a member of the undercover team. I met with this person and listened to more of the story. With even a partial revelation of events, I began to be excited. By then I knew the published facts of the case, but now I had talked to someone involved in the sub rosa investigation. There was another survivor of the original group, I was told. If this person was willing to talk ... I asked if a meeting could be arranged.

Eventually it was, and during that interview I promised not to reveal real names and not to disclose locations that might give clues to the whereabouts of any undercover survivors or their families.

As more meetings followed and I sat in motel rooms, bars, and cars listening with total fascination, I learned that police penetration of the gang was accomplished by three extraordinary people who paid prices too high. One would die, another would flee the state under a different name, and the other would become a reluctant hero.

Clearly, I came to realize, their story was not a litany of arrest reports, surveillance documents, and case numbers. It was the story of a very small group of cops, and one who wasn't, who came to depend upon one another for survival. As nature compresses carbon into diamonds, intense pressure will change human beings. But not always into diamonds.

# CHAPTER 1

On September 8, 1976, Sergeant Wayne Carlander was meticulously checking crime reports written by him and by other officers working undercover in the Narcotics Division of the Orange County Sheriff's Office. He made sure that the times listed on surveillance reports coincided with times and places indicated by officers making the buys and subsequent arrests. He also reconciled cash expenses, accounted for receipts, and prepared the reports for senior staff to audit. Like most field cops, Carlander disliked paperwork—and most other things that tethered him to a desk—but he understood the need to avoid sloppiness. Someday the cases would go to court, and he did not want a felon to walk because of an inadvertent mistake in a report.

"New man for you, Wayne, more or less. Investigator Seele," Lieutenant Sim Middleton reported, appearing just inside Carlander's cubicle.

"Make up your mind. You got a new man for me or you got Seele for me." His response was posed in the form of a directive, not a question.

"Okay, you got Seele. Know who she is, huh?" Middleton and Carlander had worked patrol together before either of them became detectives. The lieutenant liked Carlander but was always intimidated, as most people were, by his size. And his take-charge personality matched his six-foot six-inch, 295-pound physical dimensions. He was deceptively quick, confident, decisive. His face belied his intensity: round, no lines, eyes that seemed to never stop laughing. His hair was like his energy, never wanting to lie down. But Wayne Carlander was an undisguised male chauvinist, and everybody in the department knew it. He ran a hard-nosed narcotics team and the people he targeted were vicious. In a daily battle for control of the county streets and parks, Carlander needed people who had ice water for blood. He needed streetwise personnel to match the muscle arrayed against them. Carlander and Middleton had discussed his "requirements" many times, and Middleton wanted to avoid that today.

"Who doesn't? Have Brad find her a nice job in his office somewhere," Carlander said.

"Are you telling the sheriff how to make assignments, Carlander?"

"No, I'm not, Lieutenant Middleton. What I'm saying is that she probably doesn't know how to write a parking ticket but Gates figures she's ready for heavy action down here in the pits. I'm trying to do her a favor." Carlander had a way of making his personal wishes sound like Socratic logic.

"Saint Carlander. We're lucky that the pope could spare you long enough to help us out here in Orange County. Don't try to do Gates any favors he doesn't ask for. Investigator Seele reports here this afternoon."

"*Investigator Seele?*" Carlander collapsed in his chair. "She's a detective already? How much time does she have on the force?"

Sim Middleton understood Carlander's indignation. Victoria Seele had risen from recruit to investigator in minimum time and without working patrol. But she was sharp at everything she had been asked to do. Besides, the command staff was not about to turn over assignment control to section leaders.

"She's coming this afternoon, so give her a job." Middleton

turned on his heel. You couldn't talk to Carlander. He knew that.

Carlander finished his paperwork and signed out of his office for the shooting range. He had put off the monthly firearm qualifying until the final day, as usual, because he found it a disagreeable task. There was nothing about guns that he liked. Except in practice, he had never fired his gun in more than ten years on the force and was uncomfortable carrying it. He often left his weapon locked inside his desk or at home, a technical violation of department rules. His size and wiles accounted for his success as a police officer, not his accuracy in shooting people.

At the range, with fiber plugs stuffed into his ears, Carlander squeezed off the necessary number of rounds and noted without caring that he had once again qualified with a minimum score. He drove back to his office on North Flower Street in Santa Ana. He had little appetite but forced himself to take a tray at the Sheriff's Office cafeteria. He took on just enough sustenance to support his less than lithe three hundred pounds. When he returned to his desk there was a woman waiting for him.

"I'm Victoria Seele," she said. She had seen Carlander around but today his size took on new meaning. She had also heard that Carlander had a brain inside his large cranium.

"Hi."

Not a talker, she thought. "I've been assigned to you, I guess."

"Uh-huh."

"So, ah, where should I . . . do you have a desk for me?"

"Sure. Right there." He nodded across the room at a cluttered desk.

"Somebody's using it, aren't they?" she asked.

"Bud Nease. Go ahead."

"Bud Nease?"

"My partner. He's on vacation," Carlander said, nodding again toward the desk. "He doesn't use it much when he's not on vacation, either."

Victoria dropped her jacket on the back of the chair. Across the room Carlander returned to his paperwork. Reluctantly, like a bather testing hot water, Victoria sat on the front of the desk chair. She began to scan dust-covered papers. Most of them had dates that were weeks, some months, old. The telephone rang at Carlander's elbow. While he talked she occupied herself with the desk drawers. She thought she might find a caseload log, case progress reports. Papers had been pushed into the drawers with no thought of order. There were wanted posters, drafts of crime reports, memoranda referencing court testimony schedules, some current, departmental directives, a paperback book, a pack of crayons, a moldy sandwich wrapped in plastic. She used two fingers to remove the sandwich and drop it into a nearby wastebasket. She looked up to see Carlander regarding her.

"Well?" she said. "What should I do first?"

"What do you want to do?" Carlander said, looking back at his papers.

"Work. That's why I'm assigned here," she said, sensing an attitude coming at her.

"I don't think I've ever heard a detective say that before." Carlander seemed genuinely curious, and Victoria wondered if this was a unique form of humor.

"Does my being here present a problem for you, Sergeant Carlander?" She had encountered male territorial conditions before. They were acute with cops. At first she had ignored them, but later had found the best way to be included was to get them out front.

"No problem you being here," he said.

"Good. Some of the male officers think female officers won't or can't measure up. Like we're too weak, one way or another," she said.

"I've been married. You don't have to tell me that women are strong." Carlander's continued blandness rankled her.

"Look, Wayne," she said, "I know that Narcotics isn't an easy assignment. They gave it to me. I didn't ask for it. But since I'm here I'll carry my share of the load. I've been working all of my . . ."

"Did you work your way through college?" Carlander interrupted.

"Yes, and I . . ."

"I don't suppose your family could help you very much, huh? See, I pride myself on being a trained interrogator. I listen to what people tell me, Vicky. Take yourself. I've been listening to you talk. I'd say you were from the Midwest somewhere. That right?"

"Yes, that's right," she said.

"Probably your family were farming people." He arched his eyebrows in expected response.

"How did you . . . ?"

"That was a guess." He shrugged dismissively. "You said you worked your way through college, so it figures your folks aren't rich, and if they weren't rich they were still earning a living, and since you were from the Midwest, I guessed that they might be farmers because that's the biggest industry there. Right so far?"

Victoria was impressed. Carlander had a reputation as an outstanding officer and she could see why. "That's pretty good," she admitted.

"Experience. After a while it gets to be a part of what you bring to work. You know, like your shirt and pants. Or skirt, your case. You need that here in Narcotics. But I'm not against college. Most everybody's going to college nowadays. Before they come here. I think it's damn good. What'd you study? Law enforcement? Penology? Criminal psychology?" The eyebrows arched again.

"No. Ah, sociology," she said and wanted to add that she was no social worker. She believed in a firm stance on lawbreaking, and she would never pat a killer on the shoulder because he had had an unfortunate childhood. "At the time I didn't know I was going into police work." Victoria understood that a supervisor had to know something about the people who worked under him. She cautioned herself to have patience—as long as it was going somewhere.

Carlander managed to convey surprise. "No? How come you're here, then?"

"I was an office employee at . . ."

"Secretary?"

"Yes, kind of a secretary. At an insurance agency. I . . ."

"Got bored?" he asked, eyebrow not yet lowered.

"Matter of fact, I was bored."

"So here you are," he said, smiling pleasantly.

*God,* she thought, *is he putting me on?* She had gone through sixteen intensive weeks at the police academy and graduated at the top of her class. He had to know that. It was on national television news. Plus months working in the County Jail. And Burglary and Juvenile. "It doesn't take a genius to understand your implication . . ."

"Implication?"

"Yes, your implication that I'm on a kind of lark here. I'm not. I've been assigned to Narcotics and if that gives you a problem then it's all yours. Not mine."

The eyebrows extended even higher. "You're right, Vicky. There is a problem, and you're right that it's mine. We spend a lot of time in the streets. It's generally shitty out there. We do business with hypes, dealers, some heavy types. I don't see you in a sewer, and that isn't any kind of knock against you."

He waited for her to respond, but she would not. If he wanted to be a chauvinist he could dig his own way out.

"Well," he said, reaching for a small bag that Victoria recognized from her drug education classes, "I gotta go over to the jail. Just make yourself at home."

As he passed her on his way out of the office, a folder with her name on it caught her eye. Without qualm she reached into his IN basket and opened the envelope. It contained photocopies of her personnel file. She didn't have to read them to know that they included her formal education, place of origin, and family background. She did not know at whom she was most angry: Carlander for lying to her about his "brilliant" Midwest deductions or herself for her naiveté.

The jail was right across the street. The modern building was four stories high, its bars recessed into window declivities so that it was in architectural conformity with the other civic buildings and courthouses around it. The roof, surrounded by industrial-strength wire mesh and topped with razor wire unseen from street level, served as an exercise yard. The second and third floor each had three separate housing areas and a main control room where a sergeant and one deputy could direct inmate traffic, operate doors by remote switches, and maintain communications with the rest of the jail. At the jail entrance Carlander stepped inside the first electrically operated steel door. After it closed behind him he placed his pistol into a steel box, closed the cover, and locked it with a key that he left with a green-uniformed deputy sheriff.

"Hi, Wally."

"Hello, Carlander. Here to see Mowery?"

"Yeah. Drug test."

"He's in B-4. Mean son of a bitch. Have a problem, call out." The deputy actuated controls to operate a second sliding door that opened onto the main floor near the central control room. Also on the main floor was a holding cell and interview rooms.

Carlander stood in front of B-4 until the door slid open.

"Who the fuck are you?" Clifford Mowery demanded as Carlander entered, his eyes taking in the detective's examination kit.

Carlander thought the prisoner was as "buffed" as any man he had ever seen. He not only had bulk muscles, he was sculpted. Carlander reckoned Mowery had had an athlete's body to begin with, and years of assiduous pumping iron had created rugged beauty.

"Sergeant Carlander," he announced casually. From his bag he withdrew a flashlight and pupillometer. "I've got to test you for possible use of drugs, Cliff," he said easily. "Means we've got to draw some blood . . ."

"Not getting blood out of me, asshole."

"Not my idea," the big detective answered, his voice devoid of antagonism. "The lab tech will do it."

"You got bad fucking ears or something, man? I said you're not gettin' blood out of me. You want blood, you better send for help."

Carlander stopped his preparation and turned to regard the ex-con in front of him. As all good street cops know, either the bad guys control you or you control them. If a cop backed down from a crook when challenged, Carlander believed, it was time to get into a different line of work. Besides, buffed or not, this guy was beginning to anger him. Carlander moved the drug kit to one side, then calmly eyed the tattooed man in front of him. "Feel froggy, Cliff, go ahead and jump."

Mowery was not used to resistance from a lone opponent.

"Start yelling right now for your partners," he said, but did not move.

"Don't need 'em, Cliff. You feel froggy, go ahead and jump."

Mowery did not detect bluff in Carlander's eyes. Instead of jumping, the convict shrugged. "Hell, what's a few drops of blood?"

"Good choice," the detective said, careful to keep any hint of sarcasm from his voice. He then motioned for a technician waiting outside.

After the lab tech had done his work, Carlander took Mowery to an examination room, where he turned off the lights. In total darkness he used a small flashlight to test dilation. There was no contraction of the pupils at all. With the room lights turned back on, Carlander noted this on his forms. He also made notes of injection sites. He knew by needle tracks that Mowery was a "chipper," an occasional user of heroin.

He also noticed that Mowery was licking dry lips. Excessive thirst for water is a strong indicator of heroin use. "Can I get you some water?" he asked.

"Naw, not thirsty," Mowery lied.

Carlander charted thirty-two tattoos. Among them were "LOVE MY BROTHER," "HARLEY-DAVIDSON," "DEATH BEFORE DISHONOR" (a Marine slogan though Mowery had never been in the service), "BORN TO RAISE HELL," "I LOVE MY SWASTIKA," "LOVE SUE." A hangman's noose occupied a large part of his chest, as did Harley-Davidson motorcycle wings, a detailed picture of the Grim Reaper with "DEATH IS CERTAIN" over the top, and a cross (Mowery was Catholic), among others.

"Like to ride bikes, Cliff?" Carlander asked, the germ of an idea forming in his mind.

"Sure."

"Harleys?"

"Hell, yes. Wouldn't ride a ricer," Mowery said, referring disparagingly to Japanese bikes.

"Who's your parole officer?"

"Keith Taylor."

"I know Keith," the detective said.

"Never met him. Didn't have a chance." A twitch at one corner of the outlaw's mouth revealed a quick, ironic sense of humor.

"How about your parole agreement? What are your parameters?" Carlander would compare actual parole papers against Mowery's response. All parole violators knew this, including Mowery, but in Carlander's experience most parolees lied anyway.

Mowery shrugged. "Get a job, report twice a week," he said. "Usual bullshit."

"Stay away from your old biker buds?"

Mowery shrugged again, looked away. "I don't remember nothing like that."

A lie, Carlander knew.

"Drugs?"

"No drugs."

"Anything else? Liquor?" Carlander pressed.

Mowery pursed his lips as though trying to remember, then shook his head.

Another lie.

"Can I get you anything? Cigarettes? Candy bar?" Carlander asked as he rose from his chair.

"Yeah. Both of them." Mowery could not hide the sound of surprise in his voice.

"I won't put handcuffs on you when we go back to your cell if you promise you'll walk."

Carlander knew that being treated with respect was a major item of importance in any jail. One did hard time or easy time as it was meted out by one's fellow inmates. A man who received respect always earned it, and it served as a warning to the inmate population that a respected man is not easily trifled with. In this case Mowery would walk at the detective's side with his hands and feet free. He nodded his willingness to comply with Carlander's suggestion.

The two men walked out of the examination room together, and Mowery was locked into his cell.

With an idea still formulating, Carlander wanted to talk with Mowery, get to know more about him. Purchasing a pack of cigarettes and a half-dozen Snickers bars, Carlander returned to the paroled convict's cell. Concerned with the appearance of bribery, thus insulting Mowery, Carlander left the candy bars on the hard jail bed.

"From around here, Cliff?"

"Yeah."

"Where 'bouts?"

"Around."

"Tustin? Huntington Beach? Yorba Linda? Fullerton?" the detective asked.

"Yeah."

Carlander chuckled in appreciation for the tough-guy image Mowery chose to maintain. It was a reputation no doubt well earned. The convict wore scars like decorations. Only two inches under Carlander's height, Mowery had cut marks on his chest, forearms, and hands. His nose had been broken several times, Carlander guessed. His square jaw bore signs of torn flesh, as did his neck below the hinge of his jawbone. He wore his brown hair long, touching his shoulders, which gave him a piratical, romantic appearance. Even with the damage that had been done to him over the years, the man was handsome, a magnet for women.

"CHP says you were at Soledad. What for?"

"Armed robbery."

Armed robbers were regarded as the *crème de la crème* of convicts. They were the toughest of the tough. Carlander did not doubt Mowery's word on this but decided to look it up.

"Married?"

"Divorced."

"Kids?"

"Boy. He's six, but they don't let me see him. Bad example, they said. Guess they're right about that," Mowery admitted.

"What were you going to do with the gun they caught you with?"

"Protection."

"Not going to do a holdup?" Carlander probed.

"Naw."

"That's good." Carlander was amused at the consistency of the lies that Mowery offered. As if he was reading the detective's eyes, Mowery smiled.

"Follow baseball?" the cop asked.

"Why? You selling tickets?"

"I played pro baseball out of high school. Signed with the Dodgers," Carlander said. He waited patiently for a reaction that would establish a common interest.

"I always figured baseball players were bed wetters," Mowery said, his attention wandering.

No bonding there.

"You run from many fights, Carlander?"

"Not too many."

"Well, me neither."

"It's my job. They pay me for it," Carlander rationalized.

"Bullshit."

"What's bullshit?" Carlander said.

"You like it, man. Anybody can get a job. Don't have to be kickin' ass or getting yours kicked. You like it."

"I like my job a lot better when people don't get mean," Carlander said. "I can be laid back as anybody."

"Only so long. Then you get bored. Right? Then you need some action. Arresting somebody. Gives you a pump."

The noise of the jail was beginning to get on Carlander's nerves. There was a constant undertone of talking, occasional shouting, the clatter of steel against steel rattling or banging. Music from a dozen radios created a cacophony that the detective remembered with displeasure from his own duty assignments to the jail. Carlander's mouth turned up slightly at the edges. "Would you believe I like most of the people I meet at work?"

"Sure." Mowery nodded his head as he leaned back against the wall of his cell. "They're the action. I know who you are now."

"That right?"

"Yeah. You busted the Hessians. Was you, wasn't it?"

"Guess it was," Carlander admitted.

Five years earlier, when Carlander had been a patrolman working alone one night, he had been called to investigate reports of a wild party at Trabuco Canyon at Cleveland National Forest. There he had found a motorcycle club called the Hessians. They had a nasty reputation among law enforcement agencies for drugs, alcohol, and guns.

They were using drugs that night. "You're all under arrest," Carlander called out before he had thought the matter through. There were more than a hundred Hessians and he could hear urgings from out of the night like, "Let's take him."

Carlander wished then that he had never made the demand. But if he backed down, the word would spread that he was yellow and his effectiveness as a cop would be over. Most cops at least once in their careers try a John Wayne approach to trouble. That night was Carlander's stage debut. Squaring his jaw, he hooked his thumbs over his Sam Brown belt and said, "I got a .38 that holds six rounds. If you wanna make a play, I'll use it."

Carlander looked again at the evil faces arrayed around him. He saw no fear in their eyes. So he added, " 'Course, I'll shoot the women first."

After a pause that seemed a lifetime long, there was laughter. Carlander had slowly let out his breath when he heard guns, knives, and packets of illegal drugs being tossed into the darkness. It had taken his backup a full hour to arrive, but when they had, along with two buses and several patrol cars, the Hessians were lined up and ready to travel.

"Ever hear of a guy named Ray?" Carlander asked as he zipped up his examination bag. "Rides a scooter."

It was a name he and his partner, Bud Nease, had squeezed out of a busted pusher. What interested them about the man was the quality of methamphetamine that he provided wholesale to pushers. Carlander would give a lot to find the manufacturing plant supplying the southern California biker gang community. When pressed, the busted dealer had been more afraid of the man called Ray than going to jail. That made him even more interesting to Carlander.

"Ray," Mowery pretended to think. "What kind of bike?"

"Sportster."

"Lot of guys ride Harleys."

"Hell, yes. But not Sportsters. Heard of him?"

No response.

"Well, I gotta go. Good luck, Cliff." Carlander stood by the door and signaled Control. The cell door clanged shut. He nodded his head to the prisoner inside and walked away.

Without having all of the pieces clearly in place in his mind,

Carlander knew that he had had rare assets come under his experienced control: a respected outlaw biker and a cop who might be placed on the back of a motorcycle without drawing the suspicion of the motorcycle gangs. He felt that beneath her genteel background and smooth college veneer, Victoria Seele was tough. She would need to be if his idea was to work.

# CHAPTER 2

As Carlander left the jail he mulled over his plan. Instead of going directly to his office, he stopped by the main squad room for Criminal Investigations. He was not at ease with operating computers, so he asked a civilian technician to retrieve the information he wanted. In less than five minutes an auto-flow machine had produced the requested data and printed out five sheets. He quickly scanned their contents and smiled in satisfaction.

He strode purposefully into his Narcotics Division office and was pleased to find Investigator Seele seated at her new desk, now noticeably neater, going through "squeal" files and crime reports. He stopped in the middle of the room, sizing her up. She was movie star good-looking: blonde hair, blue eyes, tall, with well-toned legs. She had been a lifeguard for three summers in a small town in Nebraska. And she had stated at her initial interview when applying for police work that one of her hobbies was dancing.

Funny he hadn't seen it all before. Then again, there hadn't been the usual storytelling about the hot new lady deputy. So if she was hot, it wasn't around the other cops.

Carlander knew she was married. "So. You're married."

"Yes," she said, looking up. "My husband's name is Bill. I'm sure you know his age and occupation from my personnel file."

"Yeah. Electronics business. That's what he does, I remember now."

"Electrical. Bill does electrical contracting. Wires homes, stores, and office buildings." Her voice was correct, not warm.

"Yeah, well, we're talking about your file, background, you're Catholic. Me, too," he said, smiling.

"We're not going to say rosary together, are we, Sergeant?"

"Hell, no. I'm just wondering what you think about doing some of the stuff we have to do. You know, earlier, I said we work in the street because that's where the drug action is. Think you can do it?"

"Yes," she said.

He waited for elaboration. There was none. *Suits the hell out of me,* he thought. *She's on for the ride.* "Okay, read this guy's sheet. I'll be back in ten minutes, and then we'll take a walk." Carlander dropped the five-page computer printout on her desk and left the room.

Victoria began reading the first page:

> *Clifford Paul Mowery, a.k.a. Paul Mowery;*
> *Cliff Moury, Shane Mowry. Arrested by Fullerton*
> *PD, Anaheim, Newport, Santa Ana, Orange*
> *County, S.O., Los Angeles PD . . .*

The rap sheet listed charges with convictions for assault with a deadly weapon, theft of a vehicle, armed robbery, narcotics possession and narcotics possession with intent to sell, intimidation of a witness, credit card fraud, battery, malicious mischief, arson, and homicide.

Additional charges included DUI, violation of parole, vehicle accident(s), failure to appear, etc. All before age twenty-six. And there was the appended *For vehicle accidents and time served see attachment B.*

She finished reading within a few minutes, including a parole jacket that included a detailed report from his parole officer of three years earlier. He had observed that while Mowery was a man others gravitated to, powerful in many ways, he was not a good risk for rehabilitation. He was, according to the officer, a sociopathic personality, a compulsive liar, physically assaultive, and therefore did not have his recommendation for return to society.

While Victoria read the folder, Carlander used another office to make a telephone call. It was to Keith Taylor, Mowery's present parole officer.

"Got one of your guys down here at County," Carlander announced blandly.

"Talking about Mowery, aren't you? Figures that he couldn't stay out long," Taylor responded without enthusiasm. "Desk officer called me this morning. Well, I'm running my butt off today. Be late until I can get there."

"Hey, it's Friday," Carlander said, needing more time to put his embryonic plan into operation. "Might as well leave him over the weekend. It's not like he's going anywhere. We have a hold order on him."

"Okay, good idea. I'll get him out of there Monday."

Carlander replaced the telephone and walked back across the hall to his own office.

Victoria refolded the material and raised her eyes to see Carlander studying her. She said nothing.

"What do you think?" he asked.

"About what?"

"Mowery."

She shrugged. "Not much. Career criminal. What am I supposed to think?"

"I think we can use him," Carlander said in a tone that invited dissent.

"For what?" she asked.

"CI," Carlander said.

"Never met him. You'd know more about that than I would."

Confidential informants came in all shapes and sizes, she knew, but if Carlander thought he would be able to use a convict with Mowery's record of violence, then maybe she had missed something in the report.

Carlander stood eyeing her for several long moments, saying nothing.

"Did you do okay in Burglary?" he asked at last.

"Yeah. I think so." She had done more than all right, and she knew Carlander had checked.

"How long were you over at the jail?"

"Ten months. Mind if I smoke?" she asked.

"Mind if I get sick?"

"Sorry," she said.

"Naw, go ahead."

"No, I can wait." She was not offended. She planned to quit.

"Ever make a drug buy?" he asked.

"You mean for myself?" Victoria realized that she was not making life easy for Carlander, but it was important to establish independence.

He laughed. "From anybody. That's what we do. We make a lot of drug buys."

"No. Never have."

"School go okay?"

"Everything was just fine, Sergeant Carlander. Do you have an assignment for me?"

"Why don't you take the rest of the day off?" he suggested.

"Huh? Look, Sergeant, I'm not tired and I've already used up my comp time from Burglary . . ."

"Now that you're here," Carlander said, "I can see that you can handle the job. I didn't know that before because I hadn't heard much about you. But hell, assignments like we get dumped on us takes somebody who can think. We don't go around shooting people or beating 'em up. You can do this job just fine. Dynamite."

"Well, that's good to hear. I'm glad you feel that way," Victoria said.

"So go home," he said, nodding his head vigorously.

"Really?"

"See you tomorrow."

Carlander turned back to the papers on his desk. Victoria retraced her steps to her chair, feeling his words of welcome lifting a weight from her shoulders. She walked out of the building feeling that the department's celebrated misogynist wasn't such a bad guy after all. She could use time off. She would surprise Bill and take him to an early dinner and movie.

Although it was his day off, the next morning Carlander drove from his home in El Toro to visit Mowery again. He brought more cigarettes and M&M chocolates.

"Thanks for the nails," Mowery said grudgingly.

"The lab's going to come up drug-positive on your blood, Cliff. You're going back to Soledad. You know that, don't you? How much time you got left?"

Mowery did not answer.

"Let's see, ah, twelve. Yeah, I remember, now. Twelve years. You'll have to do 'em all now."

Mowery's eyes dropped and for long moments he gazed at the concrete floor of his cell. He picked up an already opened package of cigarettes, put one into his mouth. He didn't have a match. Carlander made no move to light it.

"How old did you say your boy is now, Cliff?"

"Six." Mowery's eyes remained fixed on his hands.

"Cliff, I wish you didn't have to go. I really wish that. Your boy is going to be almost ready to leave home by the time you finish your slide. If you finish. Hell, you're tough, no question. Tougher than tough. But sometimes ... Hey, let's quit talking about that." Changing the subject, Carlander asked, "Who'd you use to ride with? Diablos, wasn't it? Knew a guy by the name of Pig Lapp. He rode with the Diablos. Know him?"

Mowery was lost in thought but slowly began to nod his head. "Knew him. Yeah. I knew him."

"Pig could ride a damn bike. Busted him once for receiving. Small world. He ever tell you that? Chased him in a patrol car through Santa Ana out to the beach. Time I got there we had bikes and cars after him. Pig took an exit around eighty, put the bike down at fifty-five I'd guess, maybe sixty. He went over the overpass, ninety-degree turn, and I went straight ahead. Took out a speed sign, me and a couple motors with me by then ..." Carlander laughed at the remembrance. "He ever tell you that one, Cliff?"

No response from Mowery.

"Pig could ride a scooter. How about you? Can you run a chopper?"

Mowery slowly lifted his eyes to meet Carlander's. "Hell you want from me?"

Carlander considered for a moment, then took a deep breath as he made the decision to lay it out. "I'm after bikers. We're getting big-time crank on the street, and that tells me it's bikers. I want their methamphetamine plant."

"Who?" Mowery's eyes held Carlander's.

Carlander shrugged. "Whoever it is. Like you say, there's a lot of bikers out there."

Mowery's mouth twisted. "I ain't no snitch. That's number one. Number two, go fuck yourself."

"I like that," Carlander said. "Ever see Cagney films? James Cagney. Used to play gangsters in the movies. He'd say stuff like that. 'I ain't no rat,' he'd say. He'd call other people dirty rats, too. 'You, you dirty rat,' he'd say. Tough."

Carlander turned toward the open door of Mowery's cell. The detective stepped outside, paused at the bars. "You should see some of his pictures. Cagney's great."

Carlander had thought to go to the sheriff's home in San Juan Capistrano to present his idea. But this Saturday morning he found Sheriff Brad Gates in his office. Gates was wearing his favorite off-duty clothes: jeans, loafers, and a sport shirt open at the collar. He was nearly Carlander's height but weighed eighty pounds less. His fiery red hair matched his zeal for a job. He still had, at age thirty-nine, the energy of a rookie.

Carlander had a lot of respect for his boss. Brad Gates wanted to be sheriff of Orange County from the time he was given a cap pistol by his father in 1942 at the age of five. When he played cops and robbers as a lad with his preschool friends, young Brad always played a cop. His ultimate hero was John Wayne, a tall man like Brad would be, a relentless foe of those who lied and stole from the helpless. It was perhaps not ironic that as the chief lawman of Orange County, Brad Gates became John Wayne's nominal protector and a close friend of the family in the actor's later years when the film star bought a home in Newport Beach. Gates majored in criminology at California State

University–Long Beach and took a master's degree there in that same discipline. By the time he was elected sheriff in 1975, little more than one year before, he had worked the streets and the jails for fourteen years, going nose-to-nose with criminals as well as sitting through chicken dinners and meatloaf lunches with politicians throughout the country. His eyes had never focused on anything but attaining the job that he now held, and holding on to it by doing it honor.

Gates invited Carlander inside but continued working on a desk piled high with papers. Carlander outlined his idea, finishing, "He doesn't want to go back inside."

"Who does?" Gates leaned back in his chair, fingers interlocked behind his head. Carlander could tell that he had the sheriff's interest.

"I mean he wants to stay out bad. He'll work for me."

"He say so?" The sheriff continued to regard his detective skeptically.

"Not yet."

"The man is a load, Wayne. I mean a real damn day's work."

"I can handle him," Carlander said with a measure of confidence that he wished he felt more deeply.

"How about Victoria?" the sheriff wanted to know.

"What about her?" Carlander had known the question would arise. The idea he had in mind was weak because of her vulnerability, but the plan would succeed only because of it. He needed to sell the paradox to Gates.

"It's a shit job."

"They're all shit jobs in Narcotics. She can either do it or she can't."

Gates knew this very well. He had spent fourteen years working in every department before he had been elected county sheriff. There weren't many posh jobs in his department.

"How much did you tell her about what you need her to do?" Gates asked.

Carlander shrugged. "Nothing yet. I need you to say yes."

"I want to think about it. And I want to talk with Victoria Seele."

"We find us a manufacturing plant, Brad, we hurt 'em bad."

"I know."

"Keep that in mind. Okay?" Carlander could tell that Gates liked the idea of knocking off a meth operation even more, though he wanted to keep outlaw bikers out of Orange County.

Carlander exited his boss's office pleased. He felt that if Brad Gates was going to talk to Investigator Seele, he would likely go for the operation. Now there was Mowery. And Taylor. Push and shove.

Carlander's next call took place Monday morning. He had to crack Mowery before his parole officer arrived in the afternoon to sign the papers that would return him to the penitentiary. Once he was back inside the joint, getting him out again would be extremely difficult. Nor could it be done without attracting the attention of other prisoners and creating suspicion about Mowery that could be fatal.

Carlander checked his gun again inside the main entrance, then walked to the control room of the County Jail and was let inside. He walked down the polished concrete floor of the isolation block until he appeared once again before Mowery.

"Cliff. Can I come in?"

"Yeah," Mowery answered.

Carlander nodded toward the control room deputy, and the steel door to Mowery's cell rolled smoothly open. It remained open behind him as he entered.

"All set for the ride back?" Carlander asked.

Mowery did not respond, and Carlander took this as a glimmer of hope. "Cliff, if you go back inside the slide I might not be able to get you out. Understand? You're let outside for any reason, any excuse we could think up, it isn't going to look right. Cuts the legs out from under us and maybe gets you dead."

Carlander waited. Mowery stared at a point fixed in space.

Like a salesman assuming the customer had already bought, Carlander pushed for the close: "The way to keep you out of there is never to let you get inside. But I have to work fast."

Carlander thought he perceived the smallest slump of Mowery's muscled shoulders. "I told you I don't rat."

"I know that."

"So take a hike."

Carlander believed that Mowery was being hard-nosed to cover up a weakness he was clearly feeling about spending the rest of his youth behind bars. "I wouldn't ask you to do anything you don't want to do, you think isn't right."

Mowery sat silent for long moments. Then, "What would I have to do?"

Carlander exhaled slowly. "Ride your chopper . . ."

"I don't have one," Mowery said.

"We'll get one," Carlander said, beginning to feel confident that it could work.

"That's it? Ride a hog?"

"And take somebody with you."

"Who?" Mowery's eyes reflected faint interest.

"Deputy sheriff."

"They'd kill him," Mowery snorted.

"Won't be easy, but it's your ticket out of the slam," Carlander said, rising to his feet. "Will you think about it?"

"Maybe."

"No maybe, Cliff. Think about it." Time was running out for the detective. He had to be firm, exercise control.

"Okay," Mowery agreed, his head falling to his large hands.

"Call me tonight. I have to know tonight because you're due on the bus in the morning. Call me at home and I'll call the jail. We'll hold you on new charges, that'll clear you with the others."

Mowery did not respond.

"Make sure you call, Clifford," Carlander said. He stepped out of the cell and signaled to the control room guard.

The door slid closed.

Keith Taylor received Carlander's idea with extreme skepticism. Taylor was a fair but no-nonsense parole officer who believed in giving convicts assigned to him reasonable chances to make mistakes without going back to prison. But, Taylor pointed out to Carlander, Mowery had blown more chances than most. Furthermore, because of his history of violence, Mowery was an unusually high risk.

Carlander understood Taylor's concerns but managed to convince him that he was capable of watching Mowery closely enough that the public at large would be safe. For his part, Taylor realized two positives. If Mowery succeeded in infiltrating an outlaw motorcycle society, he could yield a wealth of evidence about criminal enterprises. Second, Carlander was tough enough and smart enough to handle Mowery if anybody could. The question in Taylor's mind was the latter: if anybody could. Still, he agreed that if Sheriff Brad Gates signed a letter approving the operation, he would go along with it.

"The Parole Board will probably go along with it if I say so," Taylor said, "but if we have to bust Mowery he goes straight back to prison. He forfeits his Morrissy rights." Under California's Morrissy law, a parolee has the right to appeal his parole revocation to the parole board. "I want Mowery to sign a letter to the effect that he understands that, too. Okay?"

Carlander nodded. The detective was confident that Mowery would sign anything that would keep him out of prison. That is, if Mowery agreed to Carlander's plan at all. And that was far from certain.

Carlander arrived home to a silent house. He had recently been divorced from Sandy, his wife and high school sweetheart, mother of his three children. He was now living with Judy, a beautiful woman ten years Carlander's junior who would become his second wife. Wayne Junior was fifteen years old and tall, like his father, a promising athlete. Terri Renee was eleven, Kimberly Ann eight, all with their mother. He missed them sorely, especially at night after work.

Judy arrived home with two bags full of groceries. He took the bags from her arms and accepted a kiss on the cheek. "Any calls today?" he asked.

"Not while I was at work. The machine was on all day."

He usually called his children every night that he arrived home at an hour when they would still be awake. But tonight he would not. He would keep the line clear.

He turned on the news but watched without seeing. He flipped through a number of channels but nothing appealed to him. He looked at his watch. Almost midnight.

The telephone rang.

Carlander picked it up. "Hello?"

No response.

"Hello? Cliff? Is that you?"

Click.

Carlander looked at the dead instrument in his hand. He replaced the receiver, picked it up again. He rapidly dialed a number from memory.

"County Jail, Styles," came a curt voice at the other end.

"Monty, this is Carlander. Is Mowery in his cell?"

"Yeah."

"Been out tonight? Used a phone maybe?" Carlander asked.

"Not since chow."

"Okay. Remember what I said?" the detective reminded Styles.

"Sure, we all got it. He wants to call, he can call," Styles said.

"That's right. Anytime."

Carlander fell asleep watching a sports channel, and the ringing of the telephone woke him. It was daylight but still too early for Judy to be out of bed. He punched off the television with one hand and reached for the receiver with the other.

"Hello?"

Mowery's hoarse, unmistakable voice resonated over the wire. "Bus leaves in twenty minutes. I don't want to be on it."

Victoria Seele had been seated at her desk reading open cases for more than two hours when Carlander came into the office. Lack of sleep did not show on his face. He was smiling like Sylvester with Tweety in his mouth. "Hi, Vicky. Ready to work?"

"Yes, but my name is Victoria. Take a minute or so out of your life to learn that," she said.

"Hey, nobody's gonna hire me to build a rocket, but Victoria is not hard to remember. C'mon, let's go look in on Mowery."

By the time they reached the jail entrance Victoria was in step with her new boss. She was thinking over a background report she had recently read. The rap sheet contained nothing that indicated, at least to her, that Mowery was a source of information. He was a classic cop hater, a tough guy's tough guy. But somehow Clifford Mowery, soon to return to finish his full prison sentence, was connected with Carlander's obvious good cheer. She was looking forward to finding out why.

Just inside the front door they checked their guns, and he said to the deputy, "We're here to see Clifford Mowery."

The officer referred to a clipboard. "He was scheduled out on the bus. Should be gone by now."

"Call the sergeant of the guard. We got more charges to hang on him," Carlander said by way of explanation.

The deputy picked up a hotline to Control and spoke into the phone. "Got a detective here to see Mowery. He's gone, isn't he?"

Victoria experienced a tinge of resentment at the identification of "a" detective rather than two.

"Yeah, okay." To Carlander: "He's here."

"Bring him to the attorney room."

Victoria walked with Carlander into the attorney-bondsman room. The room contained three chairs, a table, a second door, and bars on the window. Carlander did not speak and Victoria chose not to be the first. It was, she thought, his show. Finally Carlander turned to her. "You're my partner now."

"You work with Bud Nease," she responded.

Carlander correctly took her reaction as a question. "Bud's not going anywhere. Fact is, me and Bud need help," he said pleasantly.

"What kind of help? You mean from me?" Victoria was flattered but suspicious.

"Yeah. We're plodders. Four yards and a cloud of dust. That's us," he confessed. "I never thought women would work out in our line of business. Sure glad I was wrong."

Victoria still didn't believe him, but she decided to say nothing. She wasn't one for head games.

The sound of a door unlocked from the other side caused them to look up. Mowery entered and his eyes widened with appreciation at the sight of Victoria. Even in conservative clothing appropriate to an investigator, she was smashing: young, striking, effortlessly elegant.

"Well, hello there, li'l girl," he said with his most seductive aw-shucks eye twinkle.

The effect seldom failed. But Victoria returned his gaze with all the interest of a social worker watching a human disaster in the making.

"Investigator Seele," Carlander said in the way of introduction. "Clifford Mowery."

"I want to talk to you," the convicted felon said to Carlander.

"That's why we're here," Carlander said pleasantly.

"You. Not her," Mowery jerked his head toward Victoria.

"Her," Carlander responded patiently, "is my partner. So, talk."

The muscled biker looked away. He had to surrender a large slice of machismo in talking with Carlander; to do so in front of a woman, a young one, was hard. But it was talk or ride. "What do I have to do?"

"It isn't what you have to do, Cliff," Carlander explained. "You don't have to do a thing. Nothing. It's what you want to do that brought me and Investigator Seele here. We only want to find out what you think you might do for us so that you don't have to go back to the joint. That's all."

Carlander waited. Mowery shuffled his feet on the floor. "Okay, I guess I could do some stuff."

"What?"

"Hell, I don't know. You gotta tell me what you want," the convict said, trying to avoid personal involvement in a cop's plan as much as possible.

"We want to send bikers to jail. The ones selling crank. And PCP. Receiving stolen property. And guns," Carlander said, stating the obvious.

"Don't want much." Mowery was almost smug.

"Those are the guys. Can you do 'em or not?" Carlander pressed for commitment, feeling he was on firmer ground now.

Victoria watched her senior partner with interest.

"What do I get out of it?" Mowery asked.

"Too soon for you to ask," the detective said. "We'll see what kind of work you do."

"Trust you, huh?" Mowery scoffed.

"That's right, Cliff. I know you can do it, but I gotta hear you tell it to me and then I gotta see you do it."

"Some things I'll do, some I won't." Mowery's response revealed a certain convict's intuition for exploiting a situation. He was probing to see how much Carlander needed him. Or at least what the detective was willing to give for Mowery's cooperation.

"Don't be telling me you're not going to do things. I'm going to call the shots, not you."

"Don't come at me with a hard-on," Mowery said.

Carlander leaned back in his chair and studied the convict. There were times to force a showdown and times to wait it out. Carlander's continued silence tilted Mowery slightly off balance.

"So how do I do it?" Mowery asked by way of covering his belligerence.

"You do what you been doing most of your life," the detective said. "Except that you don't do any more armed robberies or stolen cars or any of that shit. You ride a scooter."

"I guess I could dig it. I ride around, I see something go down or I hear something, I call you."

"That isn't the way it's going to work," Carlander said, almost amused at Mowery's clumsy attempt to begin skating over rough spots. "Investigator Seele and me aren't gonna sit around the Sheriff's Office waiting for you to drop a dime." Carlander chuckled. Mowery grinned. Victoria smiled.

"So? Okay, what do I do?"

Carlander could see a glimmer of curiosity in Mowery's eyes for the first time since they had met. "First of all, you're still doing jail time. When you're not riding a bike and setting up buys exactly the way we tell you to do, you're back in your room under arrest. Understand what I'm saying? You don't even leave the motel we're gonna put you in, you don't leave the room. When you park the bike at night you give the keys to me or Investigator Seele here."

"Hell, yeah. No sweat there," Mowery lied easily.

"Phone rings, you pick it up by the second ring," Carlander continued.

"Yeah? That'd be okay."

Victoria could hardly keep from laughing at Mowery's agreement to rules that he had every intention of breaking. She as yet had no idea of how dedicated Mowery would be to that resolve.

Carlander had Mowery's attention now. "No booze. Just like your parole papers say that you lied to me about. No drugs. Exception is beer when Victoria is with you and you're socializing with suspects. But no getting drunk. I catch you drinking on your own or chipping, you go right back to Soledad on the next bus out of town. No Morrissy hearing. Investigator Seele's got the same authority. She sees you step sideways, she pulls the cord and you go down the toilet like a homesick turd."

Leaning against the wall, attempting to make her confusion appear to be boredom, Victoria was trying to imagine how, indeed, Carlander planned to employ the ex-convict.

"How's it gonna go, then?" Mowery asked in genuine bewilderment.

"Like I said, you're going to ride a chopper. Investigator Seele's going to be riding with you." Carlander nodded toward Victoria.

The room suddenly fell silent.

Mowery raised his hand, pointing a large finger in Victoria's direction. "Her? You crazy? They'd kill her. They'd kill a cop in a damn heartbeat."

Victoria's heart, as though in support of Mowery's assessment, began to thump. The casual, matter-of-fact way in which Mowery stated that she would die had put a chill in her.

"If they find out," Carlander agreed rhetorically, "but they're not going to find out."

"And they're gonna be hitting on her. Damn, she don't look like a biker woman . . ." Mowery shook his head in disbelief.

"Sergeant Carlander," Victoria interrupted in what she hoped was a calm, modulated voice, "see you for a minute?"

Carlander followed Victoria out into the lobby. She turned to him and said, "Is this a joke, Sergeant Carlander? Did you and the other narc detectives go to all this trouble to set me up for a gag just because I'm new and I'm a woman?"

"Why would I do that?" Carlander could, however, understand why Victoria might think that.

"Because policemen do crazy things," she said. "First week I was on Burglary, somebody called the station and reported a panty bandit. I think it was Chuck Hockney. Just a guess. But I think you're behind this one and I think it sucks."

"I don't pull jokes with my badge." At least not like this one. "You through?" he said.

Victoria looked up at him levelly. "Okay, you're not kidding. Well, neither am I. I know something about the limits of volunteering for hazardous duty and I do not volunteer for this one."

"I know it looks a little scary . . ."

"Scary?" Victoria interrupted. "God, didn't you hear the man? He's right. Do I look like a biker's girl to you? I can't stand motorcycles. They terrify me. And I can't stand that tatooed holdup artist in there. They'd see through it in a second."

"So you don't like him. County doesn't pay us to arrest just people we like." Carlander spoke with a conviction that took Victoria momentarily aback.

"I'm talking about pulling it off," she said in a reasonable tone. "They would know. Everybody would know."

"I got a hell of a cover story for you," Carlander said simply, then turned and walked back into the attorney room, leaving the door open for Victoria to follow.

"Like I said," Carlander said to Mowery, one foot resting on a chair, "Investigator Seele's going to be on the back of your bike every time you ride. And you ride when we say and where we say."

"Man, come on . . ." the convict began.

Carlander shook his head for silence. He glanced over his shoulder and saw that Victoria had reentered the room and was standing against a wall, arms crossing her chest. Her body language signaled defiance, but at least she was still there. "Listen," he said, "she's getting a divorce from an executive and she's waiting for a property settlement. She needs extra money until they sell the house, so she buys whatever dope she can get and sells it to her rich girlfriends. See?"

Victoria could see.

"And," Carlander continued, "she's away from her old man and runs across Mowery. She's not in love but . . . riding on the back of a chopper is fun."

"Yeah, well," Victoria said, shoving off from the wall, "that might be a hard sell." She had such a real fear of motorcycles that she was certain she could not hide it from anyone, much less a biker gang member.

But the rest of the story was simple, even commonplace. Carlander imagined that he saw a slight change in his new partner's skeptical eyes. "She doesn't know anything about where to buy drugs, but you do," he added.

Victoria admitted to herself that Mowery and men like him

were every woman's fantasy outlaws. He had male magnetism, an incredible body, and when he put his mind to it, according to the record, he could smooth-talk a blind woman out of her Seeing Eye dog. She touched the back of her neck with a finger as though to rub away the niggling sensation that had started there.

"Yeah, well," Mowery said, "they're gonna be all over her, gangs you want to get into. You ready for that?"

He had directed his question toward Victoria, but Carlander supplied the answer. "Your job's to see that doesn't happen. Anybody tries to lay hands on Victoria Seele has to go through you."

"I'd be fighting the whole gang every day," he protested.

"Make damn sure you win 'em all," Carlander said. "You'll need a new name," he said to Victoria.

She shrugged. *God,* she thought, *why am I even thinking about this?* "How about Samantha? Samantha ... Cook." The words seemed to escape from her mouth before she could stop them.

"Okay with me," he said without taking Mowery's vote. By this time Carlander knew more about Mowery than anyone except Keith Taylor. He also knew that the flaws in the plan were many and they were obvious.

But no one in the room brought them up.

Outside the Orange County Jail, Carlander turned to Victoria. "Gates wants to see you."

"Sheriff Gates? What about?" she asked.

"About this assignment. Don't worry. I'm going to be right there when you need me. Me and Bud Nease'll be behind you all the way."

"Then why don't I feel better?"

Brad Gates had read Carlander's plan for what he unofficially called "Operation Hog." The budget was modest enough but still needed some blue-penciling. What appealed to Gates was the operation's simplicity, a potentially large return on a relatively small investment. Carlander insisted, and Gates concurred, that the deployment would be conducted on a need-to-know basis. In addition to his hand-picked group, Lieutenant Sim Middleton, Sergeant Skip Mitchell, and Captain Robert Griffith were nominal supervisors. To forestall leaks, the pervasive terror for any undercover operative, no other law enforcement jurisdictions would be advised.

Sheriff Gates greeted Victoria at his door and remained on her side of his large desk as they took seats and talked.

"It's important for you to understand, Victoria," he said easily but sincerely, "there's no pressure on you to do this job. If you don't think you're up to it, if you think the risk is too much, say so now. There won't be any hard feelings. I mean it. No black marks on your record. Not officially and not unofficially, either."

Victoria had been looking for an excuse to change her mind. The reasons Gates had suggested sounded pretty good. She wasn't sure she was up to the operation, and she thought it was dangerous. But now that Brad Gates was offering her an honorable way out, she found herself saying, "I'm sure I can handle it, sir."

"Not worried about the risks?" he asked.

"Yes, sir, I am concerned about the risks. But I think they're acceptable."

Sheriff Gates was impressed. His confidence in his first female deputy investigator was well placed. Her answer damn sure sounded professional. "How about Sergeant Carlander? You two get along all right? You have to have trust in the people you work with in undercover programs."

"Yes, sir. I trust Sergeant Carlander can do what he says." *I hope he can do half of it,* she thought to herself.

"Fair enough. So do I," Gates said. "He's the key to dealing with Mowery. Carlander has guts and he never does anything stupid. Now," he said, changing gears, "how about Bill? Police work is hard on marriages. Undercover police work multiplies normal stress at home."

Victoria's answer was automatic. "Bill's one hundred percent behind me. He's a dream."

"You know, things are going to go bad on this job," Gates said matter-of-factly.

"What? Bad?" Victoria was surprised. She wondered if Gates was trying to shock her.

"Undercover work is like that. It always goes bad. Sooner or later. Somebody gets suspicious. Or you get recognized. Or you come unstrung. Something always happens. Otherwise, under-cover operations would go on forever."

Victoria had never thought of it that way. She swallowed but said nothing.

Gates regarded her for some time, as though trying to mea-sure something intangible. "Okay," he said, "we'll put it in gear. But I want you to speak up if things start to go down the toilet. Understand? If you find yourself getting up in the morning afraid to go to work, that's the day we pull you out. Don't hold it in. And if things get rough for you and Bill, tell me. We don't want any assignment to tear up a marriage. I mean that, Victo-ria."

"Yes, sir," she said.

With those two fateful words in October 1976 began an un-dercover operation the likes of which, according to experts, will never again be duplicated by any law enforcement agency. There was no way Victoria could know what leading two lives, one of them extraordinarily dangerous, could do to her psyche or her marriage.

# CHAPTER 3

Marriage and the notion of family were always the bedrock upon which Victoria had built her life. In a town like the one she grew up in, population seven hundred, everyone was close.

Her mother, Kathleen Avis Seele, had been gravely ill when Victoria was in the fourth grade. Victoria was the oldest of three children (to eventually become eight by the time Roberta Fay, the youngest, was born in 1970) and deeply felt the responsibilities that came with that position of trust in the family.

She and her two younger sisters, Laura, seven, and Julie, six, were boarded in a Catholic parochial school until such time as their mother recovered—or did not recover—from her sickness. Her father, Howard Seth Seele, had a farm to run that took a day beginning before dawn and lasting well after the sun set during the long planting season. Victoria was never to learn why her father, perhaps unable to care for the girls, banished her and her sisters to boarding school. The school was dank and seemed threatening to Victoria, who made a special effort not to reveal her inner terrors to her sisters lest they suffer more than they already were. Most of the food that the school's children ate was donated to the institution by charitable farmers in the area. Following each meal of the day, the students would wash, dry, and put away the dishes, pots, and pans. They would make their beds, care for their clothes, and sweep the floors of the vast three-story red brick building that turned into a monster with each nightfall. The nuns, while caring, were stern and did not replace the affection and warmth that Victoria and her sisters were accustomed to receiving at home. Victoria often heard her sisters, and other girls, cry themselves to sleep.

As fall stretched into winter the huge school grew colder with each day. Victoria felt pervasive depression but knew that she was the bridge back to their real home from this foreign, threatening environment into which they had unwillingly been sent. It was the family's worst Christmas ever. While Marian Seele languished in bed, her children dwelled within cold walls only a few blocks away. Yet it might have been thousands. They were not allowed to visit. Only after staying in the boarding school for most of a year that included a sad Christmas were the girls allowed to return to their home. Marian Seele was now out of her sickroom and about, weak but gaining strength. The "sickness" was never revealed to the children, never referred to. To Victoria and her sisters, the reason they were separated was less important than the fact that they were reunited as a family, that public school and old friends were once again central to their lives. The lost Christmas was brought back to Victoria vividly every yule season that followed.

Her family was happy for her and not a little excited when she announced that she was leaving the state to find a job in California. Victoria had no prospects at the time, but with her crisp new college degree she felt confident of finding employment. In a worst-case eventuality, she could always return home to family and farm.

As expected when she applied to the Sheriff's Office, Victoria began her police career after academy graduation working in the Orange County Jail for female prisoners. While she labored forty-plus hours of the week learning to deal with unfortunate, desperate, sometimes dangerous people who were unlucky enough to serve time in County Jail, Victoria enrolled in Cal State–Fullerton to earn a teaching credential. As one of the few female graduates of the academy and the only one to graduate at the top of her academy class, she was asked to speak to various civic groups. After overcoming nervousness the first couple of times, she found that she enjoyed lecturing. She was frequently asked to address law classes. Her teaching activities combined with a full work schedule left her little time for socializing. Until she met Bill.

One Saturday afternoon in 1970, when she was still living at Huntington Beach, an area noted for easy living, young hardbodies, and sun-tinted hair, a volleyball game was being played on the sand as Victoria emerged from the ocean. As she dried her hair she watched the game for several moments, noting that one of the four players doing dives and jumps for a wind-blown volleyball seemed to have a permanent grin on his face. For a moment their eyes met. After Victoria gathered up her towel and walked toward her apartment, she glanced over her shoulder. She saw that the smiling player was watching her progress up the sand. He waved. She returned his smile and his wave but continued walking.

During the next several days she found herself thinking about the smiling volleyball player. The following Saturday she returned to the same location on the beach, arriving earlier than usual and staying later, but she did not see the guy. She came to the beach the next day, Sunday, swam until she was tired, watched more volleyball. No smiling player.

By the end of the following week she was forgetting about him.

On Saturday night she and her roommate, Gerry Owens, threw an impromptu party, inviting neighbors and whoever else was hanging out. It was the waning days of August and to gather a crowd for a party of beach lizards the girls had only to open their windows and pass the word. The apartment and large pool area were quickly jammed with dancers, swimmers, and drinkers.

Victoria had taken a huge bite of a taco, sending a stream of salsa down her chin and neck. She was looking quickly for a napkin when she heard a nearby voice say, "Hold still." Before she could react, the trail of spicy tomato sauce was gently sponged. When she shifted her eyes, there was his face. The grin was still there. His teeth were even and white. She felt enormously relieved, almost giddy.

"Guess I need a bib," she said.

"Close," he agreed. "What you need is a Bill."

"Is that your name?" she asked.

He nodded. "Decker. I play volleyball and wipe chins."

He had soft blond hair and was tall, lithe, assured. "How did you find this place? Did you just hear the music or do you know somebody?" she asked.

"Gerry Owens. She's a buddy of mine," Bill said.

Her own roommate. "Gerry? You mean I've been looking for . . ." She stopped herself. No way was she going to admit she had been trying to find the smiling volleyball player. That wouldn't be cool.

"Looking for what?" he asked.

"Ah . . . my notebook. I put it somewhere, can't find it now. Maybe Gerry knows where it is."

Bill considered for a moment. "Oh, I thought maybe you were going to say that you've been looking for me, because I've been looking for you."

Victoria and Bill became constant companions. They endured sixteen weeks of frustration, however, when she entered the academy and needed almost all of her waking hours to deal with its challenges. She worked hard physically and studied the California Penal Code, basic police procedure, arrest techniques, tactics, patrol routine, high-speed diving, self-defense, firearms qualification, and the myriad other requirements for keeping the peace in southern California.

Within days of her graduation they were living together. Bill was romantic, a gentle man who cared about her feelings. To him, Victoria was one of the most beautiful, intelligent women he had ever met. Even considering California beaches as a baseline, he thought she was a ten. Three months after sharing a mutual address they eloped to Las Vegas.

The wedding plans were too spur-of-the-moment to invite family or even friends. Victoria called her family in Nebraska and talked for two hours. Bill had to speak with every member of the family before, sweating, he passed the phone back to his bride.

Their life was almost idyllic, Victoria thought. The deeper she got into her work the more interesting it became. Her home life with Bill could not have been better. Her parents and siblings visited her with enough regularity that she never longed for home, never felt far removed from them.

In 1976, after five years, their marriage had lost no magic. On the contrary, the energetic pace with which they approached their careers made what time they had together special. Victoria was aware that marriages among other cop families broke up with frightening regularity, but she believed that she and Bill were immune. They had something that other couples did not, she thought. He was her anchor and she his. Before she allowed her job to damage her marriage, she would give it up without a second thought.

Bill by now had become a project manager for a large electrical contractor, and the demands put upon his time equalled that of a man in business for himself. He supervised three trucks and their crews, and had little spare time.

He was scanning blueprints for the next day's work when Victoria brought him a cold beer. The night was hot and he took it gratefully. "Thanks."

"I have an assignment. Undercover," she announced.

"Yeah? Doing what?" Bill was interested.

"The department's after a biker gang. They're doing bigtime drugs and stuff." She began to arrange her thoughts in a way she thought would sound reasonable to Bill, but the more she considered, the less reasonable her explanation sounded.

"So?" he said.

"So, I'm going to ride with them," she said simply.

Bill stopped working and raised his head. "I don't understand. What do you mean, ride with them?"

"A guy, Cliff Mowery, is a parole violator. Also a biker before he got sent up. We'll buy drugs," she said. "That's all. I'll buy drugs from them and get evidence."

Bill was silent for long moments as he looked squarely at his wife. He waited for further information about her assigned job but didn't get it. "You are shitting me, aren't you?"

"No, and I really don't think it's such a big deal. I mean, it sounds worse than it is."

Bill's unreceptive face was beginning to harden. "Who is Cliff?"

"I told you. He's a biker we busted for parole violation. Armed robbery." Simple enough for anyone to understand.

"That's it?"

"Yes, I guess so." Victoria could feel her own attitude stiffen.

"What do you mean, you're going to ride with them?" he repeated.

"Kind of hang out. Get in with them," she said.

Bill appeared incredulous. "Hang out? You mean socialize with them? Go to their parties?"

"Yes, but I'll always be with backup. Carlander will be there. And Bud Nease." Sounded good, the way she said it, even to her own ears. If Bill knew what she knew about Mowery, the conversation would get a lot more intense in a hurry.

"And this guy Mowery? He'll be there?"

"He's part of the plan. Sure." She shuddered to think how big.

"Victoria . . ."

"Yes?"

"This is something we should talk over," Bill said with a kind of finality that meant that nothing was final at all.

"It's my job," she said. "Do you expect me to come to you to ask your permission to do my job?"

"You're twisting what I said. Walk around to twenty guys in our neighborhood and ask them if they care if their wives go partying with bikers. They'd go ballistic. Think I'm being unreasonable?" he demanded.

"Twenty guys in our neighborhood don't have wives who are cops."

"Victoria," Bill began with visible effort to restrain his frustration, "these people pass women around like catsup for their hamburgers. They're animals. I don't want you near them."

"I'm nobody's hamburger. Not even yours. You sound like a

redneck ordering around his woman." Immediately she wanted to take back what she'd said.

Yet Bill did not flinch. "Arresting them, that's one thing," he insisted, "but hanging out with them, partying with them, is a whole different game."

It was true. Victoria did not like the idea herself but had avoided delving into the details of what biker-gang girls are expected to do. Well, she intended to set her own rules on how she would conduct her life in spite of cops, gangs, or anything else. She was going to have to take care of herself, even if she was not at all sure how she would do it. Carlander was her safety net. And Bud Nease would be there, too.

But Mowery was the one it hinged on. If he failed her and Carlander was out of reach . . . She shook her head, unwilling to finish the thought. "I'm sorry, Bill. It's a shitty assignment. And I hate to say it, but . . ."

"You're not going to say somebody has to do it, are you?" he interrupted.

"Somebody has to do it." She tried to smile, but the effort was strained.

The weather in the Midwest where she grew up did not promote year-round motorcycle riding. And what she knew about motorcycles she instinctively did not like. She was not looking forward to her first undercover operation.

The Orange County Sheriff's Office was like most law enforcement agencies throughout the United States: It had too little money, too few personnel, too much crime. The anti–biker gang program provided just enough funds to get the show on the road. Had the operation begun a few years later, in 1982, after laws were passed providing for confiscation of property and cash from illegal drug activity, different kinds of traps would have been set for their quarry. As it was, their drug buys were necessarily small. They would pass up opportunities to score heavily against big out-of-country drug cartels and concentrate on buying from gang members who, in their large numbers, posed an equally deadly threat to communities within the counties of Orange, Los Angeles, and San Bernardino.

One of the first big-ticket items on Carlander's slender budget was the purchase of a Harley-Davidson motorcycle. People like the Hell's Angels set the standard for what was "righteous" to ride, and that was an American motorcycle. All others were foreign and therefore scorned. Since the United States boasted only one motorcycle manufacturer, the bike of choice was Harley-Davidson. With $2,700 provided him by the Orange County Sheriff's Office, Mowery picked out a used chopper.

The next order of business, accomplished within an hour of buying the bike, was ensconcing Mowery in a motel where he could give the outward appearance of living a "normal" biker's life. The Sixpence Motel, located in Tustin off Redhill Avenue and Interstate 5, was third-rate, in keeping with the general neighborhood. Carlander repeated Mowery's instructions about his living restrictions. He was not to operate the motorcycle without permission and he was not to use drugs under any circumstances. He could use moderate amounts of beer in the performance of his undercover role. Carlander knew that he, Victoria, and Bud Nease, and sometimes others, would have to watch Mowery virtually twenty-four hours a day, especially in the early stages of the program, and come down on him hard if he attempted to break the rules.

He was still in custody, still on parole, was not to leave his motel room unless granted permission. The county was therefore required to maintain Mowery's minimum living needs such as toiletries, apparel, and cooking utensils. Carlander deemed it appropriate for Victoria to accompany Mowery shopping for these items, since Carlander did not trust Mowery to spend public money wisely and he wanted Mowery to have no excuse to leave his motel room for a "necessity."

The relationship between Victoria and Mowery had not begun well and did not improve as they prepared to make their first motorcycle ride together.

"Get on," he ordered after he had swung a leg over the saddle of the black lacquer and chrome chopper and kicked the starter pedal. Victoria had ridden only once before and was not looking forward to her second experience. She was self-conscious of her body as she placed one of her shapely legs over the bike and perched behind the big convict. There was sensual clarity in the act of straddling a powerful machine. She could immediately feel heat coming up from its growling innards, enveloping her thighs, then being briskly chased by the wind as Mowery directed the bike across the Sixpence parking lot.

She thought the footrests were high—she had to bend her knees sharply—but they turned out to be surprisingly comfortable. And there was a backrest, small but providing support in just the right place. At the edge of the street Mowery accelerated the bike abruptly forward before she had found a place for her hands. She grabbed for Mowery's body. He braked the bike at the corner, dropped his strong legs easily to the ground, and effortlessly balanced the bike at the intersection.

As the bike waited she found places to grasp on the side of the saddle. She had hardly closed her fingers firmly when Mowery again gunned the engine, popped the clutch, and laid the bike over sharply as it exploded into the street.

"My God . . ." But the words were unheard, at least by Mowery, as the wind tore them from Victoria's lips. She experienced vertigo as she looked downward at pavement zooming by. She hung on tighter.

Mowery hardly slowed for traffic. Instead he drove between long lines of stationary lanes of cars caught in routine California traffic jams. Mowery drove swiftly to the head of each line waiting for lights to change. When it turned green he was the first out of the blocks as Victoria struggled to avoid whiplash.

"Lean with the bike," Mowery yelled over his shoulder.

"What?" she shouted in return.

"Lean with the bike. You're riding like a sack of shit," he said, turning his head so that she would hear.

"You drive like one. That's the problem," she yelled into the wind. It was as close to admitting fear as she would come. She understood that Mowery was maneuvering the bike purposely to frighten her, to assert his domination over her on his turf.

Mowery turned into a large shopping center, found a place near the mall entrance, and put the bike near a metal light pole. He wrapped heavy chain around the pole and the bike, securing it with a padlock.

"You don't drive a bike. You ride it," he said.

"Okay."

"You have to know that stuff," Mowery said knowledgeably.

"Okay." She could understand the logic but didn't like it.

"Biker ladies are into bikes, too. Just as much as the guys. Have to know your shit about that," he added.

"Mowery, I'm not into bikes. I have no plans to get into bikes. I don't have tattoos, either. My cover is that I'm a country-clubber." She wanted to stick as closely as possible to that cover.

"Tell you something else," Mowery said. "Don't be talking shit to me in front of the people 'cause that's not supposed to happen. They'll be looking at me like I'm not real. Or you're not."

As they walked toward a supermarket Carlander parked his car and walked behind them at a discreet distance.

Victoria understood what Mowery was getting at: Don't show me up in front of anybody. His milieu was the jungle of the streets, the biker's road, and he was the big cat. To survive he would have to dominate other men and certainly women.

Victoria had no intention of being compliant. Her training as a law enforcement officer stressed the need to take charge, be firm, decisive. The need to maintain a composed demeanor under all conditions was a fundamental requirement. And she represented the Sheriff's Office of Orange County, California. She had to call the shots, not him.

At the same time she understood that Mowery could not be emasculated among his group. He would be worthless to her and to Carlander. Worse, it could cause the operation to be discovered. She knew that she would have to appear to be subordinate, with Mowery apparently in control. The dichotomy in their relationship would, until its explosive end, continue to resemble the danger of a spark near an ever-expanding pool of gasoline.

Mowery lagged behind like a truculent child as she pushed a shopping cart and plucked items from shelves. "What kind of shower soap do you like?"

Mowery shrugged in disinterest. Victoria picked out a half-dozen large bars. She found a plastic package containing a safety razor and blades. "Okay?"

Again a shrug.

"How about this stuff?" She held up a can of shaving gel. "Or do you want something else?"

"Naw."

"Naw what?" she demanded.

"I don't like that kind."

"You only shave every third or fourth day, anyway. What difference does it make?" Victoria said.

Mowery did not choose to reply but instead made an elaborate inspection of all the shaving creams and soaps while Victoria moved down an aisle. She loaded into the cart a frying pan, a couple of kitchen pots, a set of plastic dishes, a coffeepot, knives and forks, paper napkins. Mowery trailed behind her, his face a mask of resigned disapproval. He became more attentive when Victoria began to pick out food.

"I don't drink that stuff," he said truculently.

"You don't like orange juice?" Victoria thought everybody liked that. "How about milk?"

He shook his head. She reached for eggs.

"I don't want them," he said.

As they toured the store, very little food was added to the grocery cart. Victoria began to wonder if the county had any obligation to keep Mowery alive if he refused to eat. "How did you get so big without eating?" she asked.

"I eat."

She was fresh out of patience. "Okay, you get what you want and I'll watch."

Mowery made no move toward the shopping cart. In frustration Victoria looked toward Carlander. He sauntered down their aisle, pretending to read the label on a package while keeping his back to them. "What's the problem?"

"He won't eat," she said.

"I eat," Mowery said defensively.

"Apparently not food," she said.

"Kind of food do you want, Cliff?" Carlander asked.

"Whatever's on the menu, man. I don't cook," the biker said.

Victoria's anger showed on her compressed lips.

Carlander was unfazed. "Then pick out whatever it is you can eat raw 'cause you ain't going out to eat, my man."

"That so? How long do you think it's gonna take me to finish the cooking lessons the county's gonna give me? Two three weeks? Couple months? Man, I can't cook."

"I'd recommend carrots. Lots of them. Apples and bananas

are good. Grapes. Bread. You can eat 'em raw." Carlander moved toward an exit.

When Mowery's two shopping carts were processed through a checkstand they contained a number of frozen meals and a large number of canned food products.

Nothing was easy with Mowery, Victoria thought. He resisted authority in even its mildest form. She wondered if he would respond to her badge if she had to use it. And she was certain that such a time would come.

Confidential informant Clifford Mowery, dressed to go to "church" (as Hell's Angels refer to their weekly business meetings), in scarf, T-shirt, black leather jacket, and black leather vest. *(WAYNE CARLANDER)*

Victoria Seele in the tactical office at Orange County Sheriff's Training Academy, dressed in uniform of the day for tac officers. *(WAYNE CARLANDER)*

Wayne Carlander at HQ, Orange County Sheriff's Narcotics Bureau. *(WAYNE CARLANDER)*

Victoria Seele attempting to identify property in forensic science building. *(WAYNE CARLANDER)*

Victoria Seele at inspection, the beginning of each day of academy. *(WAYNE CARLANDER)*

Victoria as tac officer at graduation ceremonies. *(WAYNE CARLANDER)*

The Hell's Angels meet at Bruno's house to include Cliff Mowery in their group. *Clockwise from left:* Michael Lee Mason, aka Bruno; Cliff Mowery; Ray Glore. *(BUD NEASE)*

More Hell's Angels gather to meet with Cliff Mowery. *Top:* unidentified member; *bottom:* Pineapple. *(BUD NEASE)*

Cliff Mowery and Victoria Seele en route to a drug buy. *(WAYNE CARLANDER)*

Orange County Sheriff Brad Gates is currently serving his fifth term since 1975. *(BRAD GATES)*

Victoria Seele receiving an award from the Optimist Club for her outstanding contributions to law enforcement.
*(WAYNE CARLANDER)*

Victoria Seele and Wayne Carlander receiving one of several awards and certificates, this one from the American Legion.

# CHAPTER 4

The next morning, November 12, 1976, Carlander and Bud Nease sat in a parked pickup truck in a middle-class neighborhood in Anaheim. In the back of the truck were a few gardening tools. Per arrangement, Victoria and Mowery, in the saddle of the chopper, pulled up next to them. Mowery killed the engine.

"This is Bud Nease," Carlander said by way of introduction.

"Hi," Nease said pleasantly.

Nease was olive-complexioned, wore a full mustache, and could be any age from early to late thirties. Victoria could understand why Carlander felt Nease could pass as any of many southern California ethnic groups. He had not shaven for at least two days. He could have been a hype, a laborer, an artist. Anything.

"Hi, Bud, glad to meet you. Glad you're here," she said.

"He's here because his goddamn vacation couldn't be longer. Had his way, he'd stay gone, because he hates to work. That right, Bud?" Without waiting for Nease to answer, Carlander continued to give directions to Victoria and Mowery. "Want you two to book it over to the Sportster Shop on Westminster Boulevard. That's where most of the work is done around here on Harleys. Me and Bud'll have you in sight. You know what to do, right, Mowery? Hang out. Get to know the folks. Don't be too obvious and don't go askin' stupid questions before you know who the hell you're talking to. Okay?" Mowery, Carlander knew, was a lightning rod that would attract electricity without making a conscious effort. "All right," Carlander said.

Ten minutes later Victoria and Mowery stopped the bike at Bruno's Harley-Davidson Sportster Shop. It was a gathering place for a wide range of bike riders, though no foreign machines were serviced there. Bruno's Sportster drew the kind of people Carlander was interested in.

Mowery pushed his machine through open doors into the shop. Bruno was friendly enough to Mowery and, while Victoria stood discreetly nearby, asked his muscled customer conversational background questions.

"Haven't seen this bike before," Bruno said.

"I been away," Mowery said, his natural taciturn personality serving him well in his new double life.

Michael Lee Mason, a.k.a. Bruno, did not know Mowery, but they were kindred spirits and sensed this in each other.

"Traveling?" Bruno asked.

Victoria watched from her oblique vantage point in the shop. Bruno was in his mid-twenties, with a round face and receding hairline, though his hair was long. His bearded Santa Claus face almost glowed with good cheer, belying cold eyes that missed nothing. He wore what Victoria was yet to learn was standard biker garb: black engineering boots, denim jeans with a chain securing a wallet from belt to rear pocket, a T-shirt, sometimes with writing or a caricature. Bruno's T-shirt had a splotch of black "hair" attached to it with the words "YOU ARE WHAT YOU EAT" stenciled below. He carried the ubiquitous buck knife at his belt and his arms were fully tattooed.

"Staying put, mostly," Mowery answered.

"Chino? I spent some time there," Bruno said openly.

"Soledad," Mowery said.

"I know some folks up there, too. Arnie Dent. Call him Hess. Know him?"

"Sure. Mean little bastard."

"That's him. Gets testy, people call him that to his face. Little. Friends call me Bruno."

"Mowery," Cliff responded. Neither man offered a hand to shake, no offense given, none taken.

"Nice-looking bitch, man," Bruno said, nodding toward Victoria, who was pretending to look at motorcycles.

"Pays the bills," Mowery allowed.

"She got a name?" Bruno wanted to know.

"Yeah. What time can I pick up my bike?" Mowery asked.

Bruno took another measure of Mowery. The man did not curry favor. Bruno liked that.

Bruno scribbled on a work ticket. "Give me a couple hours. If it ain't anything serious it'll be done. San Francisco Bar, couple doors up, serves beer if you want to wait. Good people there. Bartender's a friend of mine."

Outside, Mowery made no move toward the San Francisco. Instead, with Victoria at his side, he crossed the street and began walking.

"Seems like the bar would be a good place to meet people," Victoria opined but not with the force born of experience.

"Yeah, well . . ." Clearly Mowery didn't want to meet people.

"There they go," Carlander said as he and Nease watched Mowery and Victoria exit the Sportster Shop and begin walking east on the boulevard.

Mowery chose a bar a block away from the San Francisco and ordered two beers. He drank his from the bottle.

"Pretty quiet in here," Victoria observed.

"Play some music," Mowery offered as a solution.

"I don't mean that," she said.

Mowery took in the scene with disinterest.

"Tell me why we didn't go where Bruno suggested," Victoria asked.

"Beer's beer." Mowery shrugged.

Victoria did not like the answer. "We're not here just to drink beer." She considered insisting that he take her to the San Francisco, but they had just started working together. She did not want to become an irritant to her reluctant partner.

Mowery and Victoria picked up the motorcycle that afternoon, paying the bill from cash that Victoria provided. Bruno was not in the shop at the time.

That night Carlander conducted a short debriefing at a restaurant with Nease, Victoria, and Mowery, a practice that would become a daily routine. None of the undercover team save Carlander would go near the station house during the course of the undercover operation.

"So, how'd it go?" Carlander asked as a waitress brought sandwiches and French fries to the table.

"Okay," Mowery said.

"Quiet," Victoria added.

"What's this guy Bruno like?"

Victoria waited a moment to give Mowery a chance to describe the shop owner, but the biker just stared at his coffee.

She described Bruno's physical characteristics. "He seemed like he wanted to be friendly. He said we could wait for the bike at the San Francisco Bar, couple doors up the street, but Cliff didn't want to go."

"That right? How come, Cliff?" Carlander asked.

"Don't want to be pushy," the convict said.

Carlander thought about it. "That's it? Thought it wouldn't look right?"

"Yeah."

The cop nodded his head. "Okay. Lot of things we're doing we got to do by feel." He was quiet for a moment, then said, "See anybody around looked interesting? Besides Bruno?"

"Naw," Mowery responded.

"Vicky?"

"No way to get much feeling where we were," Victoria said dryly. She and Mowery exchanged looks.

"Bud and I got license numbers," Carlander said. "About five bikes we're gonna run, plus a couple cars. We keep putting people and machines together, Cliff, someday we start to make some interesting matches."

"Real police work," Nease said.

"That's right. Remember names," Carlander reminded his charges. "Always remember names. Street names, real names, any names. Give 'em to me and I'll run 'em." Carlander had little insights to offer on today's assignment but always came away with something by making routine a virtue.

Mowery twitched a smile.

"Anybody hear the name Ray?" Carlander asked. The others shook their heads. "Well," Carlander continued, "probably a lot of Rays, but keep your ears peeled. We find Ray and we might get us a factory. Then we all go to heaven. Guaranteed. Tomorrow we pick up where we left off today. Drop into the San Francisco, Cliff, you and Vicky."

"Time?" Victoria wanted to know.

"Let's say eleven. We're gonna be up late every night, so there's no sense starting too early." Carlander and Nease would be up and at work early but would not join Victoria and Mowery in the field until midmorning.

Victoria arrived home a few minutes before ten that night, at the end of what would prove an unusually short workday. She opened their back door leading in from the carport and was at once struck by a delicious smell of garlic toast. Immediately her mouth watered. She had drunk coffee all day but had not eaten much solid food.

"Hi, you righteous bitch," Bill laughed. "That's what they call you now, right?" He had a candlelit table set with salad, pasta, and red wine. Garlic bread occupied a wicker basket on the table. Without speaking, Victoria put her arms around him.

"What a man to come home to," she murmured. "And real food, too."

"I figured you were probably tired from beating up other gangs with chains, popping wheelies and stuff. Or whatever you gang members do," he said, pulling out a chair for her at the table.

"Whatever we do can be wiped away with good wine," Victoria said as she tasted the delicate Pinot Noir.

He kissed her on her still-wet lips. "What do you do all day? Typical biker day, I mean."

"I'm not really sure," she said, falling heavily into a chair. "Some of them have jobs, I guess. This was our first real day in the field and nothing much happened."

"Expect to see a crime happen every day?" he wondered aloud.

"I guess we do. We look around for a drug buy," she said. "When somebody sells us the stuff, we bust him. Or her. No, actually, we don't bust them right away; we make two and sometimes three buys. Qualifies them as a dealer that way. Anyway, that's the plan. I haven't pulled one off yet. How long have you been waiting dinner?"

"Got home at seven," Bill said.

"I love you," she said.

"You have every reason in the world," he agreed.

"And I'm glad you know how to cook." She was feeling bone-tired. Her nerves continued to jangle even after she was safely at home, where she was out of sight and hearing of suspicious people who would kill her if they knew who she was. Tension created a dull pain between her shoulder blades. Her drift from middle-class security had begun.

Carlander was still at his desk at the OCSO narcotics squad room at midnight catching up on neverending paperwork. Official crime reports were kept on each contact or drug suspect. Each crime report was underpinned by a surveillance report that recorded precise times that contacts were made, drug deals went down, other crimes were observed. Every surveillance report was annotated in minute-by-minute chronology so that when indictments were drawn up it would never be one investigator's word against a suspect's, but corroborated by a second and even a third officer of the undercover team.

Simultaneously, each investigator kept a personal diary of every facet of his or her operation for the day, every person contacted, every license plate run through the records computer, every name mentioned by any suspect that was checked out. Diaries were written in a kind of shorthand so that if the book was lost or stolen, it would be of little value except to its author.

He left the station after midnight, drove back to Mitchell Street near Edinger, and parked his truck where he had a view of Mowery's motel. He methodically worked his way through two bags of sunflower seeds and started on a third. By three o'clock he decided that Mowery would sleep through the night. He closed the seed bag, started the engine, and drove to his apartment. He hadn't called his children because they were already in school when he awoke. He would try to spend the entire weekend with them, he decided.

He paused, thinking over what he was trying to protect his kids from. Everything grew easily in sunshine and the prospect of an easy life in Orange County, named after its most fecund crop, enticed families who flocked west to escape the drought of the thirties. But it was World War II that had ignited a California economy that exploded in the late forties and continued expanding. For a considerable time Orange County escaped Los Angeles's smoke-belching, smog-clogged arteries of commerce on streets and freeways. Its beaches lay white, pristine, just far enough out of the madding way to provide unequaled weather and attendant good living for its prosperous residents.

Santa Ana in 1950 had a population of only 15,000. Since that date it had become a city of over 400,000, and the metropolitan population of Orange County mushroomed from 176,000 in 1950 to 1.8 million in 1979.

The county flourished as an idyllic residential and resort area with just enough light industry to support a slower-than-L.A. population expansion. But citrus orchards were sold off, replaced by glass-fronted buildings erected by international corporate giants who sought to provide a clean living and working environment for employees yet remain close enough to the financial markets of Los Angeles to be convenient.

In the late fifties upwardly mobile black middle classes found affordable homes in Cypress, Los Alamitos, Garden Grove, Stanton, and Fullerton. White flight followed, creating the first outlines of erosion around shores of entrenched communities of Anglos. When African-Americans settled in those same communities in the late sixties, Latino ethnic groups, never easy neighbors of blacks, moved farther north into Los Angeles County.

Predominantly white neighborhoods shrank into discrete communities. The abrupt end of the Vietnam War brought an

Asian influx in the eighties that changed the demographic character of Orange County dramatically. It became possible to drive for miles along main streets and imagine one was in a foreign country. While Vietnamese, Thai, and Japanese cultures brought a highly motivated immigrant dedicated to enriching American shores with unique art and commerce, it also created a tsunami of crime. Closed Asian gangs, insular because of their language, confounded Anglo police who were, and are, ill prepared to deal with people they could not understand either in language or customs. In June 1992 the *Los Angeles Times* reported that 51 percent of the Los Angeles population could not speak English.

The trend southward, toward San Diego via Orange County, became the number-one topic of conversation among any gathering of southern California's shrinking Anglo residents.

Old-money whites had retreated into revetments around coastal communities like Laguna Niguel, Newport Beach, Huntington Beach, and San Juan Capistrano. Within the central confines of the county are parts of Fullerton, Yorba Linda, and Villa Park, where affluence in the form of manicured lawns—cared for by minority labor—and upscale shops could still be found.

Everything seemed easier under the sun, including crime. There were tourists to fleece, racetrack patrons to hustle, beaches to prowl. Temperate nights obviated the need for accommodations requiring expensive heating. A blanket tossed anywhere provided enough comfort for sleep, while the very atmosphere people breathed in southern California reeked of party time, easy money, easy riding.

When Victoria and Carlander arrived at Mowery's motel, they knocked on his door without getting an answer. Mowery had been cautioned that when his telephone rang he was to answer no later than the second ring. They did not want him wandering down a hall where he might meet someone to deliver drugs to him or would in some other way find time to engage in a criminal enterprise.

"Hold it," came Mowery's recognizable voice from the other side of the door.

"Open up, Cliff," Carlander ordered. "Right now."

Still the door remained closed. Carlander was not a patient man, and he was suspicious. He inserted his duplicate key into Mowery's door and opened it.

Mowery was still in bed. There was something else inside the room: the maid's pushcart. The bathroom door was closed.

"She's cleaning the bathroom," Mowery said blandly.

"She forgot to take her uniform in with her," Carlander responded, equally bland. "Come on. You're late for work."

Victoria was dressed in jeans, white tank top, and navy-blue windbreaker with a red bandanna folded and tied around her blonde hair. She leaned against the chopper while Carlander and Nease waited in a plain car parked at a far end of the motel's parking lot for Mowery to make his appearance.

"Man," Nease said to Carlander as they surveyed the area. "That woman looks good."

"Yeah."

"We shoulda got a dog," Nease said.

"Huh?"

"We shoulda got a dog," Nease repeated. "To go out with those assholes. She looks too good."

"We didn't have a dog," Carlander said.

"He's going to jump her bones," the detective ventured.

"No, he isn't."

"How do you know?"

"Because he'll go back to the joint to do serious time. He knows that." Carlander thought it was obvious.

"That's very good, Carlander. We should spread the word. Break the law, go to jail. Get rid of crime that way."

"Shut up," Carlander said.

At Carlander's insistence Mowery and Victoria returned to the San Francisco Bar. The inside was dim, even at midday. Posters of motorcycles and their owners adorned the walls, along with pictures of women in various stages of nudity. Trophies won at motorcycle contests donated by their winners over the years rimmed the entire premises. There were two pool tables in the back and a small dance area along with tables and chairs by the bar.

Victoria sat at a table while Mowery bought two beers. The

clientele was a mixture of biker and working-class folks, all of whom were white. Outlaw biker gangs would not share space with minorities. There were fewer than a dozen men drinking beer and munching sandwiches. Victoria was the only woman. Often, she noticed, someone would look over a shoulder to appraise them, then turn back to his drink.

"Nice place, huh?" Mowery asked.

"If it has the right folks, I like it," she said, speaking as a cop.

Someone put money into a jukebox and strains of a Willie Nelson song caused Victoria and Mowery to raise their voices slightly to be heard.

"Like country-western?" he said.

"No."

"Not any?" he asked.

"Well," Victoria replied, "I admit that I haven't heard it all, but I think my answer would be pretty general."

"Good music," Mowery assured her.

"They sing through their noses for some reason," she said.

"That's style," he explained.

"I'll listen more carefully," she said dryly.

Mowery finished off his beer and bought another. He returned to their table. "Well, you're gonna hear a hell of a lot of it before we're through ridin' around together."

"What?" Victoria asked.

"Country music."

"Why do they wear those big hats indoors?" She was not really curious but felt she should try to see whatever Mowery and his coconspirators saw. "They don't even take them off when they eat. I've seen them in restaurants."

At first Victoria attempted to monitor the amount of beer he consumed. The last thing she and Carlander wanted was a confidential informant getting bombed on the job. They knew that everything that they said, every aspect of their conduct, was going to be examined in retrospect when arrests were made and they were called upon to testify in court. If they got that far.

Mowery almost defied belief. He did not appear to be drunk long after Victoria lost track of the number of beers he had consumed. After a while she gave up trying.

"Hey. Shane."

Mowery looked to his left to see a familiar face. "Tank. Hell, man, where you been?"

Mowery and Tank shook hands with elbows bent, hands clasped thumb to thumb. Tank was about thirty years old and wore a leather vest with no shirt underneath. His chest and arms were covered with tattoos, including the kind sometimes received in prison, where the work can be amateurish. His thin black hair hung straight and long, and when Tank removed the cigarette from his mouth Victoria could see that the upper lip was scarred. The effect was to give its owner an air of angry arrogance. "Been right here," Tank said. "Last six months, anyway. I know where you been, too. Hell you got going for yourself now?"

Mowery turned his back squarely on Victoria and faced the bar. It seemed to her that she was being removed from the conversation, a notion that Tank apparently shared. He turned away, too, and their voices became inaudible to her. To maintain her place in bikedom's male-oriented milieu, she had to sit, wait, and watch Mowery guzzle beer.

Within minutes a girl walked from the ladies' room and joined Tank and Mowery.

"This is Lisa," Victoria heard Tank say. "Baby, this is Cliff Mowery. Told you about him."

"Oh, yeah, he talks about you, Cliff." The girl appraised Mowery. "Yeah, God, you're just as big as Tank said."

Laughter.

"He's that big all over, better believe . . ." Tank chuckled.

"Guess I'll just have to believe what you two're saying," Lisa teased.

Victoria sat at her table watching the threesome at the bar enjoying a leisurely day of relaxation. She felt foolish, ignored. But was this the correct reaction for a biker's girl? She wasn't a biker's girl, she reminded herself. Her cover story was that she was from the other end of the social spectrum. She would therefore not be expected to act like a biker's moll would act. She made up her mind that it was important to stay within her own character, to rely upon who she perceived herself to be inside her cover story.

She rose, turned, and walked out of the San Francisco Bar without glancing in Mowery's direction.

Outside she walked east, a course that would bring her into Carlander's and Nease's view. She had gone only half a block when she noticed Bud Nease keeping pace with her on the opposite side of the street but not looking her way. She walked past a parked car with Carlander seated behind the wheel, his newspaper opened to the sports section. She turned a corner and slowed her pace as she heard a car engine start. Within a minute she saw Carlander's car coming toward her from around the block. It stopped and she quickly got inside. Nease occupied the front seat while Victoria slid low in the back for several blocks until Carlander was sure they were not being followed.

"What happened?" he wanted to know.

"He met somebody at the bar he used to know. White male, about thirty, name of Tank . . ." Victoria recited.

Nease jotted notes as she spoke.

"What'd he look like?" Carlander probed.

"Stringy black hair," she said, picturing the man in her mind. "Crushed upper lip that didn't heal very well. Black velvet hat with a feather sticking out of the band. Jeans, boots, leather vest."

"Any club sign on the vest?" Nease asked.

"No," she said. "Picture of a grinning werewolf with blood dripping from its mouth, but I didn't recognize a club and there wasn't any printing on it. Cliff turned his back so I couldn't hear them talk. Then a girl joined them . . ."

"Name?" Carlander asked.

"Sounded like Lisa but I'm not sure." She did not want to guess.

"Ever see her before? At the jail, maybe?" Carlander was alert for women who had done time in County Jail when Victoria was assigned there. The world of criminals is a small one; the women's world is smaller yet.

"No. Anyway, I sat there waiting, but Mowery didn't introduce me. I felt that he never would, so I left," Victoria finished.

"Hmmmm."

"It was the right thing to do," she asserted.

"Okay. No argument," Carlander agreed. "Here's a key to

Mowery's place. Meet us there. Bud and I will go back to the bar and wait for him to come out."

Victoria paced Mowery's room, stopping only to stub out a cigarette, then, to her own disapproval, lighting another one. She was acutely aware of the disgust in which smokers were held by nonsmokers. She stabbed the hardly smoked butt into a tin ashtray and then, feeling guilty lest she appear a weak addict to Mowery, dumped the contents of the ashtray into his already overflowing kitchen garbage container. She wanted to empty the damn thing, to tidy up, but she refused to help Mowery to avoid even this simple chore. If he was ever to stay out of jail, he would have to learn to take responsibility for himself.

She heard the snarl of the Harley more than a block away. She was looking out of a window when the big convict leaned the bike over, gunned his way across four lanes of traffic, and arrived at the entrance to his parking lot inches ahead of oncoming cars. He raced the engine once again, the last infusion of power enough to catapult him smoothly toward a parking slot near his room.

As Mowery slowly, gracefully dismounted from his chrome and stainless steel steed, Victoria saw Carlander and Bud Nease bouncing in their Orange County undercover car. Carlander parked in the middle of the lot among other cars. When he and Nease were certain they had not been followed, they opened their doors and walked quickly toward the motel room.

Victoria said nothing as Mowery entered, Carlander and Nease shouldering their way inside two steps behind.

"Sit down," the detective snapped.

Victoria wanted to sit as though in reflex to an order issued by her father when he was angry. She realized in time that Carlander was addressing Mowery. The convict leaned defiantly against his vinyl-covered table.

"What the hell's going on?" Carlander said.

"What do you mean?" Mowery asked, his eyes not meeting Carlander's.

"What I mean is, you turn your back on your partner, Vicky here, blocking her out of a conversation you're having with one of your old buds. That's what I mean about what the hell's going on." Carlander's anger was always out front. He wanted people to know what they had done that disturbed him. And it was intimidating.

"Hey, she's the one who left. I can't do much if she . . ." Mowery began.

Carlander cut him off. "She left because you made her look bad. Don't play innocent shit with me, Mowery. You can't insult a class lady in public and expect her to take it. You know better than that."

"She's uptight, man," the parolee insisted. "She walks in the place with her nose in the air, everybody sees her nose up there, thinks what the fuck is she doing with a chopper rider, like I am, and she wants everybody in the place to kiss her ass. She doesn't like Willie Nelson. You know that? She's the first person I ever met, man or woman, didn't like Willie Nelson. C'mon. She's got to put out, too."

Victoria and Carlander shared glances, then looked back at Mowery.

"And you're not doing shit to make her feel welcome in the bar. Listening to me? She's not at home in places like this. That's part of the cover. She's not your get-down biker girl. You know that, so don't dance with us." Carlander knew that everyone, especially Mowery, would need attitude adjustments as the operation went along. The beginning was crucial so that rules and techniques were understood.

But Mowery had a point, Victoria realized. She understood that Carlander could not afford to let Mowery win the argument, could not cut him any slack, but it was certainly possible that she had seemed hostile at the San Francisco.

"Who's Tank?" Carlander changed the subject.

Mowery shrugged. "Just someone I know. Used to know."

"Last name?"

"Don't know. Just Tank is all we ever called him," Mowery said.

Carlander considered. Mowery could be telling the truth. It was entirely normal for biker associations to be carried on for years with neither party knowing the other's legal name, first or last. "You ride with him?"

"Sometimes. Not a lot." Mowery shrugged.

"You holding anything back?" Carlander was sure that he was.

"Like what?" Mowery challenged.

"Like he's an old buddy of yours, and maybe you don't want to see him get into trouble. What's he do for a living? Carlander studied Mowery's face to detect the slightest movement or tic that would show he was lying.

"Why don't you ask him what the hell he does for a living? I didn't have time 'cause she's staring at my ass and you're trying to peel off what's left. Her, then you. Too much, man," Mowery said in a low, even voice.

"Don't push me," Carlander said, sensing that this encounter was headed for a showdown.

Mowery rose, fists doubled. Carlander rose, jutting his face toward the convicted felon.

"Don't do nothing here," Nease put in nervously.

"Let's go outside," Mowery said.

"Let's go." Carlander followed Mowery out of the door.

By unspoken mutual agreement the two huge men walked purposefully around the motel and stood in an alley. They turned to face each other, Mowery hunched in a coiled position to throw a kick. Experienced street fighters seldom use their fists. A kick delivers more force, far more damage. But Mowery could see that the cop was not preparing for battle. Mowery could see something else in Carlander: He betrayed no signs of fear.

"Take care of yourself, asshole," Mowery snarled as he moved toward Carlander. The cop did not move, did not change his expression.

"So what are ya gonna do? Shoot me?" Mowery said, still tense.

"Nope. We're gonna bang it out after you take your best shot. I'll handle myself. Then you go right back to the penitentiary. Express."

The parolee's face turned white, his lips the same color. Carlander knew that Mowery was now at his most dangerous. Someone whose face is red is not yet a serious threat. When battle tension begins to mount the parasympathetic cortex rapidly sends blood to parts of the body that may become wounded in the upcoming battle. During this process a person is not yet ready to strike. The real danger comes when the same automatic command system prepares to minimize trauma where the body might be torn. So it "holds" blood in place. Hence, whiteness.

Then color slowly began to return to Mowery's face. Prison. That was the magic word.

Carlander bent over and picked up several stones. "See that telephone pole?"

"Yeah," Mowery grunted.

"Best out of five." Carlander hefted his rocks.

Mowery picked up a handful of rocks. "I'll go first."

As Carlander had guessed, Mowery was a good athlete, with a better than fair arm. He was not surprised that Mowery missed on the first four tries, however. On the fifth throw he hit the wooden utility pole.

"Just barely," Carlander said as he stepped up to take his turn. The first missed. The second missed. The third missed. He flicked a glance in Mowery's direction to see the convict struggling to keep a smile from his face. Carlander used a slight windup and this time nicked the pole. His brow no longer sweating, he threw his last stone and grazed the pole.

"There," he said, greatly relieved.

"Luck."

"Wasn't luck. I used to be a pro," Carlander reminded him.

"Barely hit it both times." Mowery was smug.

"That's like barely winning the World Series," Carlander pointed out. "Or barely winning the Super Bowl. See what I'm saying? Winning is winning, losing is losing, and you lost."

Carlander and Nease had seen Tank when he exited the bar.

"Son of a bitch was lying," Nease observed about Mowery when Carlander, Victoria, and he met at a Sizzler restaurant that night. "See his tats? This dude Tank was a Diablo, man, and we know Mowery rode with the Diablos."

"We don't have a choirboy," Carlander said. "Don't want one. Not saying anything like that. Hell, look at me, I'm the nicest guy I ever met and I tell lies sometimes, but I don't lie to my partners, no fucking way, man."

"He's not a partner," Victoria observed.

"Bullshit," Nease put in. "You work with a CI like Mowery, going out on ops, you gotta trust him. Tips are one thing. Tip's a tip. But when you go through a door together, man, you got to know this dude ain't shooting you a line of bullshit. What time is it?"

"Why?" Carlander asked.

"My daughter's birthday," Nease explained.

"So? She has one every year, doesn't she?" Carlander said.

"Yeah, and she wants her daddy there," Nease said defensively.

"Kids aren't supposed to get everything they want, Nease," Carlander said. "You give kids everything they want and they grow up thinking they ought to have everything. Thing to do is show your kids some goddamn disappointment once in a while so they'll grow up realistic about the world. Probably what happened to Mowery. Spoiled as a kid, probably. Grows up thinking he can have anything he points his finger at. Pretty soon the finger's a gun."

"My kid's six and she hasn't robbed a bank yet," Nease pointed out.

"How do you compare Bud's baby girl with Mowery? I think that's lame, Carlander," Victoria observed. She was fatigued herself.

"I gotta go," Nease said, leaving abruptly.

As Carlander tried to catch the eye of a waitress, Victoria asked, "Are you worried about Mowery?" She was. She had re-read his police records for at least the tenth time. And she had made discreet calls, queried people who knew him. She was more than curious about the man into whose hands, Carlander's promises notwithstanding, she would put her life.

Clifford Mowery's father lived in South Gate, in Los Angeles County. A man of limited education from a rural community in Arkansas, Jack Mowery worked as a heavy equipment operator for a machinery company in El Monte, where he was considered dependable. He always showed up, always worked hard. He was well enough thought of that he had always gotten his son rehired by the company when he was released on parole or termination of sentence from various youth institutions, jails, and eventually prisons. Clifford's mother, also from Arkansas, had once been an attractive woman. She was quiet, forever vexed by an only son who seemed rebellious and mean for no reason that she could fathom. She was mystified that a boy provided an adequate home could hand out such a heavy load of misery to everyone he met.

Nor could Mrs. Mowery understand why her married and divorced daughter, Roseanne Claxton, who should have been more mature at twenty-seven, would be a biker's girl. She was living with a man called Dago Paul, who was a member of the Hell's Angels, a man whom not even Clifford trusted. Mrs. Mowery could not ask Diane questions about Dago Paul or what his real name was without sending the girl into a tirade.

Mowery also had a six-year-old son, Shane, whom he professed to love but hardly knew. Mowery, Victoria knew, solved all of his problems with booze, drugs, or fists. It was one thing to say that he loved his son but not enough to stop drinking, fighting, and stealing long enough to present a positive role model. Victoria didn't expect Clifford Mowery to compare with Bill Decker, but how would he act if their lives were on the line?

Elaine, Clifford's ex-girlfriend, was an exceptionally attractive woman who had been unfortunate enough to be drawn to Mowery's animal magnetism like countless other women. Yet he treated her no differently from them, which was disdainfully, even abusively, especially when he was drinking.

"So, tell me. Are you worried about Mowery?" Victoria repeated.

"He's stroking us. Trying to see how little he can do and still stay out, ride the bike, party, eat a doughnut for breakfast. That's his life. I'll wait, then I'll land on him with both feet." Carlander sounded certain.

"I'm going home," Victoria said, suddenly struck with utter exhaustion.

"We've got reports to fill out," Carlander protested.

"I'm too sleepy tonight. 'Bye, Carlander." She rose from the table, moved wearily toward an exit.

"You'll be too busy in the morning. Then you'll be too busy tomorrow night. Then the first thing you know . . ."

*It's Carlander's call,* she thought as she drove home, *but unless Mowery has a change of mind and attitude, the operation might be over before it starts.*

# CHAPTER 5

Victoria had been assured by Carlander that she was doing a good job. Yet she was new to the game of undercover and she felt that every move she made around Mowery's underworld contacts was forced, perhaps clumsy. She was self-conscious. She wondered if she would ever feel at ease in an intensely male environment.

Several days went by while Mowery drank beer with some old running buddies and some new. Victoria continued not to be privy to conversations involving drug deals, auto thefts, arson, and extortion. She debated about reporting this feeling to Carlander, but she decided to keep her own counsel. She would give Mowery more time.

Carlander was of two minds as well. Though he was willing to be patient while his undercover team socialized, he was disappointed with their progress. He said as much to Mowery. "It isn't looking too good, Cliff."

The convict looked up from hot cereal and a powdered doughnut he was eating in a corner booth at the Kit-Kat Kafe in Anaheim. "What isn't?"

"Whole thing. Maybe I was wrong," the detective lamented theatrically. "I thought we'd be onto a whole lot of junk by now. Hell, these guys aren't clean, I know, but before we started hanging around with you me and Bud were making buys every day. Right, Bud?"

"Yeah. Sure were," Nease confirmed.

"We could set Victoria here up with street hypes," Carlander said, dismissing Mowery's value to the project.

"Damn, you gotta give it some time, man . . ." Mowery said.

"Up to me, I'd say sure, take all the time you need," Carlander mused aloud, "but Gates thinks we're going nowhere. Maybe he's right. Maybe we ought to wrap it up."

"Wrap? Ah, what about me? I mean, I thought we had a deal," the parolee argued.

"We do, Cliff. And I damn sure intend to put in a good word for you." Carlander glanced at his watch.

Victoria and Bud Nease exchanged looks. She was not as familiar with Carlander's psycho-ploys as Nease. She was not familiar with Carlander at all, as far as that went.

"Saw a hell of a picture last night," Nease said to Victoria. "*Rocky*. Seen it yet?"

Victoria shook her head. "No."

"Good picture. About a fighter. Nobody. Sleazy asshole but he kills himself to, you know, get to fight the champ." Nease picked at his breakfast plate.

"I don't like stories about fighters," Victoria said.

Mowery stopped chewing his doughnut. "I got the name of a dealer. Got it last night," he said.

"Who from?" Carlander asked.

"From, ah, Little Dee," Mowery answered.

"Who's Little Dee?" Carlander wanted to know.

"You seen it yet, Carlander?" Nease continued talking and pushing his food absently. "Huh? This Italian guy, the actor, they say he's a pretty good fighter, too. Like, really, I guess. Big enough, looks like. But he could be wearin' elevator shoes like Alan Ladd used to do."

"He's, ah, a guy I met at the Backdoor. You know him." Mowery turned toward Victoria for confirmation. She shrugged her shoulders.

"What's the seller's name?" Carlander asked.

"Name is Link," Mowery said.

"Connected to a biker club?" Victoria asked with awakening interest.

"I like fight pictures," Carlander said to Nease as though hearing him for the first time.

"Want to go?" Nease asked Carlander. "I'll see it again. We can go today."

"Toros. Good club," Mowery said almost desperately. "Lives in Huntington Beach. We could do him right now. Okay?" he said with a sense of urgency.

All eyes shifted to Carlander. He pursed his lips. "I guess. Hell, I don't have orders to wrap it up yet. Just letting you know ahead of time. Me and Bud'll follow."

Victoria and Mowery rode to Huntington Beach while Carlander and Nease trailed behind. On this day Carlander used Colorado license plates on his unmarked car. As usual, it was an uneven struggle for Carlander to weave his way through traffic while Mowery used the chopper to run between lines of cars and trucks. But Carlander, too, was known to be wild behind the wheel of a car.

He watched the two contrasting figures, a beautiful blonde, finely chiseled nose, high cheekbones, straddling the saddle of a roaring chopper driven by a hulking, tattooed man whose hair was as long as his woman's, wearing greasy jeans and an open denim jacket with sleeves ripped off. The two attracted attention from pedestrians as well as other drivers as they wove through traffic. They seemed to personify what was normal in southern California, a place that daily redefined outrageous.

Mowery had no trouble finding Banff Avenue in the beach town. He parked his chopper in an alley behind a bank of lower-middle-class apartments. As he and Victoria stepped off the bike and began to look for an apartment number, they became aware that they were not alone in the alley. Victoria was already nervous. She spun in the direction where she sensed another person. A young man, barely in his twenties, reed-thin, neat and clean, but with darting eyes, was watching Mowery and Victoria attentively.

"Looking for somebody?" he asked in a voice on the verge of cracking.

Mowery eyed the young man, quickly sweeping the alley for others who might be about. He saw no one else. "Fuck's it to you?"

The young man smiled. He was used to Mowery's type. "If you're lookin' for Link he's not around."

"Where is he?" Victoria asked.

"Out of town a couple days. We're feeding his cat," the thin young man said, apparently not affected by the biker's aggression.

Mowery moved toward his chopper. "Okay," he mumbled.

"I can help you with a buy," the young man said. "My name's Danny."

Mowery glanced at Victoria, then back to the young man. "All right. Whatcha got?"

"Depends on what you want. How 'bout some white powder?" Danny asked.

"How much?" Victoria wanted to know.

"Eighty-five," Danny said.

"That's high, man," Mowery said.

"Because it's good stuff. Shit you get on the street's stepped on more than the sidewalk," Danny said matter-of-factly.

Victoria was certain that Danny was a cokehead himself and that eighty-five dollars per gram reflected his upscale commission. "Okay," she said. "Where is it?"

"I don't keep it here," Danny said. "I can get it."

"Where?" Mowery asked.

"Close. You can wait upstairs. My lady's there. It's cool. Okay?" the surf druggie offered.

Mowery nodded. Danny led them around a corner and up two flights of stairs to an apartment at 314 18th Street.

The apartment was clean and neat, but almost bare of furnishings. Danny introduced Victoria and Mowery to Carrie, a wraith of a girl about Danny's age. The dealer snatched the cash from Victoria's hand, promised he would be back soon, and left the apartment. Carrie smiled as they occupied a sofa, one of only three pieces of furniture in the living room. Without offering her guests food or drink, she took a chair near them, folded her hands in her lap, and sat quietly. Victoria sensed that Carrie not only felt herself to be the guarantor of Danny's return but that she had been through a similar routine many times.

"You're cops, aren't you?" Carrie said, startling Victoria.

"No. No, we're not cops," she responded.

"Oh, that's good," Carrie said, her desolate smile still fixed. "Danny got busted a while back. Two pounds of grass."

Danny was back in less than ten minutes. Victoria had timed it. He likely had not left the apartment complex, and if he had, Carlander, watching outside, would have seen him.

He turned over a double-strength Baggie containing white powder, which Victoria tasted on her tongue but declined to snort. Danny urged them to call again, gave them his telephone number, and reminded them that he was in business anytime.

In a Bob's Big Boy restaurant Victoria turned over the evidence to Carlander, who tagged the bag.

"Kid's name was Danny. License number on his car was ULU-344," Victoria recalled from memory.

"Run that number, Bud," Carlander said to Nease, who slid out of the booth in search of a telephone.

"Looked like a juvenile delinquent to me," Victoria said.

"Wasn't the dude we were after," Mowery said. "Link. Remember that name I gave you? That's the dealer. This kid Danny, he intercepted us because Link wasn't around, he said. So, hell, you know, it was a pretty good backup bust. I figure."

"We'll wait a few days, week or two, we'll make another buy from him. If Danny's in the business with both feet . . ." Carlander opened his hands.

"Let's try for Link tomorrow," Victoria said.

"Suits me," Mowery agreed.

"That could be one," Carlander allowed as he bit into a hamburger. "One, but we gotta have more. Two, three a day. We're hanging out plenty. Party every night for you, Cliffie. Me and Bud sit in alleys while you party, and that gets old fast. I lose interest. Make that guy Link one for tomorrow and then try to have a couple more."

"Balls. Three? You don't want much, man," Mowery said.

"We're tying up a lot of manpower." Carlander pointed out the obvious.

Bud Nease returned. "Car belongs to Edward Philip Spooner, age twenty. He's got a sheet but only one conviction because most of the busts were old ones. He was booked once six months ago for possession of marijuana along with Janet Naomi Royster, nineteen. Sound like the girl?"

"Yes," Victoria said. "Carrie was the name."

"All right," Carlander agreed, hitching up his pants. "You two go ahead of me and Bud. Tomorrow we'll park up the street from Fat Albert's in Bolsa Chica. Say, one o'clock. Hey, Cliff. Two."

"I'll try, man," Mowery said.

"Two," Carlander repeated.

Victoria led the way out of the restaurant. She zipped up her windbreaker while Mowery swung himself into the saddle and kicked the starter pedal.

"Turkey's a mess. Never saw a cop wasn't," Mowery said of Carlander. "Worst than most."

"He's one of the best. Maybe the best." It was no effort for Victoria to support Carlander. Watching him operate every day was an education.

"That's your opinion," the convict grumbled.

"Professional opinion," she corrected.

"Yeah? Well, I'm giving you my professional opinion," Mowery snapped.

"Your professional opinion isn't worth much. Not about Carlander. Or any other cops." Victoria could feel her temper rising.

"You don't think so?" Mowery gunned the engine, let in the clutch, and effortlessly laid the bike over into a flow of traffic. They made two lights through Fullerton before they had to stop.

"Life I live's exciting," he said. "Last car I had was a Porsche. New one. Did you know that? Hundred and sixty miles an hour that car would go. I spent more money in six weeks than you're gonna make in two years busting hypes and saluting faggot suits and calling them sir."

Victoria raised her voice, her mouth close to his ear. "You had so much excitement you decided to take some time off to rest up in Soledad."

The light changed to green, and four lanes of cars stabbed accelerators at the same moment, cutting off conversation. Mowery screamed out in front of all other traffic, made a sharp righthand turn, and roared down a side street past a city park. He made a left and rode three more blocks until yet another red light held them up.

"Price of living your life. Oughta try it sometime," he said.

"I don't call doing time in a six-by-ten-foot cell, staring at a wall, the right price," Victoria sniffed.

"What do you know about time?" Mowery sneered. "It's not what the big hand's on and what the little hand's on. That's not time. Time is what you're doing when you do it. Time's different for everybody. I don't do time like you do time. You know who does time pretty good? Carlander. I'll say that for the son of a bitch. He's on the edge. No back-down in that dude."

Victoria could see definite similarities in Carlander the cop and Mowery the lawbreaker. They were both big, macho, and, in a perverse way, in the same business. They clearly enjoyed living on the edge and they both enjoyed the violence connected with crime that was never farther away than the next dealer or the next thief. She was not yet comfortable in Carlander's world and she was acutely aware that she did not fit in Mowery's. Unlike her two undercover companions, she was frightened.

Victoria arrived home a few minutes after 1:30 that morning. The neighborhood, newly developed tract homes with professionally planted saplings placed symmetrically along pristine sidewalks, was absolutely quiet. Inside their house of eight months, Bill had long ago gone to bed. He would have almost half of his workday completed by the time she awoke around eight hours later. She quietly opened their bedroom door, hoping that by some chance he would be awake and they could talk. But Bill was lying on his side, apparently asleep. With her new schedule she had not seen him for three days. She felt a pressing need to talk with him. Yet she couldn't wake him up every night, she reasoned, and she knew that this would not be the only night she would want him but not have him.

\* \* \*

Victoria had no appetite the following day. Instead she had butterflies in her stomach, which had replaced food as the morning norm. She stuck with black coffee.

Mowery had a buy set up, he told Carlander, Victoria, and Bud Nease at a coffee shop.

"Yeah? Who?" Carlander asked.

"Bobby, they call him. He could be big," Mowery said.

Victoria watched him closely. She would be meeting the people he steered her to, and she wanted as much advance information about them as possible. Part of learning about them, she felt, was to study Mowery.

"You mean he's fat?" Carlander jabbed.

"You know what I mean," Mowery said, the corners of his mouth beginning to turn downward in what would become his normal daylong grimace.

"I don't know what you mean, but we're going to find out, Cliff. Where's he live?" Carlander seemed to be challenging Mowery. Victoria thought maybe that's what the biker needed.

"I'm supposed to call. Hang on." Mowery rose from the table and made his way to a public telephone.

"See," Carlander said to his team, "I worry about Cliff. He's short on American work ethic. He can only remember dealers when he's threatened."

"Gets old, too," Nease observed.

Victoria watched Carlander sip a glass of milk as she burned her tongue on hot coffee and yet another cigarette. She cursed herself silently for scalding her tongue.

"Ever think about quitting those things?" he asked.

"Every day," she said.

"Well?" Carlander pressed.

"Well, what?" Victoria knew what was coming and was already tired of the lecture.

"Why dontcha quit?" he pressed.

"Because I don't want to," she said dismissively. There was certainly denial in the way she used tobacco, but she would quit in her own time.

"Then why do you think about it every day?" Carlander needled.

Victoria chose not to respond.

"One hour," Mowery said as he arrived back at the table. "Place on 9th Street, Buena Park."

"Bobby?" Carlander asked, all business again.

"Yeah, that's his name," Mowery confirmed.

"Okay, Bud and I'll go ahead of you. Look the place over . . ."

"Problem, maybe," Mowery said.

"Yeah?" Carlander's tone was suspicious.

"His old lady did time at County. Don't know when so what I'm thinkin' is she could recognize Samantha Cook here."

Victoria felt the butterflies again. She would gladly step back from this buy but wasn't sure what kind of signal it would send if she was too quick to run. She waited for Carlander.

Carlander considered. "Ah, then you ride with me in the car, Vicky, let Bud make this buy."

Victoria felt a sense of relief, but she wondered briefly if replacing her in the overall operation could be accomplished with the same ease. She believed that the old saw that said no one is indispensable did not apply to her, at least in this case. She left Carlander to pay the bill as the foursome strolled into the restaurant's parking lot. "Better go in your car, Bud," she heard Carlander say. "Show up riding on Cliff's bike with him and you'd look a little funny. No problem with me, because I know you and Mowery here are straight, but . . ." Carlander chuckled at his own innuendo.

The area was lower middle class. Twenty years ago this had been a neighborhood of wage-earners who put time and care into their houses and their surroundings, but they had been replaced by ethnic minorities who were deprived of regular employment and did not tend lawns or paint their houses. Nease had been in a thousand places like it. Cars, sometimes five and six at a time, were parked on front lawns. Broken toys were left where they had been tossed by children.

Mowery turned the chopper into the address on 9th Street, put down the kickstand, and shut off the engine. Nease stopped his Camaro Chevy at the curb, got out, and joined Mowery. Robert Starks, "Bobby," strolled boldly down the walk in front of his house with a fistful of Thai sticks in a thin plastic bag. He smiled easily at Mowery, whom he recognized, unconcerned by the presence of Nease, who fit the company of Mowery and the neighborhood.

"This what you want?" Bobby asked.

Nease took the Thai sticks, removed them from the bag, and smelled them expertly. "How much?"

Down the block Carlander had arrived in a pickup truck. His hair was messy, hanging down one side to an ear, and he wore a denim workshirt and lightweight jacket. He seemed not to look in Nease's direction. Next to him, slumped into the seat of the truck, was Victoria. Carlander caught her profile out of the corner of his eye and stifled a laugh. She looked like a boy. She was wearing his navy blue knit cap pulled over her ears, bright blonde hair stuffed underneath. He watched for other vehicles cruising by lest Nease be set up. A lone Ford LTD, fifteen years old with four Chicanos inside, drove slowly past. The car slowed near Robert Starks's house but picked up speed again when the occupants' eyes focused on Mowery's intimidating presence and Nease's street-tough looks.

"Ninety-five," Starks was saying to Nease.

Nease counted out five twenties and handed them to Starks.

"You ain't got ninety-five? I got no five," the drug dealer said.

"No, man. What you got is it," Nease said, laid back and obviously unconcerned about the discrepancy.

"Then I owe you a nickel," the dope peddler said, relieved that Nease was easy to get along with.

"Cool by me," Nease said, pocketing the Thai sticks. "I like doin' business with a man at his house. Makes me believe he's goin' to be around. Next time you owe me."

"I can dig it." Starks turned to Mowery. "You Mowery, right?"

Mowery nodded his head without speaking. Then he said to Nease, "Let's go."

But Nease was in no hurry. "What else can you get?" he said to the pusher. "I got customers if the price is right. Coke? Mary Jane?"

"I could get it to you, yeah. Anytime, anyplace."

Nease judged Bobby Stark to be small fish but he could know people who weren't. "You take care," Nease said.

Mowery fired up his chopper, let the bike roll backward until it reached the street, then shifted gears and was gone.

Nease watched Mowery round the corner on the bike. He climbed into his car, pulled into the street, and as he drove on shot Carlander a look as though to say, I don't know where the hell he's off to.

Victoria was anxious to find out how the Starks buy had gone. She called Carlander's private number and got his answering machine. She left directions for Carlander and Nease to meet her at a greasy spoon appropriately called The Hangout on Chapman Boulevard in Garden Grove.

Once assembled, the group talked for thirty minutes about the day's activities, including the Starks buy and license numbers that Victoria had picked up while Nease did the buy. She also said that Carlander's surveillance had been barely adequate.

"We were too far away," she noted.

"Half a block. Less," Carlander said. "Close enough."

"How fast could you cover half a block if Starks pulled a knife? Or a gun?" The question was a challenge to Carlander, a very real concern about security.

"He isn't gonna pull shit," Nease said. "Starks is a punk."

"Punks don't pull guns?" she pressed.

"What're you going for, Vicky? We get much closer and the suspect sees us. There was never a problem. Right, Bud?" Carlander said.

"They were standing outside so we could see them easy," she said. "And nobody, especially Starks, is going to mess with Bud and Mowery. But it won't always be that way."

"We have to get closer?" Carlander asked incredulously.

"I think so." Victoria didn't simply want her hand held. She wanted to know what would happen when the balloon went up. She remembered Brad Gates warning that all undercover operations end sooner or later because they degenerate.

"Well, we can't," Carlander said with finality.

"Sometimes we could," Nease said, disputing Carlander.

Mowery offered nothing to the argument. He couldn't have cared less.

"That's what worries me," Victoria said. She wished she had

used another word. "Worried" sounded like a mother waiting for her kids to come home from the late show. She did not want to be tagged as somebody who had to be babysat.

Carlander looked around for a waitress who could refill his iced tea. Nease checked his watch. Mowery was disinterested, too, anxious to leave.

Victoria saw three people enter the restaurant, two men and a woman. They were tattooed, including the woman, and they wore the biker's uniform of jeans, denim vests, boots, and Buck knives in sheaths attached to their belts. The dining area of The Hangout was built in an L shape, with a salad bar bisecting the room.

"Don't turn around," she heard Carlander say in a conversational tone across the table. "They're Hessians." She had seen them, too. Were they at Trabuco Canyon when Carlander arrested the entire gang? She watched the motorcyclists as they sauntered into the room and seated themselves at a table. *They must have seen Mowery's chopper outside on their way through the front door,* she thought, mentally kicking herself. She should have had him park in the rear of the building. The butterflies in her stomach were back.

The newly arrived bikers glanced around the room, expecting to see one of their own: whoever owned the chopper out front. The back of Mowery's head could be seen from their vantage point, but Victoria was not visible to them. If they were to use the restrooms before leaving, and Carlander was certain that they would, they would pass right by the table.

"Are you sure? They flying colors?" Mowery asked in reference to club identification.

"Yep," Carlander said as he slowly chewed his sandwich. It might be that these riders would not know Mowery, but they would almost surely know him. For Mowery and Victoria to be seen in his company could be a disaster for the program at best and at worst the death of one or more of those seated at this table.

"What are we going to do?" Victoria asked.

Carlander shook his head. "In a half-minute I'm going to get up. I'm gonna stand by the table like I'm counting money. Nease slides out, stands next to me, facing me, back to the dudes. The dudes, maybe the girl, too, will look at me for a few seconds, then they'll look back to their food. I give the word, Mowery stands up behind me. I give the word again, you jump for that door there, Cliff." Carlander nodded toward an entrance to the kitchen. There was a tray and cart parked near the door. "Walk through the kitchen. Don't run. Vicky hangs around here for a while, until you're sure they're gone." Carlander raised his eyebrows toward Victoria. "Everybody got it? Okay."

Carlander slowly rose from the table, looked down as though studying the bill, reached into his pocket, and retrieved cash. He allowed his eyes to glance casually around the room, as though looking for a waitress. Then his attention went back to paying his bill.

Nease, on cue, slid out from the table, stood next to Carlander. He, too, glanced around the room. "They're looking . . ." Then he said, "Now."

Mowery rose, taking cover behind the huge cop, his belt buckle pressed against the small of Carlander's back.

"Wait," Nease said.

One of the bikers and the woman sat with their backs to Carlander, but the second man faced them. A waitress arrived at their table, obscuring his vision for a moment.

"Now," Carlander whispered. Mowery moved. He was exposed to the riders' view for less than a second and only from the rear. As the waitress shifted her weight from one foot to the other, the riders could see Victoria's table again. But this time Mowery was gone.

"Let's go, Bud," Carlander said. The two of them began walking toward the front, seemingly disinterested in the other customers.

Outside in the parking lot, they sat for five minutes until Victoria emerged. She walked at an oblique angle to Carlander's car, then stood near a street curb and the parking lot driveway. In a moment the roar of Mowery's chopper could be heard as he pulled up near her. She acknowledged to herself a surge of excitement, a reminder of a time when, as a lifeguard in college, she had plunged into the city swimming pool after a drowning child. She swung a shapely leg over the chopper's saddle behind Mowery and they were off.

When she had arrived home the night before, Bill was in bed, asleep as usual. It was hard to communicate.

She fell asleep watching television in a recliner. When she awoke it was morning. Bill was gone. Depressed, she wondered how Carlander did it. He seemed like a normal father while she, hardly into the job, was never seeing her husband.

Sunday was supposed to be Victoria's day off, but she was obligated to take her turn checking on Mowery. She drove by the Sixpence Inn before breakfast and checked the mileage on Mowery's motorcycle. It looked all right. She drove across town to where Wayne Carlander was watching his son playing a pickup basketball game. She knew he made it a point to watch his son's games as often as possible. She understood what Wayne meant when he said his son was destined for athletic stardom. He was almost as tall as his father and still a freshman in high school. He had been a 55 percent shooter from the floor in regular-season play, was fast, and could rebound with anyone in his high school league. Victoria caught Wayne's eye from the other side of the court but decided not to confirm that Mowery was still tucked into his room. She waved good-bye and left by a side door.

# CHAPTER 6

Mowery's ex-girlfriend called Carlander and insisted he come to see her. She was going to have Mowery put back in jail, she said as he sat on a worn sofa. She knew he had violated his parole, she said.

"I don't want him around me, understand? Huh? God, he's awful when he's drunk ..." She pushed at her hair, freshly curled at a beauty shop, and flashed gleaming nails.

"Has he been here?" Carlander asked calmly.

"Here, right in this damn house? Or the phone, or what do you mean?" she said, dancing around specifics. "He'll do anything. He'll try anything because he's nuts."

"He's not going to come here," Carlander said patiently.

"Why is he out, anyway? Parole, yeah, you told me. What kind of laws do we have ...?" the woman said in frustration.

Carlander observed that it was not possible to keep prisoners locked up forever.

"Did he say anything about me? What did he say? He'd die without me. He said that once ... And you know, I think it's true. He always comes back to me. Always." She brushed her breasts with both hands as though to clear them of breakfast crumbs.

Tough-talking though she was, good looks and strong sex appeal shone clearly through her overpainted skin. No wonder Mowery had gone for her. "He doesn't talk about his private life," Carlander said. Her breasts were ample, he thought. Not implanted. Got so everybody who could get a job waiting tables bought a new set of tits with their first paycheck.

"He must have said something," she continued. "Not that I give a shit. He's a pain in the ass. Wasn't always like that. He used to be fun. Did you know he's hung like a horse?" She suppressed a giggle. "Half the girls in school were trying to get his pants off, and the other half, you know, the rally-squad goody-two-shoes were sick that they weren't getting it from him but didn't have the guts to admit it . . . Looks good on a bike, doesn't he? But Christ, he gets boozed up and crashes through my door. Wherever I am he finds me. I don't tell him where I am and, hell, there he is."

"That why you called us?" Carlander asked her.

Carlander watched her carefully. He did not want this woman to make an official complaint to anyone about Mowery. Even a jilted ex-girlfriend could do more damage than a Hell's Angel.

"So, has he bothered you? You give me the word and I'll look into it real fast," Carlander said.

"People tell the son of a bitch everything, every goddamn thing I do somebody blows the fucking whistle to him . . ." she continued. " 'I love you, baby.' He tells me that and I say shit, Cliff, if you really loved me you'd get off that fucking bike and get a job, and I don't mean holding up a restaurant or knocking down a card game. Is that asking too goddamn . . . Not that I want him back. No way. Where is he now? He can call me, it's okay if you give him just my phone number, but don't . . ."

Carlander told her he would be in touch.

December 10, 1976. That night Carlander was not tired and had no one waiting up for him at his apartment, so he settled into a comfortable surveillance of Mowery's motel room. He had opened a bag of sunflower seeds, and he slid lower into the seat of his undercover car when, minutes later, the room door opened and the man walked outside. Mowery glanced around but did not spot Carlander, who was parked among other cars in an overcrowded lot, and approached the Harley. The keys to the motorcycle were in Carlander's pocket, but the detective moved his hand to touch them for reassurance. He watched while Mowery worked for a few moments on the bike, then rotated the starter pedal. The bike fired up.

"Hot-wired the son of a bitch," Carlander said under his breath. He started his car and accelerated quickly to cut Mowery off at the exit. The two men glared at each other for long moments.

"You getting out of my fucking way?" Mowery demanded.

He appeared to Carlander to be frustrated, but not yet determined to run the bike over the top of him. "Get off the bike."

"Big man," Mowery spat.

"Get off the bike," Carlander repeated.

Mowery seemed to consider his options. Without leaving the saddle, he pushed the bike slowly backward with his powerful legs. When the engine was shut down, Carlander pulled his car alongside.

"Where were you headed?" he said as he stepped out of his car.

"Had to get something." The convict's tone was truculent.

"What?" Carlander insisted.

"Cigarettes," Mowery said.

Carlander inspected the ignition of the chopper and his hand came up with loose wires. He considered his predicament. For Mowery to be out of his room was a violation of his parole contract. Not only that, he had tampered with the motorcycle, which did not belong to him and which he was forbidden to ride except with permission. But Carlander had known from the get-go that it would be like this.

"If you want to walk down the street for a pack, I'll walk with you," he offered, certain Mowery was lying about cigarettes. What he wanted more than anything else was to be able to run free, find his buds, maybe a woman. Anything but the company of a cop.

"Guess I could do that." Mowery tucked his thumbs into his belt and started walking, Carlander at his side. Both were aware of the intimidating sight they made on a nighttime street in the middle of gang turf. Side by side, their shoulders covered the entire sidewalk. They stepped with the assurance of men who had seen violence in most of its forms, who had received and administered pain, who therefore understood it.

"Ever play ball in school, Mowery?"

"Never spent much time there," the felon said.

"Oh, yeah, that's right," Carlander said in feigned recall. "Well, can't blame you for that. Nothing they teach you in high school gets you ready for knocking off liquor stores."

"Bet you went, though," Mowery snorted. "Must of got free lunches or something. Cops don't pay for a fucking thing."

"You're right about that, Cliff," the detective said. "As long as I can get free chocolate eclairs down at Lovelette's Bakery I'm never gonna quit the Sheriff's Office."

"No difference between me and you. Only thing is how much." Mowery looked away from Carlander, surveying the street scene.

"Ever hear of a cop stealing from a collection plate, Cliff? We had a cop did that. Stole money out of his church box. Wasn't but maybe ten bucks in the box and he hit it twice." Carlander laughed fully. Mowery slowed his pace and regarded Carlander for a long moment.

"You admit that? A cop?"

"Sure," Carlander nodded easily.

"All right." Mowery's eyes revealed triumph. "Then you admit it that cops are slimeballs. Like those freaks who get on television and tell old ladies to send 'em money so God will love 'em."

"What's wrong with that?" Carlander raised his eyebrows.

"What's wrong? Hell do you think, what's wrong? Fucking thieves is all they are," Mowery said.

"Victimless crime," Carlander said. "People who send in money are happy because they think God wants 'em to. Those guys in the robes with the choir and the flowers behind 'em, they're happy to get the money. Everybody's happy. Victimless crime."

Mowery laughed with Carlander, but he quickly sobered. "I

can maybe understand you being a cop. You're not smart enough to do anything else. But her . . ."

"Victoria."

"Yeah. Hell, if I had a body like hers I'd be rich in a week," Mowery said.

"That's a problem you got, Cliff. Price tags. I knew a guy once who said, 'What good are friends if you can't buy 'em and sell 'em?' "

"That's bullshit," Mowery said with what Carlander had come to see was his certainty that most issues are black-and-white.

"I don't bullshit. I have to lie sometimes, but I don't bullshit," Carlander corrected.

They continued in silence. Then Mowery asked, "So, where did you find her?"

"It's not like she was hiding and we tracked her down, Cliff. She joined the department. Applied." She didn't expect anything like this, though, Carlander admitted to himself.

"Yeah? What's her old man like? Must be an asshole," Mowery said, certain of his assessment.

"What makes you say that? To you everybody's an asshole."

"Come on," Mowery snorted.

"Come on, what? What's that mean?"

"You want your old lady running with these dudes?" Mowery turned to regard Carlander fully. "Woman looks like she does? Talks like she does? Been to college, you said."

"Yeah. Well?"

"Well? What kind of dickhead lets his old lady do that?" Mowery looked challengingly at Carlander.

"She's a cop. She's not out having a good time, Cliff. She's working."

"That's what I'm saying." Mowery was frustrated. "Would you let your old lady work at this shit? I mean, what kind of man would do that? He must be an asshole."

"As a matter of fact he's a great guy," Carlander said.

"You know him, huh?" Mowery was not willing to be convinced.

"Naturally," Carlander exaggerated. He had met Bill Seele at an OCSO picnic. "Great guy."

Mowery grunted in skepticism. "She was my woman, it'd be different."

"Like how? You guys would do things together?"

"Sure."

"You'd get her her own gun," Carlander envisioned. "Tape the grips so she wouldn't leave fingerprints because you care about her. You'd maybe get her a little bigger saddle for the chopper because you want her to be comfortable on those long trips out of town, away from the heat after a job. You'd teach her how to work on the bike so's you could drink a cold beer while she's setting the timing . . ." Carlander laughed again.

"Hey, come on now . . ." Mowery laughed, too, but then said, "You think it's funny, man, but what happens when the brothers want to do their thing? Huh? 'Hey, baby, initiation time for the club . . .' You want me to get near the big clubs, right? Inside, even. Well, nothing is for free, Carlander. Did you tell her that?" He seemed genuinely concerned as he waited for Carlander to answer.

The detective slowed his pace and turned toward Mowery. "I'm going to be there. All the time. That's not going to happen to her."

"I look like I got sawdust leakin' out of my ears, Carlander?" Mowery spat. "Who are you trying to shit? You may be big and ugly and maybe your mother tried to sell you to some nice Mexican family and couldn't, but even you aren't that dumb. You don't believe that your own damn self."

Carlander's face appeared frozen in the reflection of a nearby streetlamp. Then he said, "I told you before. I don't bullshit."

"You also said you lie," Mowery reminded the cop.

They arrived at an all-night service station where a clerk sat behind six inches of bulletproof glass. He passed a pack of Camels to Mowery through a small opening that received cash and credit cards. Cop and convict walked the six blocks back to the Sixpence Motel. As Mowery inserted the key into his door, he asked, "Got any kids?"

"Boy and two girls," Carlander replied.

"They proud of you?" Mowery sounded genuinely interested.

"I think so." Not because he was a cop, Carlander knew, but because he loved them and cared for their needs.

"I don't guess my kid thinks much of me," Mowery allowed.

"He's real young. Lot of time left for him." But would there be any time for the father? Carlander would not bet his pension that Mowery and his son would spend long, happy years together. Carlander wondered about life without his children. It would be bleak.

Mowery nodded his head and unlocked his door.

"Cliff," Carlander said, "tomorrow look for three buys."

"Three's a lot," Mowery objected.

"Naw, not a lot. Look for three."

It was almost 3:00 A.M. when Carlander arrived at his apartment. He showered and went to bed.

A few minutes before noon the next day, Victoria parked her car three blocks from the San Francisco Bar. She had arrived late, but Mowery was not there. She went to the ladies' room and did not hurry washing her hands and brushing her hair. She examined her makeup, what little she used, then returned to the bar. She tried to decide whether to order a beer, opting for coffee when she saw Bobby, the bartender, making a fresh pot. Before she could add cream, Mowery entered.

He slowly removed his sunglasses as he scanned the room purposefully, challenging everyone within. To Victoria he appeared to be the biggest cat in the jungle and, she had to admit, a beautiful animal. He saw her and sauntered across the room, fully aware that he was being watched by every pair of eyes in the bar. "Two," he said to the bartender. He pushed aside her coffee cup as the bartender provided two longneck bottles of beer. Mowery took a chair at Victoria's table and smiled. She was surprised at this touch of social behavior.

"I'd like a glass," she said, and waited. Mowery regarded her for a moment. He rose, stepped to the bar, and returned with a glass.

"Thank you," she said. She found herself comparing him with her husband. Bill was handsome, attractive, and intelligent. Intelligence was important, she told herself. Most important, Bill was thoughtful and caring. By contrast, Mowery was egocentric and arrogant. He had left a litter of broken lives on either side of him as he rolled along on life's stolen wheels. Like most cops,

Victoria was familiar with homosexuality behind prison bars, and she tried to imagine Mowery participating. It didn't seem possible.

"Big dude comes in here. Night Train. Heard of him?" Mowery asked, his eyes scanning the room as though she were of secondary importance.

Victoria shook her head.

"Got picked up in Paris, France, wallet full of American Express cards. Supposed to be selling 'em but he decided to use 'em instead. There he was, sitting on his fat ass on some famous street right there in Paris, bottle of expensive champagne in his hand saying to girls walking by, 'Hi, there, Cheree, wanna fuck?' Might've got laid, not on his good looks but because there are a lot of horny ladies in the world, Paris too, except he was a puke-looking turkey. Jeans hanging down around his ass, motorcycle boots, big chain on his belt, other end to his wallet full of American Express cards all with a bunch of people's names, sitting on the bench when the French buzz busted him. He's dealing again. We can make a buy."

"Do we travel to France?" Victoria said dryly, wondering if there was a point to all this reminiscing.

"No, hell, he's out now. Comes in here," Mowery informed her.

"Does he belong to a club?"

Mowery shrugged. "Don't know. Used to be," he said, signaling for another beer.

"Which one?"

Mowery shot Victoria a hostile glance.

An hour later, she was still nursing her first beer while Mowery had consumed at least a half-dozen. He was shooting pool in the bar when Bruno walked in. The motorcycle mechanic liked Mowery and went out of his way to be friendly with Victoria as well. She had made up her mind to take advantage of the situation by somehow striking up a conversation with him. She saw her chance when, after retrieving a beer for himself, Bruno turned to survey the room. His scan stopped when he saw Victoria. She smiled, and he walked over to her and sat down.

"Damn, girl," he said, "every time I lay eyes on you makes me think about how I could have Cliff there killed for fifty bucks. Then I'd swoop right in and offer my deep feelings of sorrow about your loss." Bruno laughed evilly. "Only reason I don't is 'cause I'm five bucks short. Borrow it from you?"

"Lots of days I'd put up the whole fifty. Keep checking with me," she said as she smiled.

"He used to ride with the Diablos, didn't he? How come he's not picking up with them again?" Bruno asked.

Victoria touched her beer bottle to her lips while she thought of a plausible answer. "He tells me that they don't have a strong club in Orange County. Says they're . . . pussies."

"Well, guess he'd know that. Man like that should have a club."

"Do you have one, Bruno?" Victoria asked.

"Yep. Called the Jungle Bunnies. Got to be black to get in, so I'm on the waiting list." He chuckled at his joke. Victoria joined him but was aware that he had avoided her direct question of club affiliation. She was careful not to insist on an answer.

"Did you close up shop for the day?" she said, wanting him to talk.

"Got Steve keeping the place open. I'm waiting here for Ray Glore. Know him?"

The name "Ray" caused a bell to ring inside her head but, as the group had said many times, there were a lot of Rays in Orange County and probably many who rode motorcycles. "Ray Glore? I don't think so."

"You don't think so. Well, if you'd met him you'd know. If you don't know, you don't know." Bruno's eyes held no humor.

"Who is he?"

"Runs a club, sort of. Into a lot of business." Bruno winked as though all things would be revealed in their time.

"Like what?" she asked.

Bruno shrugged. "Massage parlors. Sells some stuff."

"Sounds interesting," Victoria said, trying to sound impressed without being inquisitive.

But Bruno had said all that he would say about Glore. He suddenly seemed to remember who he was talking to and changed the subject. "Been a whole week since I've had your chopper in the shop."

"God, what's left to go wrong with it? Are all motorcycles this bad?" Victoria was genuinely aghast at the amount of time the chopper had been in Bruno's shop, which did not include the time Mowery had spent keeping it running.

"Harleys are all good. Some's just better than others," Bruno assured her. "Here's the man."

He abruptly rose from her table and moved toward the long bar. Although he attempted to look nonchalant, Victoria could tell that he was not. Her eyes swept beyond him toward the front door. Bright California sunlight blurred images as people entered the bar's darkened interior. After her eyes readjusted she could see that the new patrons were four in number and that one of them was a girl. The girl was in silhouette, as were two of the men. The fourth had his back to her. It was this man to whom Bruno gave his attention.

After several moments of conversation Bruno turned, looked to the back of the room, and called out. "Shane. C'mere, man. Want you to meet somebody."

Mowery leaned his pool cue against a wall, took up his bottle of beer, and walked languidly toward the bar. Bruno offered his hand in a palm-up position, interlocking thumbs. "You know Vern, here . . ."

Mowery nodded and spoke to Vern, who returned his greeting.

"And this is Ray Glore, Butch there behind him," Bruno said, completing the introductions without mentioning the girl in their company. Ray Glore was not as tall as Mowery but was well muscled in spite of evidence of dissolution at his beltline. He was dark-complexioned, and his bottomless eyes, Victoria thought at the time, sent a chill through her as they flicked over Mowery, then over her. He was asplike, with nostrils that seemed to sense the air around him. Victoria almost expected a forked tongue to flick through a slit that served as a mouth. During the following weeks Victoria would have more opportunities to watch Ray Glore.

The man scared her on sight, as he did most men. Victoria believed he was Indian. He was hard, intense in everything that he did, even in the way he moved. He did not speak much, but she noted that when he did it was in the form of a quiet command to which everyone around him listened carefully and obeyed without question. His eyes missed nothing, she thought. And he was always listening. So intuitive was he that Victoria's abiding fear when she was around him was that her face, by some involuntary gesture, would betray thought within her and he would read it correctly. She forced herself to meet his eyes, never a comfortable action for her.

Even Mowery was on guard. He was not easily intimidated, but Glore had a reputation for being more clever, far more evil, than his fellow bikers. He also had a reputation for a quick, fierce temper. Two Angels had spoken in hushed tones to Mowery about a girl who had worked in one of Glore's massage parlors. Believing she was turning tricks on his time, he slashed her with a knife, rendering her unfit for future employment. Glore was also fixated with guns, a fact that Victoria would learn for certain.

Neither Mowery nor Glore offered to shake. The two men nodded to each other, acknowledging wary respect, not friendship.

"Bobby," Glore said to the bartender, "bring Cliff another beer. Treat you okay up there?" he said to Mowery, revealing that he was well informed about everyone who mattered.

"Pretty good. Spent some time locked down. Makes you buggy, some," Mowery grunted.

"Mowery," the man they called Butch said, "hell, I remember you. You rode with the Diablos. We kicked your ass."

"You didn't kick my ass." Mowery's look fixed Butch squarely.

"Soledad, were you?" Glore interrupted.

"That's right."

Victoria knew Mowery was tense. He seemed resentful, antagonistic, and she did not understand why.

"We got a hack on our payroll up there," Gore said casually. "Delivers meth. Name's Pollard. Know him?"

Mowery was about to raise his bottle of beer but slowly put it down.

"Something wrong with the beer?" Glore asked.

"What's wrong with the beer is who bought it." Mowery's voice was low and menacing. "If there's a guard at Soledad name of Pollard they hired him yesterday. I don't like your ugly fucking face and I don't like the queer-looking asshole standing behind you, neither."

Sounds of pool balls clicking, glasses clinking, all conversation, stopped. Victoria's first thought was to summon Carlander and Nease, but she knew that she would not make it through the door without being restrained by Glore's bikers. Her thoughts turned to the gun tucked into her jeans behind her back, and even though she knew that practically every patron of the bar had some kind of weapon, she decided to use the gun before she let Mowery go down, certainly before hands could be put upon her.

Then soft laughter. Vern, moving easily to Mowery's side, patted him gently on the back. "Told you this man's got a short fuse," he said to Glore. "Hell, Clifford, lighten up a bit. Ray likes to check folks out his own way."

"I love it," Glore said through crooked teeth. "I fucking love it. You're right about Butch there being a queer."

The entire room exploded in laughter. Pool balls clicked once more, conversation resumed. Even Butch, not known to accept an insult even as a joke, took it meekly from Ray Glore.

Victoria expelled her breath at the release from tension, but a mild current went through her as she heard a reference to "Butch." She could not immediately put the street name together with police interest, though she was now certain that she was at last among the big league of biker gangsters.

She felt a hand on her arm and she turned.

"I'm Toni." It was the woman who had entered with Glore. Toni was young and sexy, with an air of self-confidence beyond her years. "Come on, I'll buy you a beer."

Toni led Victoria to a table and motioned to the bartender with her hand.

"I'm Samantha Cook," Victoria said.

The women appraised each other. Toni had dark eyes that matched long brown hair. Several inches shorter than Victoria, she wore jeans that appeared to be sprayed onto her hips. She wore a tank top that clearly flattered her full figure, and no bra. Men referred to her type, Victoria knew, as "spinners."

"You're not acting real smart," Toni said, matter-of-factly.

"Me? Why not?" Victoria felt the immediate clutch of cold in the pit of her stomach that was to become a constant companion the entire time she would spend around the Hell's Angels.

"Hanging around the guys," Toni said, her eyelashes fluttering theatrically. "Keep that up and somebody's going to find out who you are."

Victoria was surprised that when she opened her mouth, she sounded so casual. "That's no secret."

"Oh, yeah? Bet you paid seventy-five bucks for those jeans. Shirt's fifty and the jacket's another hundred. What're you doing in this shithole?"

"I'm with Cliff." Victoria was still trying to catch her breath, then shift mental gears while guarding against Toni's stilettolike probes. Immediately she began to inventory her clothing, wondering whether she had made a horrible mistake. She had tried to think of everything . . .

"So you're fucking the big stud?" Toni asked, looking toward the bar.

"I . . . I guess so," Victoria said, unable to keep the indecision of what to say from her voice.

"You guess so? He's sticking it halfway in?" Toni pinned Victoria with eyes that derived their authority from Ray Glore's power. Victoria realized that Toni enjoyed instilling fear in others.

She laughed at Toni's imagery. "Do you know Mowery?"

"Not yet. Bet he's got a dick that won't quit. Reminds me of Sonny," Toni said, reappraising Mowery from a distance.

"Sonny?" Victoria was not familiar with the name.

"Where the fuck have you been? He's president of the club." Toni turned her attention fully on Victoria.

"Oh, sure," Victoria said, feigning knowledge that she did not have. "I mean, I've never met him."

"Well, no shit, honey." Toni gave Victoria a particularly penetrating look. "He's been away for a while."

Although Victoria was cop enough to recognize that "being away" meant being in jail, she did not yet realize that Toni was speaking of Sonny Barger, national president of the Hell's Angels. He was doing time in Folsom Prison, convicted in 1973 of a host of criminal activities including extortion, loansharking, selling and receiving stolen property, and aggravated assault.

"Don't they have a new president?" Victoria asked, opting to take shelter behind her cover.

Toni snorted. "Shit, Sonny's the president now, always will be. What the hell difference does it make where he presidents from?"

*Interesting,* Victoria thought, *that Sonny Barger is still running a club from inside prison.* She felt sure this information would not be a revelation to police intelligence departments. Still, she would mention it to Carlander.

"How'd you meet him?" Toni asked.

"What?"

"Mowery. How did you meet the guy?" Toni rolled her eyes upward impatiently.

"Oh. In a motorcycle shop," Victoria said, trying not to swallow. "He was looking at bikes, scooters, he calls them, and so was I."

"You married, Sam?"

Victoria experienced a momentary chill. "Ah, no. Well, I'm going through a divorce." She remembered Carlander's urging not to volunteer information. The less of her story she revealed the less chance of mistakes.

"Yeah? Asshole got any bucks?" Toni's eyes remained fixed on Victoria's face.

"He makes a good salary. I miss it. Are you Ray's lady?" Victoria asked, wanting to turn the subject from herself.

"Yeah. Except I like to spread it around. He likes to make movies, too, so it works out." Toni smiled with what she intended to be humor.

"Really? The kind of movies you sell?" Victoria felt she was not thinking ahead, that she was a step behind the curve.

"Yeah. And I'm the star," Toni said, smiling.

"Who are the . . . actors? The guys?" Victoria asked.

"Angels, sometimes. I don't dig all the Angels, you know? So I don't do any of 'em I don't want to. Ray'd cut their nuts off."

"I guess Ray's pretty important in the Angels," Victoria ventured, relieved to be on a bit more solid ground.

Toni fixed Victoria with a look that alerted her once again that she had said the wrong thing, or had been too direct.

"Sam, let me have the keys to your car."

Victoria looked up to see that Mowery was standing at her side, hand out. She grasped at the opportunity to escape from her precarious situation. "I'll go with you," she said.

"Naw," Mowery insisted. "Me and Bruno's going for a ride. Be back real soon. You stay here with . . ."

"This is Toni," Victoria said.

"Ray's squeeze," Mowery acknowledged.

"More or less," Toni revised.

Victoria was caught in a no-win situation. She dared not demonstrate control of any kind over Mowery in public. So she remained sitting, concealing her frustration, as Mowery picked up her purse, extracted her car keys, and walked out the door with Bruno.

"You in the phone book?"

Victoria realized, with surging apprehension, that she was not in the telephone book. Nor was her fictitious estranged husband. Anywhere. "No, I . . . moved out. Why?"

"I might want to call you," Toni said, her eyes leaving Victoria's and taking in the room.

Victoria let out her breath slowly but wasted no time in finding a pencil. She wrote *Samantha Cook* on a napkin and added a telephone number. Carlander had a special phone line hooked into a room in the sheriff's office for exactly this kind of situation. It was answered by Lynn Young, an administrative assistant to the team. When Lynn was not available to take a message, an answering machine would pick up the call. As Victoria pushed the napkin toward Toni, she hoped that this was not part of a Hell's Angels identification process.

# CHAPTER 7

Mowery was now in the company of the heavy hitters of motorcycle gangs. He was clearly respected by Glore, Bruno, and other Hell's Angels with whom he had come in contact. Now he was expected to diligently use his position inside the Angels to turn them in to the law. This set up a powerful tug of war inside his mind. He wanted to stay out of prison but, in the process, was he prepared to rat?

It was argued later that Mowery was, after all, charged with the responsibility of infiltrating motorcycle gangs as fully as possible and was therefore not responsible for crimes he may have committed with them. There was no such thing as partial allegiance to the Hell's Angels. Full membership required that the prospective member become active in criminal life, even if only as an accessory to crime. But when did an accessory become a perpetrator? Carlander and others knew in advance that they would be faced with this dilemma sooner or later as Mowery spent more and more time with the gangs. Mowery had been a criminal since he was a juvenile. He had never expressed remorse for his victims, never given Carlander reason to believe that reform was part of his future plans. On the contrary, Mowery had revealed in words and deeds that a life of crime was his idea of a good time.

Shortly after Mowery left Victoria at the San Francisco Bar, she left as well. Walking down the street, she looked neither left nor right but appeared disinterested in her surroundings. She was confident that Carlander and Bud Nease would have her under surveillance. She crossed at an intersection and waited, as though for a bus. Carlander pulled up at the red light near her, and Victoria got into the car.

"He took the keys to my car and split," she said.

"How?" Carlander wanted to know.

"Picked up my purse and did it. I couldn't show him up in front of the others. He knew it. Bruno went with him." Victoria was not sure whether her decision to play the role of a biker's compliant woman was the right choice. Maybe she should have insisted that she go with her car.

"Know where he went?" Carlander asked.

"No."

"Shit," Bud Nease said. "Knew I shoulda watched the back door."

"I should've thought of that, too," Carlander muttered under his breath.

"So? What now?" Victoria asked.

"So we find him," Carlander said without enthusiasm.

"You're kidding," Victoria said. "You mean Bud takes five cities in west Orange County, I take the cities in the north and you get the rest?" She assumed there were times when one's losses were cut and the waiting game was played.

"Something like that," Carlander said.

"Well, not me," she said. "I'm going home."

"Good idea," Nease said.

"Not a good idea. He won't be there," Carlander contradicted.

"Take me home," Victoria said to Nease.

"Goddamnit, I won't have any mutinies," Carlander growled. "You're a flake, Nease. You're working, too, Victoria."

"No, I'm not, Captain Bligh. Let me out. I'll take a cab." Victoria was adamant. She was already two hours into overtime.

"Captain who?"' Carlander said.

"Bligh, man," Victoria snapped.

"I don't know him. Highway Patrol or something?" Carlander's face was blank.

Mowery and Bruno drove to a remote location in San Bernardino County, where Bruno received a number of military weapons from young men with flat-top haircuts. Mowery assumed they were Marines, possibly stationed at nearby Barstow Marine Barracks, the principal supply depot for Camp Pendleton and El Toro Marine Corps Air Station. The weapons consisted of semiautomatic rifles, grenades, and C-4 explosives. They were loaded into the trunk of Victoria's car, then driven to an address in Fullerton.

In appreciation for Mowery's help, Bruno supplied his muscled friend with a full ounce of methamphetamine. In addition, each of them snorted a line and Bruno opened a bottle of whiskey. Mowery drank most of it and left Bruno's house around ten o'clock. Bruno was in no shape to get farther than his own couch, upon which he collapsed shortly before Mowery drove off.

Mowery was suddenly gripped with the need for a woman. In explicit violation of his parole agreement, he tried calling his ex-wife. She was not home. Instead he contacted a girlfriend whose husband was pushing a ten-wheeler over the Rocky Mountains. They drank more whiskey together. But before they could settle into a quiet evening at home, Mowery found himself engaged in a quickly escalating argument with a neighbor. The man on the other side of the disagreement retreated back into his house, short of a physical confrontation, and Mowery drove off.

Heading south on I-5, he had gone no more than three miles before he spun the car and crashed into a guardrail. It was by then early in the morning, and traffic was light. Mowery stepped over the guard rail and began walking toward downtown Santa Ana. By the time light was beginning to creep over the Tustin hills, Mowery caught sight of a pastry shop and decided that he was hungry.

"Doughnuts," he said to a girl behind the counter.

"What kind would you like?" the girl asked.

"I don't give a fuck. Just make sure they got holes in 'em," Mowery said.

The owner emerged from the kitchen. "Say, we don't need that kind of language in here."

"Okay," Mowery said and turned back to the counter girl. "Give me some doughnuts. Don't give a fuck if they got holes in 'em or not."

"That's it. Out. Get out right now!" the manager said, his face red.

When Mowery's doughnuts were not forthcoming he reached into his pocket, extracted a handful of crumpled bills, and dropped them on the counter. Then he walked around a glass case and helped himself to several handfuls of assorted doughnuts, ignoring the refinement of a bag to carry them.

"I called the police. Better get out of here, fella. Your last chance. The police are coming," the frustrated manager railed.

"I'll have some of that coffee there," Mowery said to the girl, ignoring the protestations of the manager.

"I called the police," the manager sputtered.

The counter girl, police or no, filled a large coffee container and served it to Mowery, who smiled in gratitude through a mouthful of doughnuts.

He was still sitting at a table, picking his way through crushed doughnuts, when two uniformed officers stepped inside. One of the officers paused briefly to speak to the manager before approaching Mowery.

"Would you mind coming with us, sir?" the officer said.

"Why, I'd just be fucking delighted to my eyeballs to step outside with you two young ladies," Mowery responded.

Officer Rudi Fleck was a twelve-year veteran of the streets and his partner had been on the force five years. Fleck was savvy enough to understand the problem of arresting a man of Mowery's size and temperament and chose to ignore the insult.

"Manager'd rather you leave," Fleck said, his voice devoid of challenge.

Mowery smiled, not moving a muscle.

"Shit," Fleck said under his breath, realizing he and his partner had no way out. Then to Mowery: "How about it, man? Can we do it outside?"

As Mowery was walking outside with the policemen, the manager trotted to the door. "He didn't pay for his coffee."

*Not smart,* thought Officer Fleck. *Thing to do is shine the price of coffee.* But he tried to use the new complication as a way out of an otherwise certain confrontation. "Tell you what, sir," he said to Mowery, "pay for the coffee, then you can go."

"Fuck the coffee," Mowery said as he balanced himself on the balls of his feet.

"Okay, my treat." Fleck reached into his own pocket and paid the manager for Mowery's coffee, hoping that his last desperate attempt to avoid a fight would be successful.

"I don't want your money, Officer," the manager said. "I want that wiseguy to pay for it. Only right."

Fleck ignored the doughnut shop manager. "Sir, take the money. Please, it's the easiest way."

"Take the asshole's money," Mowery said to the manager, "first thing the prick's paid for since he put on that monkey suit."

"Call the station," Fleck whispered to the manager. "Tell the dispatcher that officers need backup. Fast. Give them this address."

Fleck sank his baton, end-first, as far into Mowery's gut as possible, intending to stun him long enough to get hand and leg cuffs in place. The force of the thrust was well delivered and caused Mowery to stumble a step backward. But while the blow was painful, it was not crippling. The convict caught the baton in a viselike grip with one hand while the heel of his free hand shot toward Officer Fleck's neck. The punch missed slightly but caught Fleck in the collarbone, partially paralyzing his left arm.

The second cop quickly attacked Mowery's right side with his baton. He jabbed below Mowery's armpit, but the convict was familiar with fighting more than one attacker at a time. One martial arts technique consists of maneuvering one's opponents so that they are required to go through or over their own members to get to their target. While Mowery made uncomplicated movements with his feet, he was able to inflict heavy punishment on whoever was in front of him. With only two men, it was a piece of cake.

Fleck and his colleague went to their Mace. While not permanently scarring, the chemical compound is searing, blinding, painful to whatever body area it touches. Each officer had used his entire can on Mowery by the time two additional cars carrying four more officers arrived on the scene.

It took all six policemen to subdue Mowery. He was eventually hauled to the Anaheim jail, put in an isolation cell, still shackled, and left on its concrete floor.

Within minutes his arrest record was called up from a central data base.

At 4:00 A.M. the telephone rang near Victoria's bed. "Hello?"

"This is Sergeant Hurley, California Highway Patrol. Is this Victoria Seele?" a voice announced on the other end of the line.

"Yes?" Her response was offered in the form of a question.

"We found a 1970 Maverick automobile registered to Victoria Seele wrecked and abandoned on I-5 freeway near Santa Ana. Would that by any chance be your car?" Sergeant Hurley said.

"Probably," she said.

"You mean you don't know?" Hurley's voice was taking on an edge.

"Not exactly." The line was silent for a long moment while Victoria struggled against early-morning mental fog. What the hell had Mowery done with her car?

"It says on our paperwork that you are an Orange County Sheriff's deputy. That right?"

"Investigator. That's right," Victoria confirmed.

"You're a detective and you don't know where your car is?" The CHP sergeant's voice dripped with sarcasm.

"I'm working on a case, Sergeant Hurley," Victoria said with more assertiveness than she felt. "Why don't I come in in the morning and talk to you about it? Soon enough?" she asked.

"Why, sure. What time do you think that might be, Detective Seele?" Hurley said.

"Let's say ten o'clock. And, hey, I appreciate, ah, you know . . . everything," she said, relieved.

"No problem. Car isn't going anywhere. I get off duty at eight o'clock, but I might just stick around the station to hear this one. I love great stories."

Click.

* * *

Victoria immediately called Carlander. She described the CHP's connection with the car and asked Carlander what she should do. They discussed her legal and professional alternatives. They decided that the less said to outside agencies, the better. She knew the drill.

Carlander's telephone rang again at a more reasonable hour—7:15 A.M.. It was Keith Taylor. "Santa Ana PD has him locked up at city jail," Mowery's parole officer said. "Assault upon police officers, drunk and disorderly, resisting arrest, theft . . . that one came over a cup of coffee and, frankly, I don't understand it . . . but the list goes on. You ought to let him sit for a while. Ten years or so."

Carlander drove to his office in Santa Ana. He first proofread crime and surveillance reports, submitted expense vouchers, and responded to a confidential memo from Deputy District Attorney Ronald Kreber on the progress of his investigation, omitting this morning's developments. He made several telephone calls, including Bud Nease and Victoria. Their assignments would be different today—he would have them recontact dealers from whom they had already made buys and attempt to make follow-up buys. Carlander then called nearby Santa Ana Police HQ and made arrangements to visit prisoner Clifford Mowery.

Carlander arrived at the Anaheim city jail in the late afternoon. He was prepared to give up his attempt at an undercover coup that probably wasn't possible to pull off in the first place. Expecting Mowery to abide by rules had been unrealistic. He had gone out and done what he had always done. He got drunk, wrecked a car, got into a fight.

When Carlander arrived at Mowery's cell for what he had planned as a brief, hard-bitten farewell, his temper began to ebb at the sight of Mowery's condition. His eyes were both beaten shut, fluid oozing from them. His nose and lips were swollen, and one side of his face had swollen to twice normal size. Flesh had been torn from his wrists. But worse of all were fiery burns over all the exposed flesh on his body. Blisters welled in chains up his arms and chest, his back where his shirt had been ripped off in the struggle, and all over his neck and face. A single whiff of Mace is enough to drop most men helplessly to the ground. Two shots will make tough men writhe in pain.

Mowery tried to sit up when Carlander entered the cell.

"Hello, Cliff."

"Wayne."

The response was weak, and his eyes made a feeble attempt to follow as Carlander moved to where Mowery could see him without moving his battered body.

"Well, I saw the cops. They don't look so good, either," Carlander said in a tone he hoped sounded cheerful.

Mowery showed the ghost of a smile.

"Can you talk?" the detective asked.

"Yeah," Mowery croaked.

"Doctor looked at you?" Carlander asked, feeling pity for Mowery. He could only imagine how the man felt.

Mowery moved his head slowly from side to side. It was possible for him to talk, but the task was painful, so it was easier not to.

"I'll see one checks you out. Guess you'll live, though." Carlander was beginning to feel depressed. When Mowery did not respond the detective was at a loss for words. The angry harangue he had prepared for Mowery, the repeat offender, now sounded petty. All he could feel was sympathy for a pathetic, whipped animal.

"Is it over?" he heard Mowery say.

"The program?" Carlander verified. "Yeah, I guess it is."

"Sorry."

Mowery's apology seemed genuine, Carlander thought. "Hell, me, too. I had a chance to be a hero," Carlander joked feebly.

Mowery's head moved slightly in appreciation. Then his face screwed up in pain and more fluid flowed from his eyes.

"Sorry . . . Victoria, too. You know . . . the car . . ."

"Insurance will handle it, I guess. I think she can do that without giving up your name. No need to add all that crap on your sheet, either."

"Hell of a lady, isn't she?" The inmate's swollen lips caused the words to slur. Mowery licked them as though he could improve their function.

"Cliff . . ." Carlander began.

"Yeah?"

"I don't understand why you did it. What for?" Carlander knew that everyone, sooner or later, had an urge to raise hell. But Mowery's came far too often and the results were too violent.

"I got drunk," Mowery said, shrugging. "Seemed like a good idea at the time."

"You haven't done shit yet," Carlander said, feeling anger borne of frustration. "Not a fuckin' thing. All you've been is trouble. Gave us a few nothing pushers, not your buds, not the wheels in the club."

"I was trying . . ."

"Don't waste your time with bullshit." He hated to waste time, and Mowery had wasted more of it than anyone he had ever been associated with. "I told you. I can deal with lies. Hell, you lie all the time, but bullshit makes a long day. We could cut bullshit out of our workday, we'd eliminate overtime. I might still be married. So don't bullshit me."

Carlander was interrupted by Mowery's darkening face. "Why don't you get on a chopper yourself, big man?" Mowery's head fell back, his body suffering from the effort of raising his voice, but his eyes bore into Carlander's.

Carlander understood fact when he heard it. If he was to catch bad men, he would have to have the baddest on his side. But he had to remain in charge, call the shots as he saw them. "You got to try harder, Cliff. I know you haven't been throwing us the big fish. You think you can get away giving up the little guys?"

"I'm not going to kiss your ass," the biker said simply.

Carlander nodded his head. It was as close as Mowery would come to admitting that he wanted to continue the program. Carlander decided not to press Mowery for promises. He was after deeds, not words. "I'll give it one more try. They'll probably put me on the same bus with you heading up to the joint."

Carlander learned the name of the arresting officer on Mowery's case: Rudi Fleck. Good cop. Carlander hoped not too good.

Officer Fleck was scheduled to testify in a trial, so Carlander walked two blocks to Orange County Superior Court. He took an elevator to the sixth floor and found Fleck standing in a corridor talking with two other police officers. One of them, Fleck, was wearing a uniform, and the other two, waiting to testify, wore civilian clothes.

"Talk to you a minute, Rudi?" Carlander asked. He could see that Fleck had received more than one blow to the head. The brow above one eye was swollen, a cheek bruised, a lip cut. He wore an elastic bandage on his left hand.

"Can I do for you?" Fleck asked without enthusiasm.

"My name's Wayne Carlander, Sheriff's Office."

"I know who you are," Fleck said.

Carlander winced inwardly at Fleck's lack of warmth at the sound of his name. "About the collar you made last night . . . morning, really . . . Mowery."

Fleck sighed, rolled his eyes and scowled. "So?"

"I guess he was a major pain in the ass for you guys," Carlander offered.

"Pain in the ass. Pain in the ass." Fleck rolled the words around on his tongue as though trying them for context. "That's kind of funny," he said.

"How about letting Mowery go? He's working for us. I know he got out of line but we . . ."

"Working for you? CI?" Fleck asked in a monotone.

"Yeah."

"I don't see that as a problem. Get another one," Fleck said with disinterest and started to turn away.

"I can't," Carlander pressed. "Not like this one. This guy can get to the people, people we're gonna bust. I talked to your station commander. He's not in love with Mowery, either, neither am I, but he said that if the arresting officers go along with it, he could let him walk."

"Well, see? There you have it," Fleck said, almost pleasantly. "Some of your wish came through. Except for the part where 'if the arresting officers . . .' That's the part that blew you out of the water, 'cause I don't agree to let the son of a bitch walk. Cases so hard to come by at County you have to hustle our jails to find 'em? Get me a transfer. Your fuckin' department is where I want to be."

"Wait." Carlander persisted, holding Fleck's arm. "I know Mowery can be a kind of asshole . . ."

"You as crazy as he is? Take your hand off my arm. He's going back to the slammer where he belongs, and I'd like to appear at a parole hearing twenty years from now and tell the board not to let him out. I'm tellin' you, man like that has got to have bodies laying around somewhere."

"Fleck," Carlander began evenly, "I'm asking you something I wouldn't bother asking any other cop because you're the best in the city. Hell, in the county . . ."

"Oh, Jesus, please, don't . . ." Fleck said, pulling away from Carlander but finding himself facing a wall.

". . . and because you can see the big picture. You're not a small-time thinker." Carlander nodded his head in emphasis.

"I'm gonna throw up."

"Please," Carlander beseeched without shame. "We can bag some heavy hitters if you help us out on this one."

"I gotta go to court," Fleck said, turning away.

"Think about it."

"Okay, I'll think about it," Fleck agreed.

"Well?" Carlander asked.

"Well, what?"

"What do you think?" Carlander's brows shot up expectantly.

"Shit."

"Is that okay shit?" Carlander pushed.

"Hey, Carlander," Officer Fleck said, "if I call you up at three o'clock in the morning and tell you that I just shot some guy in the back of the fucking head you're going to come to wherever I am, take my gun, then go directly to the station and confess to the killing yourself. We got a deal or not?"

"Deal. I swear to God. Thanks, Fleck." Carlander turned to leave.

"Hey," Fleck said. "Don't go making the same deal with the other cops. I don't want your confession thrown out because you're runnin' around giving yourself up for five other homicides."

Carlander nodded his head in assent and turned to leave but was stopped by Fleck. "Carlander . . ."

"Yeah?"

"You really getting into these bikers?" Fleck glanced around as though a motorcycle rider might overhear. "No bullshit?"

"We got a good chance," Carlander affirmed.

Fleck thought for a moment, then said, "They had a one-eighty-seven seven, eight months ago in Huntington Beach. Place called the Capri Bar. Couple dudes blew away a nice kid. Hear about it?"

"Seems like I did. Why?" Carlander wanted to know.

"Twenty-one years old, the kid was," Fleck said. "Bartender said the shooter and his partner looked like bikers. One of the pricks didn't like the music the kid played, so he shot him. Bartender said the shooter had a name on the side of his hat. Butch."

"Got a description?" Carlander asked, interested.

"Nothing that would help," the policeman said. "About five-eight or -nine. White."

"Butch," Carlander mulled. "We'll keep our eyeballs peeled. Thanks again, Fleck." Carlander stepped into an elevator.

Kenny was just twenty-one years old. He was having his first legal beer on his birthday in a bar with his father, Kenneth A. King, Sr., when a loud voice complained about the music on the jukebox. When confronted by a scruffy-looking man with "BUTCH" written on one side of his western-style hat and "HELL'S ANGELS" on the other, Kenny admitted that he had played the music. "Well," the man said, "I don't like nigger music and I don't like you." An argument ensued and Kenneth easily knocked the man down. The man stalked out of the bar, returning within minutes. This time he had a gun. He shot Kenny twice in the chest. The man turned on his heel and left, followed immediately by a second biker and their two dates.

No one among the one bartender and thirty patrons saw anything. Huntington Beach homicide detectives had physical descriptions of Kenneth King's killers, but no names and certainly no addresses. Leads were thoroughly investigated, to no avail. The only solid clue, if it could be called that, was the fact that both men were bikers.

* * *

It took Carlander the rest of the day, but he located each officer and received angry, grudging agreements to allow Mowery to walk, persuaded by Fleck's example. Mowery's cell door would not be reopened, though, until Carlander convinced all parties connected with the case, including Sheriff Brad Gates and Keith Taylor, that Mowery's lapse should be overlooked and that it would not happen again.

Then there was Mowery himself. Carlander was still dealing with a hardened criminal who was used to having his own way. Carlander's reputation would once more go on the line. He had a time bomb that could go off in his face at any time. He might be smarter to follow Taylor's advice and leave Mowery locked up.

On the positive side was Victoria's report. She had seen a man called Ray Glore. He was likely a mega–drug dealer. Moreover, he was clearly an important man in the Hell's Angels organization. If there was a methamphetamine factory anywhere on the West Coast, Ray Glore would know where it was. Bruno was a clubmate, that was for sure. Carlander tried to remember another name Victoria took down when Mowery took her car. Wasn't it Butch? He shook his head. He'd look back in his records, but he doubted that it would be the same guy who pulled the trigger in Huntington Beach.

Still other bikers remained to be identified. Carlander never seriously questioned the value of Mowery's infiltration.

Carlander met with Sergeant Skip Mitchell, his nominal superior, and Lieutenant Sim Middleton. Mowery's violations of law—though Carlander did not yet know of his involvement in receiving guns with Bruno—were quite serious. The three men discussed their legal liability, how it would look if they were brought to answer charges ranging from using poor judgment to criminal negligence. Few cops, however, would pass up the opportunity to put away truly big-time crooks. The decision by Mitchell and Middleton was to back Carlander to the hilt.

Sheriff Brad Gates was working on papers when Carlander entered his office on short notice.

"I know what you want, Wayne," the sheriff said.

"Yes, sir. I guess you do."

Gates waved Carlander to a chair. "I talked to Captain Lagstead at Anaheim PD. He said the arresting cops were willing to shine the assault charges. How the hell did you pull that off?"

"I promised to confess to murder if Fleck decides to kill somebody," Carlander admitted.

"He hasn't done it yet, huh?" Gates asked.

"Not yet, I guess," Carlander said with a straight face.

"Mowery's reading you like a Braille book. Picking you like a banjo."

"Maybe he is, Sheriff. Except now we've got some targets. Dude by the name of Ray Glore is a big number in the Hell's Angels. Got a homicide suspect ID'd, maybe, and Victoria's spending time with some other riders that are Angels, I think." Carlander knew the word Angels would get the sheriff's attention.

"Well, so far what you have is a lot of stuff to check out. Can't you put somebody else with Victoria? Nease, maybe?" Gates liked the program even if he didn't like Mowery.

Carlander thought that Gates was beginning to come around. "Naw. Mowery's a mountain. They like the son of a bitch. He's as bad as they are. Nease is cool, but he couldn't get a foot inside the Angels."

Sheriff Gates asked about a number of matters, including the meth plant and other possible gangs affiliated with the Angels, accessories to the distribution of drugs as well as extortion and theft of property. As the two speculated on what might be uncovered, Gates was still intrigued with Mowery's potential. "Talked with Keith Taylor yet?" he asked.

"Haven't tried bending his arm up behind his back," Carlander admitted.

Gates sighed. "What the hell. I'll write another letter to the Parole Board. If we're lucky they'll turn us down."

"Yes, sir." Carlander turned to go.

"Victoria still willing to sit on the back of that damn chopper?" Gates asked, impressed with her courage.

"Hell, she's getting to love the game," Carlander lied.

"I can't believe it," Victoria said as she paced the floor in her house. "The son of a bitch did it to himself. I tried. I did what

I was supposed to do, but the whole fucking thing blew up. Carlander's favorite archcriminal lit the fuse. So now we can go back to ... to ... whatever we're supposed to be doing. Everybody knew it was going to happen. Gates told me that it was going to go to shit and it did. Fast, kind of. But that's the kind of guy Mowery is. He's so busy cutting his own throat he has to use both hands for the job. Jesus, he must love prison. Well, he's got a lot of friends there. Know what I'm going to do? I'm going to pour gas on that motorcycle and light a match. Hey, Bill? Want a beer?"

Bill was watching the obsessed stranger his wife had become. The undercover team was averaging twenty-four hours of overtime per officer per week. Bill knew she needed a break.

"Hey, I've got some time off now," she said, lighting another cigarette. She punched the remote control of the television. A network program was reviewing America's bicentennial celebration. Tall ships sailed triumphantly up the Hudson River. "Mowery's in jail. We can relax. See some movies. Lay around on the beach, if we want. The weather's good." Victoria snapped the television off, tossing the remote carelessly aside.

"Sounds good," he said. He could hardly take the time away from his job, but he had hardly seen his wife in the past weeks. They had thought that the enforced separation caused by her duties—and his—would make their time together richer, more valuable. It had not worked that way so far.

"What did he do?" Bill asked.

"Six cops got between him and a doughnut. God, he's insane. They all are." Victoria put her arms around her body as though chilled.

"Serious?" Bill wanted to know. "How long will he be inside?"

Victoria shrugged. "Who knows? He might go back to prison. He broke parole in a big way. Beating up on cops always gets a reaction from other cops. And judges."

"How do you feel about that?" Bill asked. He crossed the room to the refrigerator to find something cold to drink.

"Great. I mean it. Relieved. I'd do anything to get off that motorcycle. We ride it all day. Make a phone call to line up a dime bag of coke or a jar of meth and go tearing off on the chopper. All day and half the night. And waiting for somebody to ID me or . . ." Victoria stopped, thought for a moment, then continued, "If Mowery was back in the joint . . ." She halted again as though not clear about her thoughts.

"Is he that bad a man that you want him back inside?" Bill asked, curious. He had never met Mowery but wanted to know everything about the man.

"Depends on what you call bad. If you're in a fight and he's on your side, he's a great guy. If he's against you or if he stole the money out of your cash register, then he's bad." Victoria accepted the beer Bill retrieved from the refrigerator. She was beginning to acquire a taste for it, having drunk more beer in the past weeks than she had in her entire life.

"That isn't the kind of bad I was talking about," Bill said. He wanted to know what she thought about him, not merely his police record.

"He's self-centered. That's his biggest problem. Only thinks about himself. And sex. He screws everything that moves. Doesn't have to work for it, either. They just . . ." Victoria shrugged ". . . kind of climb all over him." She thought again. "Arrogant. For a guy who's spent so much time in jail he thinks he's got all the answers. Never in doubt."

"Does he lie?" Bill asked.

Victoria turned her head sharply toward her husband. Her voice revealed surprise. "Of course he lies. Naturally."

Two days later the telephone rang. "Mowery's out. We're back in business," Carlander reported. The news struck Victoria like a body blow.

# CHAPTER 8

High-speed rides between drug connections continued for Victoria and Mowery through the holidays. Not all of the buys were from Hell's Angels, some were from hangers-on. There were plenty of Hell's Angels wannabes and ambitious biker dealers to keep the undercover operation more than busy. By the end of December 1976 they had achieved a certain pattern to their work when a development arose that should have been a minor inconvenience. Suddenly, and without suitable preparation, a substitute for Victoria was needed.

Larry Torres was not a member of a motorcycle gang, but Mowery informed Carlander that the man was a major dealer in heroin, a product the Hell's Angels disdained to handle. The Torres organization turned out to be large, in fact, the largest heroin outlet in California at the time.

Carlander called up Torres's sheet, which included an assessment of his activities by LAPD Intelligence. It revealed that he had done state prison time as well as stops in Orange County Jail, where he had been a leader of other Latinos.

"He's got a girlfriend, Nita. She was there when you were there," Carlander said to Victoria. "Remember her?"

"Yes, real well. I checked her mail, ingoing and outgoing," Victoria recalled. "I don't think she'd remember me, though. I can do this buy."

"Too soon for a suicide mission," Carlander said.

"I didn't see her that much. I don't think she'd remember me," Victoria stated, not wanting to be excluded.

"Just when I thought you were getting smart," Carlander observed. "We'll use somebody else. Anybody got a name?"

"Ain't that much choice," Nease observed.

Victoria pointed out the obvious. "I'm the only female detective you have."

"How about Karen Higgins?" Nease suggested. "Sim says she's good."

Karen Higgins was a new officer with the Orange County Sheriff's Office. Clearly an ambitious woman spurred by Victoria's record of success, she was being trained by the department to work patrol and eventually investigations. Also like Victoria, Karen Higgins planned a long-term career in law enforcement. Her husband, Paul, was a veteran of the Huntington Beach Police Department. During his seven-year career carrying a badge and a gun, he had put himself through law school at night and was about to sit for the California state bar exam.

"Pretty young," Carlander countered, noting that she was only twenty-three.

"What am I? An old lady?" Victoria deadpanned. She thought Carlander was being too careful. What's more, she could not imagine anyone else doing it as well. "She's green," Victoria pointed out.

"I know she's green," Carlander allowed. "What do you think, Cliff? Want to go inside with a green lady?"

Mowery shrugged. "Hell, why not?"

In fact, Karen Higgins was still working at the women's county jail, a preliminary posting that every new deputy is obliged to undertake. Still, Carlander recalled that Victoria had not been a grizzled veteran before she was tapped for detective work. And, he had to admit, she handled her assignments extremely well. "Okay. She's workin' at the jail, I think. I'll pull her out."

"You're going to ask her," Victoria corrected, feeling a sense of responsibility to protect Karen.

"That's what I just said," Carlander responded.

Victoria was firm. "You can't just tell her that she's got this assignment. Explain to her what the risks are."

"What are you, now, her agent?" Carlander said.

"I know how you work. You did it to me," Victoria reminded him. "It was a done deal to ride a bike with Mowery, and I hadn't said a word. Just tell her what's involved, that's all. Christ, she's a kid."

"Hey, wasn't you brought her name up," Carlander said.

"Doesn't matter who came up with it," Victoria argued. "She's a hell of a good lady. I like her a lot. Just tell her the problems she could run into."

" 'Course I'll tell her. What am I, the enemy?"

He found her doing a P.M. shift at the jail. They talked in the lawyer/bondsman room, where they would be undisturbed. "This is probably a one-time thing," he said. "Maybe one or two or three other times if we run into the same problem, but that's all. It's not a promotion to detective . . ."

"That's all right," she said, eagerness obvious on her face.

". . . or anything like that. I don't think you have enough time in for investigator, anyway. I'm supposed to tell you about risks. Ah, be real honest, there aren't any. My opinion. Not to say that something couldn't screw up . . ."

"I'm not afraid. I know I can do it," Karen pressed.

"The worst part to me would be riding that bike. I wouldn't get on that thing for nothing."

"My brother had a motorcycle," Karen said, anxious to deal with what she considered pro forma warnings. "I like riding motorcycles."

"Well, just so you know. I gotta be out front on what's involved. This isn't a permanent thing, understand. One-time shot," Carlander reiterated. "So. Want to make a buy for us?"

"Yeah. When do you want to start?"

"I have to talk to a couple people. Sheriff Gates, one. Your captain. I'll call you in a couple hours. We got a lead on a guy sellin' heroin. Should be okay, the way we got it set up. We'll call. Anybody you have to talk to first? How about your husband?" Carlander did not anticipate a negative response here, either.

"He won't care. I mean, he's a cop, you know." Karen smiled reassuringly.

"Yeah, yeah." Two cops in a family, he considered. Not unheard of but wouldn't it be hell growing up in a house like that? Of course, they had no children yet.

"I'll call him," Karen said.

Mowery, a man dedicated to the admiration of women, was not disappointed in Karen Higgins when they were introduced. She did not have Victoria's classic features, but she was a package that would get anybody's attention. She worked at staying in shape. She had brown eyes and matching hair that was partially sun-bleached at the tips in a frosted pattern.

"Hi, Cliff," she said to him.

"Hi, there, li'l girl."

Karen Higgins looked pleased and Victoria shook her head.

"Torres lives at 13521 Sunswept Avenue, Apartment 5, in Garden Grove," Carlander said to Karen and Mowery. "All right? We're gonna be there, me and Victoria, before you get there. Tired of fighting the traffic, way you drive, Clifford. So what you do, Karen, is . . ."

"She needs a cover name," Victoria said.

"I know that, Vicky," Carlander said. "Let me get the whole rap out and then you can make suggestions. What name do you want, Karen? You pick it."

"Aubry," Karen said without hesitation.

"Aubry? That's a man's name. You mean Audrey?" Carlander asked.

"I had an aunt who was a little nutso. Her name was Aubry. Heron for a last name. Like the bird," Karen said as though it explained everything.

"Okay. Remember that, Cliff. Don't be calling her Karen," Carlander warned.

"What was that name again?" Mowery said.

He was teasing, Victoria thought. "Aubry, she said."

"Come on," Carlander said. "Let's work. Okay, ah, Aubry, so when you get to Torres's place, you knock on the door. Not Clifford here. It's you who's buying the junk, not Mowery. See, this is like a play and everybody's got a role. Mowery's role is that you want to buy narcotics to resell and Mowery, he introduces you to somebody who can provide it. You make the buy, not Mowery. Okay? Cliff isn't a police officer, so there's nothing he can do, officially anyway. So you tell Torres that you want heroin. It's not for you, tell him, it's for a friend. Couple friends. Mowery was a horse chipper once." Carlander nodded his head toward the biker. " 'Course, not anymore. Mowery's clean as a nun's datebook, but Torres doesn't know that, so he'll figure the buy is for Mowery or Mowery and his buds. Whatever. All you gotta do is buy. Okay?"

Karen nodded. "What if he offers me something else?"

"Like what? Clam dip and some white wine?" Carlander asked blandly.

"Like drugs?" the neophyte asked.

"Shit," Nease said insightfully.

"Depends. How you feel," Carlander said.

"Ask for whites, too, or other crap, and he'll get suspicious," Victoria said.

"Whites. Torres isn't a meth dealer," Nease put in.

"Doesn't hurt to ask," Carlander put in. "About anything. He might know somebody or knows somebody who knows somebody." He turned up the palms of his hands.

"But don't be stupid," Victoria warned again. She wanted to be assured that Karen could walk before she tried to fly.

"Or I'll have to kill him to protect you," Mowery said with a straight face.

"Ah, yeah, he's supposed to protect you . . ." Victoria rolled her eyes upward. "So take care of yourself."

Karen looked at Mowery. The felon met her eyes but did not smile. "Don't count on it," he said.

The response was not what Karen expected. For a moment she looked almost startled. Victoria caught the look and thought maybe the girl would pull out.

"That's right. Don't count on it," Carlander repeated lightly, as though Mowery were still teasing. "One thing more. All of you, keep your ears peeled for a bike driver name of Butch. Dude did a one-eighty-seven last year at a bar in Huntington Beach. Okay? Let's go."

Karen Higgins did not lack confidence. Carlander had warned her that in any undercover operation the officer has to possess the correct balance of confidence and fear. Overconfidence could lead to a slip, sometimes with disastrous results.

With Mowery standing at her side, she knocked firmly on the door of Torres's apartment. After a moment the door was opened by a Latino man slightly taller than Karen. He had no fat on his body, but his muscles were slack, she noticed. The sleeves of his white shirt, which was unbuttoned down the front, were rolled up but still covered his elbows. It occurred to her that Torres might be covering needle tracks.

She saw that he had a number of the tattoos that seemed obligatory for any macho hombre who has done significant time in a slammer. Among them were a glowing cross, a dagger dripping blood, a hooded skeleton, a woman's crotch, and a heart with "MARIA" in its center. Torres was a nervous type with erratic movements and eyes that never settled. He quickly appraised Karen, then looked to Mowery.

"Hey, come in, meng. Siddown. Big fucker like you gotta be tired alla time. Siddown."

The pronunciation *meng* instead of *man* told Mowery that he was a Cuban, not Mexican. Mowery distrusted Latinos, Chicanos, just as he did blacks. But Latinos, with their exaggerated sense of machismo, were dangerous, when they imagined that a deal had gone wrong or that they were not being shown proper respect.

The apartment was in a lower-middle-class neighborhood, though Torres could afford better, Karen suspected. It was the kind of place that could be quickly vacated with little of value left inside. And Torres could carry on his business without attracting unwanted attention from neighbors.

"So? Whatcha want? Somebody want a drink, eh?" the Cuban offered. "Or some blow? I can give nice samples. We got a business here, a real business for real people."

Torres pronounced people *pipple*. Mowery smiled. Torres

smiled back. "That's right, you can enjoy business or not, not fucking do it, eh? Kinda bike you ride, meng?" he asked of Mowery.

"You seen my scooter," Mowery said laconically. "Harley. Chopper."

"What I got? You ain't seen my ass on no Jarley-Shopper. People get killed on them shits, meng. Fuck 'em. Night train. Ever see 'em?" Torres offered Mowery a photograph of his customized Chev.

"Nice sled. You build it?" Mowery said without enthusiasm.

"You're fucking right, I build it from . . ." the Cuban began.

"I want to buy something," Karen interrupted.

Torres looked at Karen, then back to Mowery, jerked his head in her direction as though to say, "Did you hear something?" but continued on. "The car worth serious bucks, meng. I turn down twenty-five thou' from a dude, meng. Twenty-five. But I ain't selling . . ."

"And I ain't buying if you ain't selling," Karen said with humor meant to be taken seriously.

"Hey, we're talking something, here, lady, but you in a big hurry, okay, you can't even siddown. What?" The Cuban seemed willing to be amused by this attractive girl. Apparently Karen's assertiveness had struck a chord.

"Smack. How much you got?" she said, all business.

"Who the fuck are you? How much I got? Shit, baby, I got the world." Torres thumped himself on the chest theatrically. "You wanna buy the world? Where your money, eh? *Dinero*, baby." He rubbed thumb and forefinger together.

"Can I get five balloons for a hundred?" she asked.

Torres looked toward Mowery in amusement. "Eh? Five? No. *Quatro. ¿Habla usted 'spañol? Nada?* Four balloons. That's the price. Hundred dollar ain't no big deal, babby. 'Kay? Wait."

Torres disappeared into the back of the apartment. Two bedrooms, Karen guessed. She and Mowery sat down simultaneously, smiling at the minor coincidence. Karen did not move away.

"Better watch your young butt," Mowery warned the fledgling deputy. "You make Torres feel like you're stepping on his *cojones*, and he's liable to get mean."

"You're supposed to protect me," Karen reminded him as she batted long eyelashes flirtatiously.

"I'm not big on cops," he said in a muffled tone.

Karen met his eyes but made no other response. " 'Course," Mowery smiled, "some of 'em I don't wanta see get hurt, neither . . ."

Torres returned with four rubber balloons of the kind bought for children in any store. Karen had seen them at an academy orientation lecture. Two were red, one yellow, one blue. The colors of individual balloons were of no relation to their contents, heroin, but would be recorded on the crime report and evidence registration form. She also knew that balloons were the preferred container of heroin dealers because "mules," people who transported the dope, could swallow a considerable quantity, since rubber balloons passed easily through the gastrointestinal system. The contents of Torres's balloons would later be analyzed by a police lab and found to total five hundred milligrams, 6 percent pure heroin, a typically stepped-on load.

Torres took the handful of twenties without looking at them, stuffing the wad into a pocket while he continued to rhapsodize about his Chevy. Mowery looked at Karen. It was her call to make. She seemed in no hurry to leave, and neither was he. Mowery would have liked to take a small chip of horse but instead accepted from Torres the offer of a beer. Karen wandered innocently around the living room, poking here and there through sparse collections of car magazines, pinups of nudes, and stacks of tapes. She chose one, placed it into a deck, and keyed the music.

Torres smiled.

"You like that? Good music. I'm goin' to buy a club. Call it, ah, Médico Música. Eh? A disco. You will be invited . . ." he enthused.

"I don't see a picture of your lady. What's her name? Nita?" Karen said.

The effect on Torres was electric. He leaped from his chair and slammed the heel of his hand into the tape deck, smashing the case, rendering the machine useless.

"That *puta*. I fuckin' killed her, meng. Cut her up like a fucking rabbit. Bitch. *Puta* bitch. You laughing at me, meng? Eh?

You better not be laughing at my ass, meng," the Cuban spat at Mowery.

"I'm not laughing," Mowery said, working hard to keep a smile from his face. "Hell, I never met the lady."

"She ain't no lady. She's a dyke, meng. A goddamn lez." Torres's eyes became black holes.

"Oh, no," Karen blurted in mock horror.

Mowery looked at Karen, who sharply took in her breath and held her hand dramatically over her mouth.

"Yeah. First the goddamn woman, I bring her in here, meng," the Cuban railed, "when she was fourteen, from her shitty family, like pigs, and took care of her real good. Real good. Treated her like a fucking queen. So? I get busted eighteen months ago for PS . . ."

"PS?" Mowery asked.

"Possession with intent to sell, is the bullshit cops pushing, and then she makes the fucking slam, all I told her to keep her ass out, no need for her to work, she don't listen . . ."

"For what?" Karen interrupted.

"What? Same. Same shit, dumb-dumb, that woman," Torres snarled.

"She was dealing while you were inside? What? County Jail?" Mowery was curious now.

"That's right. Santa Ana farm. So what's the bitch do? Fucking her girlfriends. She likes 'em."

"So you killed her, man?" Mowery asked, still secretly amused at the Latino's humiliation. A man losing his woman to another woman was unthinkable to a Latino. The loss of face could not have helped his business, either.

Torres paced the room, looking at everything but his two new customers. "I'm gonna, meng. I'm gonna kill her fucking ass someday. I love the bitch, meng, and she does that to me. I'm gonna kill her."

Outside, Mowery and Karen did not talk while they mounted the chopper. They cruised by the place where Carlander and Victoria were staked out, continuing at a slow pace until Carlander was locked into a secure trailing position.

"How'd you know about his old lady, Nita?" Mowery asked Karen over his shoulder while waiting for a long traffic light.

"Everyone knew about Nita and Torres in County Jail. He wrote letters, made telephone calls, told her who to talk to and who to stay away from. That was just about everybody. 'Don't let nobody touch you, baby.'"

"But she did anyway, huh?" Mowery asked.

"Yeah. Did everybody." Karen laughed.

"Like the bike?" he asked, referring to the chopper they were riding.

"Love it." And she did.

The usual late-night foursome became a fivesome at Karen Higgins's first debriefing, and because of it there was a heightened state of expectation as they occupied a table at Love's Restaurant off the Golden State Freeway in Santa Ana.

For his part, Carlander had already called his son from a public telephone in the foyer.

"Hello?" a youthful voice answered.

"Wayne. It's me," the detective said to his son.

"Hi, Dad."

"Not calling too late, am I? Were you in bed?" Carlander asked.

"No, I was watching TV," Wayne Junior said.

"Should be in bed," the detective admonished. "How about your sisters?"

"There's no school tomorrow, Dad. They're in bed, Mom's in bed," the typical teen drawled laconically.

"Okay. All right. How's it going?" Carlander pressed.

"My grades are fine, and the team's doing great." Wayne Junior was a star of his basketball team even though only a sophomore. "Coming over tomorrow?" Wayne Junior asked.

"No, no, I can't because I've got to work." The detective had paid no attention to the day even though Christmas season was his favorite time of the year. And he made a point to spend all of it that he could with his children.

"Thursday?" the boy persisted. "We're on Christmas vacation, you know."

"Sure, I know that," Carlander said. "I ever miss a Christmas with you or your sisters? I'll be there. We got this shitty case we're doin'. . . . I just want to, ah, make sure everything's all right."

"What could be not right?" Wayne Junior poked at his father.

"Parents always worry. About everything. Someday you'll be worried about your kids," Carlander said.

"No, I won't," the boy said with certainty.

Carlander smiled. "All right, then, I'll . . . call you pretty soon. I'll come over Sunday. I don't work this Sunday so we can get together. Do something."

"USC and Notre Dame," Wayne Junior suggested.

"Wanta see the Lakers? I can get tickets," Carlander suggested.

"Could you get tickets to the USC game?" Wayne Junior was as excited as his cool would allow.

"Of course. Have I ever failed? We'll take Terri and Kimberly, too," the detective said.

"What the hell was the bang we heard?" Carlander asked at the debriefing.

"That was Torres," Karen laughed. "He told us about his love life."

"His wife? Why did he talk about Nita?" Victoria wanted to know.

"I asked him," Karen said.

"You asked him what?" Carlander injected, attentive.

"About Nita. That's why he blew up." Karen was enjoying being part of the gang, liked being the center of attention.

"Did you bring up her name or did he?" he asked.

"He did," Karen lied.

Victoria saw the glance that Mowery directed toward Karen before turning his attention back to his coffee and steak sandwich.

"Why did he do that?" Carlander did not like unnecessary complications on a case. Good undercover work meant eliminating surprises. Karen Higgins seemed to invite them.

"Just talking, you know," Karen said. "I asked him about a lady in his life, so he goes bananas. First he said he killed her, then later he said he was going to kill her next time he saw her. Something wrong with that?"

"Killing her?" Carlander asked sarcastically.

"No," Victoria said, defending Karen's actions. "Good work, talking about things like that, keeping the conversation going. Builds confidence. They have to trust you in this business."

"But you knew the girl in County Jail?" Carlander pressed. The hour was late and the restaurant was nearly empty of other customers. He did not like to be conspicuous.

"Well, I never knew her personally," Karen said. "She was gone by then, but everybody talked about Nita. She was beautiful . . ."

"That's right," Victoria said. "I used to check out their mail, both ways. He was a controlling s.o.b." Victoria remembered vividly hearing of Torres's reaction to his woman's betrayal. While she did not agree with Nita's choice of sexual partners, she could not help but feel ironic satisfaction with the total frustration of one of the most nauseatingly macho men who had ever graced the other section of County Jail.

Victoria felt a sense of discomfort about the way Karen approached her work. It was necessary to be inner directed, but there was something in her manner, especially the casual, almost intimate way she treated Mowery, that struck her as unprofessional. She could not have guessed how close the substitute detective would bring them all to disaster.

# CHAPTER 9

Days became weeks while Victoria and Mowery ingratiated themselves with bikers, the Hell's Angels in particular. They made buys in various parts of the county on a daily basis. They would do a deal for a gram of meth in Fullerton, ride the chopper to Stanton for three balloons of heroin, go to Garden Grove for two grams of cocaine, then take another ride to San Bernardino for more meth and a conversation about guns. Or stolen cars. Or hot electronics and where to sell them. And Carlander, often with Bud Nease, would follow behind them. In addition to roaring from one rundown, drug-infested neighborhood to the next, Victoria and Mowery would attend parties at bikers' houses or simply hang out in their favorite bars.

Victoria still did not fit in easily, but her presence was not challenged. Mowery was by now included as a regular, although he was not officially a member of any club. It had become common knowledge that the Angels liked what they saw in Mowery, and Vern, a vice-president, had told him that when the time was right, he would sponsor Mowery himself. Mowery was an intimidating force, a hard battler who was suited to war. His nomination took place two months after the operation started, during a party at the Roaring 20's bar in Anaheim. Four motorcycle clubs were in attendance: the Diablos, Satan's Slaves, Dragons, and, most important, the Hell's Angels. There were more than two hundred bikers and their ladies packed into a space meant to hold seventy. Music blared at full volume, beer flowed from the taps, and impromptu drinking contests sprang up everywhere. "Colors," jackets or vests depicting insignias of club affiliation, were "flown" on this festive occasion.

Although there were not enough chairs, all of the Hell's Angels were comfortably ensconced at the best tables.

"Hey, Mowery," Bruno smiled at the biker. "Heard you took apart some cops. Six of 'em, I heard."

This was information Mowery was not anxious for anyone to know, but there was no use denying the fact. The Hell's Angels learned everything sooner or later. "We went around, yeah." Mowery looked away toward the small stage where the wet T-shirt contest would be conducted.

"Well, hell, man, let's hear the damn details." The voice belonged to Mexican Kenny, a San Bernardino Angel.

"Wasn't much. Just got my ass beat." Mowery was choosing a modest, even humorous dismissal of what he'd done. For good reason. Doing battle with a cop was among the most noble of all achievements for any Angel.

"The hell'd you get out of jail so quick? Huh?" somebody asked.

Mowery did not turn toward the source of the question. He was afraid his eyes might betray him. Instead he simply jerked his thumb in Victoria's direction. Then he rubbed his thumb and forefinger together in the universal sign of money. *Dinero.*

Laughter erupted around the table. No one asked any more questions. At least not then.

Raucous cheers broke out when it was announced that the long-awaited wet T-shirt contest for the undisputed "Best Body" award would begin at once.

There were two masters of ceremonies, a hard-body type by the name of Jesse, who rode with the Satan's Slaves, and Dago Paul, an Angel from Boston. He had black hair, an ink-black beard, and dark brown eyes, a man who never wanted for female companionship. He was also a killer, Victoria would learn later.

"All right," Jesse said into a microphone over the noise of the crowd, "let's get the ladies up here. C'mon, you darlings, right up here. Come on, lovely lady, over here." Soon a collection of ten girls had come forward.

"We got all the clubs 'cept the Angels," Dago Paul said into the microphone. "Nobody. I guess we're going to have to sit this one out." He winked at the crowd.

"Can't win the prize without a lady," Jesse said, playing along.

"What's first prize?" Dago Paul asked, blandly.

"Yeah, yeah," the crowd cheered in the spirit of the game, "what's the prize?"

"First prize, Dago, is a case of beer for our queen's old man, and some lace panties here and matching bra, right here . . . and they are black, ain't that a bitch? Huh? Crazy . . ." Jesse held up a slim white box from which he withdrew the promised lingerie.

Applause.

"Well, damn, let me ask Sam here if she'll volunteer for the Angels . . ." Dago Paul said as though the idea had just occurred to him.

Ringing applause. Whistles, cheers.

"Yeah, yeah," Mowery yelled, clapping his hands enthusiastically.

"Go, Sam, baby!" Buffalo hollered.

For a long moment Victoria could not believe what was happening. While applause built and men and women whistled, Mowery leaned near her ear. "Better get that jacket off or somebody else'll do it for you."

Victoria, though, was not intimidated. *Might even be fun,* she thought. T-shirts were *de rigueur* for biker men and women, so it was necessary only for Victoria to unfasten her bra and slip it out underneath her T-shirt, with a touch of modesty that pleased her interested audience. The volume of shouts and whistles increased with every movement she made. As she rose from her table and mounted the steps to a temporary raised platform, rock music from Led Zeppelin began to play. Contestants began to move to the beat and Victoria joined in. She was an outstanding dancer and, not by accident, had been the president of her college sorority's entertainment committee. She was the tallest, the most graceful, clearly the most attractive woman on the dais.

Led Zeppelin gave way to "Satisfaction" by the Stones. The ladies on the dais undulated their bodies in the best showmanship tradition. None, unlike Victoria, seemed concerned about the effect they had on a hundred boozed-up bikers. The idea was to turn on the audience. She wondered if she was getting too much into her role.

"That's it, Dago. Do it man, do it," someone urged.

Dago Paul, assisted by one of the bartenders, began pouring pitchers of cold beer slowly over the girls. The beer used was purposely cold, to maximize nipple erection.

Noise from the bikers rose to a crescendo as the desired effect materialized. Jesse passed among the girls, pausing behind each with a hand above her head, asking for a popular vote from the audience. Each was given a spirited ovation, some spectators falling out of their chairs. As Jesse approached Victoria, there was no doubt of the winner. As he raised his hand above her head the crowd was howling in unison.

Victoria, a.k.a. Samantha Cook, was the official queen of wet T-shirts and the proud "possession" of a motorcycle gang. By approbation a cop had become the darling of the Hell's Angels.

She laughed both at the irony and from pure party enjoyment. She joined Mowery at their table while outside two girls, Sally Cuttler and her friend, Sissy, each occupied a panel truck in the parking lot where they "pulled the train" for the excited contest audience. Their reward was a full tank of gas for each van and all the meth they could snort.

Inside the Roaring 20's no one had made more noise than Clifford Mowery, who stood on a chair, clapped his hands, and whistled through his teeth while cheering Victoria on to victory. "Let's dance," he said as she dismounted from the stage, still wet with beer.

"Sure," she said, now in the mood to keep it going.

The two of them danced at first without touching, their bodies keeping time to music from Credence Clearwater. Other bikers formed a circle around them and watched with admiration while Cliff and Sam did their thing. Mowery was a good dancer, Victoria realized with surprise. Despite his musculature, he was lithe and had the coordination of an athlete. He moved nearer to her, then took her hands, controlling her steps through spins and half-steps. She moved away from him in provocative hard-to-get-but-worth-the-effort motions. He followed, then did his own coy turns away, but never let his eyes lose contact with hers.

Other ladies in the contest and their men moved out onto the dance floor. It became crowded, forcing Victoria and Mowery closer together. Near the end of a song he put his arms around her, placed his lips on hers, and lifted her easily off the floor. In the midst of the crowd she couldn't avoid him, as she understood he knew very well.

"Don't do that again," she said into his ear. "Ever."

"Acting, girl. Gotta make us look right. Nobody's gonna look like you do and not get handled." He smiled hugely.

Victoria went to the ladies' room, removed her wet T-shirt, and sponged off most of the beer, which had begun to stick to her uncomfortably. She replaced her bra, then zipped up her cotton windbreaker over it and returned to the tables. Everybody spoke to her as she passed through the crowded room.

"Damn, Sam, you looking fucking dynamite . . ."

"Oughta be in the movies, girl . . ."

"Angels never had anybody better, hell, as good . . ."

Victoria and Mowery again sat at the Hell's Angels' table, but in a more prominent position. "Okay," one of the Angels said, "hold it down here at the table for a minute, I got an announcement to make. You all know Cliff Mowery. Good man. I like him, you like him. Cliff's a hell of a bike rider and a hell of a man. None better when trouble comes, and he damn sure can hold his mud. Church meeting last week in San Berdoo I put Cliff up for membership in the Angels and . . ."

Applause immediately broke out at the table. "Right on . . ."

". . . and as Cliff's sponsor I'm here to tell you that every brother there at the meeting knows Cliff and felt just like you men here do that he ought to get his colors right away."

Vern picked up a box near his chair on the floor, opened it, and withdrew a leather vest. On the front was the name "CLIFF" tooled into the soft leather and on the back a white rocker with "CALIFORNIA" in red. Vern presented the vest to Mowery.

"Cliff knows, because I told him, that everybody who becomes an Angel gets there by being a prospect. Prospect time is a little different for different folks, but it doesn't take long, Cliff. Meantime you got all the privileges of a Angel except for church meetings." Vern was alluding to regular club meetings, referred to as "church" among the biker brethren. "You'll ride with us, do what we do and what's asked of you, talk business with all the members. Congratulations."

Vern offered his hand to shake and Mowery took it. Mowery also responded to an embrace by his sponsor and shook hands all around the four tables occupied by Angels. No speech was required or expected. He mumbled thanks and sat down, but not until he had slipped into his new vest.

Beaming, truly excited with this extraordinary turn of events, was Victoria. She knew that when Carlander received the news he would be pleased. Their man was being allowed into the workings of an organization that had hitherto been impossible to penetrate.

When the contest was over and dancing had given way to serious drinking, Victoria noticed that she was no longer excluded from "business" conversations. She was now Sam or "Lady Sam" and allowed to sit where she liked.

"Proud of you," Dago Paul said, his arm around her shoulder, where he left it when his attention turned across the table.

"T.Q.'s the man for dynamite. C-4. Ammo. Some reason he don't fuck with guns 'cause I guess he don't work near 'em . . ."

". . . have to drive the trucks down here from Sacramento. How 'bout you, Shane? Takes three people, two to drive and a shotgun . . ."

"Then we'll smoke the motherfucker," Victoria heard Dago Paul say, "he don't fuckin' see reason. It just isn't that hard to understand when I tell 'em how it is. Can't have people testifying against the brothers."

*A witness?* She wondered. *Must be a witness.*

". . . with Trudy at DMV. She's got a damn drawer full of car titles but, hell, she moves all over the office. Driver's license we pay for, too, but the main thing is that she rides and gets fucked every Sunday because her ex-old man has the kids then . . ."

Laughter. The biker was talking about Trudy Morse, a state employee in the Department of Motor Vehicles who supplied genuine papers of registration, licenses, and receipts for a price and often at no cost to her best friends and customers, the Hell's Angels. Victoria would remember her name.

". . . he knows everybody over there. Wears his colors. Go to Stanley's Gun Room on South Main and Warner. He'll take all the crank you got . . ."

". . . a desk jockey at Orange Mining Company . . . selling for us now . . ."

Victoria felt that she was sitting among the perpetrators of every crime committed in the tri-county area. She marveled at the quality of information that drifted by her like ripe fruit ready for plucking from a tree. Police intelligence units could spend thousands of man-hours attempting to glean a fraction of what she was hearing at a single beer bust.

". . . shot that little motherfucker right through the heart, man. Dead before he hit the fucking floor. . . . Damn right, 'cause I called the next day, talked to the lame-ass bartender . . . gonna think again 'fore he plays any more o' that nigger music . . ."

Victoria's head snapped around. Bugger Butch doubled over in laughter as he pantomimed the way his victim had slid to the floor. She began to watch him carefully. She had seen him around and knew that he carried a gun, like most Angels. Now she remembered why Butch had tugged at a nerve. Witnesses to the cold-blooded killing of Kenny King in the Capri Bar in Huntington Beach had said that the killer had worn a hat that said "HELL'S ANGELS" on the crown. The name Butch had been attached. This man could be him.

Victoria had the distinct impression that this was the Angels' way of revealing to her how important they were. They talked with humor about reselling stolen goods, a staple industry of theirs, and the fact that one of the "brothers" would not have to stand trial in San Bernardino County after all, thanks to the presence of Dago Paul. He casually allowed as to how he was wanted in Connecticut for essentially the same thing. Murder.

The Hell's Angels had accepted Mowery into the inner circle, and Victoria was with Mowery. She was excited at the prospects. She speculated about how long they might remain there: weeks? She would be satisfied with weeks. In fact it would be months, and those months would be devastating to a major criminal enterprise.

# CHAPTER 10

The undercover operation had been under way fully three months and Victoria recognized that she was feeling the effects of strain from long hours and the stress of being always on guard against the slip that would give her away.

The next afternoon, January 14, 1977, Victoria was beginning to feel that her cold beer soaking had been worth every drop.

At a table in the San Francisco Bar with Buffalo were Fat Mike, an H.A., and someone neither Mowery nor Victoria had met before. His name was Doug, and he was introduced as a "friend." Doug was average size, wiry, and wore a western hat and boots. He was an ex-member of the Hangmen, a club that the Angels did not like and had warned to move their act out of southern California. Doug was apparently attempting to rectify his first wrong choice in motorcycle clubs by offering the Angels a piece of his business, which was extortion from massage parlors.

But Buffalo was talking now to her and Mowery together about a different kind of deal. "I'm kind of short," he said, "so

I can't do all I want. Like I'm doing something with Fat Mike, you know, buying a club, so we got to make some big scores. Coke is where you do business enough to grab off thirty thousand, that's what we need, but not all the brothers dig coke. It is shit, but hell, we'll do it anyway, me and Fat Mike. Big fucking place, like this maybe, so we got a place that makes some money, all the beer we fucking drink we shouldn't be paying retail, huh?"

"Smart," Mowery agreed with Buffalo. Victoria wondered if he was paying lip service or if he truly agreed.

"Yeah. So we had a connection won't do us any good right now," Buffalo continued, "today, because we been layin' out all this bread to, you know, buy the club . . ."

"What's he sellin'?" Mowery asked.

"Crank. I figured you might be interested. You got some places to sell it, right, Sam?" Buffalo said directly to Victoria. It was far from the first deal she had ever done with the Angels.

"Yeah, I have some customers," she responded. "Is it good meth?"

"Wait till you try the shit. Man, it is really, really good stuff," Buffalo enthused.

"Our own. So you know it's gotta be good," Doug added, nodding his head for emphasis.

Our own. From "our" factory? Victoria felt her pulse quicken.

"So where do we get it?" Mowery asked.

"Easy Gene. Know him?" Buffalo asked.

"Naw." Mowery let his eyes drift around the room, then settle on Victoria.

"From up north. And Charlie One-Thumb," Buffalo said.

"I know that crazy motherfucker. He was at Chino," Mowery said. He looked sidelong at Victoria as though to convey "complications."

Victoria smiled at him. "I didn't know you were at Chino, darling."

"Ten months," he said.

"Ten months and couldn't remember. What a life. Travel. Friends all around you. No money worries," she smiled as she batted her eyes.

"They're gonna meet you at the Handi-Mart on Lincoln in Anaheim," Buffalo was saying.

Mowery looked Victoria squarely in the eyes. "Wish you'd been there with me."

"Hey. You in or not?" Buffalo wanted to know. "They're gonna be there tomorrow noon."

The next morning Mowery and Victoria announced the offer at breakfast while Carlander and Nease ate pancakes and listened.

"You gonna eat your sausage?" Nease asked Carlander.

"I ordered it," the cop said simply.

"No shit? That how it got there on your plate?" Nease shot back.

"Charlie One-Thumb's a rat," Mowery said.

"Think he'd set us up?" Victoria asked, concerned. The operation had to end someday. It would likely end because they were discovered.

"Sure." Mowery cynically believed anyone could—and would—set up anyone else. "I know he would."

"You already ate two eggs with your pancakes," Nease reminded Carlander.

"So? I'm bigger than you. A lot bigger. Stronger, smarter, bigger," Carlander said with finality.

"Sausage do all that for you?" Nease mouthed, striking back.

"Want some more, order it," Carlander said, regarding Victoria and Mowery.

"Why would he?" Victoria asked.

"I don't know." Mowery shrugged. "Money. Maybe just to be mean. Why does anybody do any shit? How much cash you got?"

"Enough. Buffalo wouldn't set me up," Victoria said, attempting to learn more about Mowery's suspicions.

"You an expert now? Bike riders? Reading minds or what?" Mowery said.

"He likes me. He wouldn't set me up," Victoria insisted. Intellectually she knew Mowery was right, that anybody would set up anybody else given a set of circumstances. But she did not believe that Buffalo would do it to her.

"I thought you were a whole lot smarter than that. Should be by now."

"Forget it. We're not here to pick assignments," Carlander said, settling the issue. "Man sets you up with a drug buy, meth, maybe from their factory. Can't pass on a chance like that unless you got a big-time reason."

"Getting set up is a big-time reason," Victoria pointed out.

"You know that, Vicky? What makes you think that?" Carlander said.

"I didn't say I knew it, I'm only asking because our star outlaw here brought up the subject of a possible double-cross." Carlander was on the prod today, she thought. It did not happen often, but when it did she wished they could all go home and start all over.

"Yes or no to the double-cross, Mowery?" Carlander asked, wanting to put an end to what sounded like speculation on everyone's part.

"Fuck. Who knows? She's got a gun, so what's to worry?" Mowery said, displeased that his opinion was so lightly considered.

"I love it. Victoria's gonna smoke Charlie One-Thumb," Nease said, chuckling.

"Hey, Carlander, your kid having a problem at school?" Mowery asked as the others walked outside.

"Huh? What you know about a problem? What kind of problem?"

"I'm asking you. That's all."

"So why did you ask?" Carlander said.

"Because I heard you talking about it on the phone one time. You were using the phone at the Ten-to-One. Remember?" Mowery said, an edge to his voice.

"Yeah, well, quit listening to other people's conversations. He's fine. He's an honor student. You know, just like you were in high school." Carlander saw the expression of hurt and sudden flash of anger on Mowery's face, and the detective was immediately sorry. He tried to think of apologetic words, but they eluded him.

Mowery joined Victoria, who was waiting outside by the bike. He turned the key in the ignition, stabbed the chopper into life, and, with Victoria on the back, spun out of the parking lot on their way to meet with Charlie One-Thumb.

A few minutes later Mowery had parked the Harley-Davidson in a lot in front of a convenience store.

"Where's the shadow?" he asked as they dismounted from the chopper. Victoria looked up and down the street but did not see Carlander or Nease. They might have gotten hung up in traffic, the usual hazard in the game of follow-the-leader that more often became hide-and-seek.

Victoria paused to retrieve a tube of lipstick and a hand mirror from a small leather purse she wore attached to her belt while they were riding. She pretended to look into the mirror but instead scanned Lincoln Boulevard. Nearby was a four-way STOP signal and the shoulders of an embankment of a busy cross street beyond. While she delayed by using the business of applying makeup, she saw none of the frequently changed cars used for undercover operations. She and Mowery could not continue to stand outside any longer without creating a question if anyone within was watching them. "Let's go," she said.

Inside the store they pretended to examine merchandise on the shelves. They were appraised by an employee of dark complexion who wore an earring in his left ear and had a tattoo on each forearm. He shifted his attention to a magazine he had presumably borrowed from a store rack. Victoria believed that the clerk was friendly with, if not a member of, the motorcycle alliance. Mowery and Victoria strolled through the premises until they reached a doorway leading into a storage room. As they stepped inside, Mowery was met by a familiar face.

"Shane," Charlie One-Thumb said. "Ain't seen you since when, shit, ah . . ."

"Chino," Mowery said, his gaze taking in the far corners of the back room and its array of boxes and cans.

"Yeah, yeah, hell, man, how's it?" Charlie One-Thumb offered his upraised hand in the traditional thumb-clasp. Mowery took it. True to his sobriquet, Charlie One-Thumb was missing a thumb on his right hand. He appeared to be in his forties. Mowery searched back ten years to Chino and tried to picture

Charlie One-Thumb at the time. He had been missing his thumb even then and at six feet two inches he was rail thin. He wore a leather jacket at all times, hot weather or cold, and the collar was always turned up at the neck in a fifties look. Inside the jacket, Mowery knew, Charlie carried a knife. There was likely a handgun there, too, Mowery guessed.

"I'm okay," Mowery said. "You?"

"I been cool. Out five years next month, November."

"Next month's March, Charlie . . ." Mowery corrected.

"Whatever."

"Doing good, huh?" Mowery said amiably.

Victoria knew him well enough to recognize his *pro forma* exchange. He couldn't care less about how good or bad Charlie One-Thumb was doing.

"Righteous lady, man. Yours?" Charlie One-Thumb said of Victoria as though she were property. Like a bike or a gun.

"Just renting," Mowery said smoothly.

Victoria recognized his response as proper for a biker, but she would never get used to it. Nor did she like the fact that she could do nothing about it.

"Well, you're spendin' your money right," Charlie One-Thumb said without feeling. He was nervous and, Victoria believed, was more concerned about finishing his business rather than reminiscing about old prison days.

"You ain't lying. Damn, you live good."

Victoria and Mowery turned toward the owner of the voice behind them. It belonged to a man Victoria thought was as ugly as they came. His face was pockmarked so that his nose looked as though it had been hit with fine buckshot. He had a single eye tattooed above it. A notch had been carved in one ear and a scar beginning at one corner of his mouth ran to his chin. He was under six feet tall and overweight, but there could be no mistake that muscle lay underneath.

"Know Easy Gene here?" Charlie One-Thumb asked Mowery.

"No," Mowery said. Easy Gene was not from around Orange County, he was sure.

Mowery did not offer his hand, nor did Easy Gene. A twinge of a smile touched Easy Gene's warped mouth as though he was accustomed to creating instant dislike in people he met, and might have enjoyed the effect.

"This is Lady Sam, Charlie," Mowery said, pointedly ignoring the newcomer.

"Guess we missed the show the other night," Charlie One-Thumb allowed. "Heard about you."

"No reason we can't have our own back here, huh, Mama?" Easy Gene grinned as he moved closer to Victoria.

"Let's do what we came here to do," she said, hoping her voice did not betray her.

"Hell, we can do any fucking thing we want back here. Business, everything," the evil-faced biker pressed. "Let's spread some around, baby."

She froze at the man's blunt suggestion. She realized that she was standing with three bikers, all sociopaths, in a dark room doing a drug deal. She had no way out. What would Mowery do if Easy Gene and or Charlie One-Thumb insisted on playing? Mowery would ultimately save himself if it was him or her. She could scream, but she had no idea where Carlander was located, and even if he was parked at the curb he could not possibly hear from that location near an eight-lane boulevard.

"Any goddamn reason why I shouldn't spread you around?" Mowery asked Easy Gene in a voice that was almost a whisper.

Mowery's reaction started Victoria's heart pumping again. She was now glad, delighted, relieved that he was big and tough.

"Huh? You comin' down on me, man?" Easy Gene said, clearly taken by surprise. And angry. "That ain't right."

"What isn't fuckin' right is your manners. You don't borrow my scooter, you don't take my boots, you don't make for my old lady without asking. You understand what I'm saying to you?" Mowery held his gaze on Easy Gene without blinking.

Charlie One-Thumb's eyes widened, expecting the worst. Easy Gene's jaw clenched, and his hand moved toward his side. He had a knife, maybe more. Mowery seemed not bothered in the least. "Whatever you come up with, dude, you're gonna eat it with your gums."

"Hey, man," Easy Gene said, visibly struggling to control his black anger, "I'm just telling your lady here she's dynamite. I

144 / *Michael Detroit*

don't appreciate taking shit from a prospect," he blurted as a
face-saving retort.

Easy Gene was of course referring to Mowery's proposed
candidacy in the Hell's Angels. Fighting among members was
a serious breach of club rules. Fighting over women among
the membership was simply not tolerated. It was a denial of
the brotherhood that provided the glue that held the group
together. But although the notion of communal sharing existed, in practice some men were jealous and their women protected.

Victoria looked at Mowery in wonder. He had done what he
had repeatedly said he would not do: fight the membership to
protect her. But the confrontation ended when Charlie One-
Thumb became impatient. He wanted to be rid of the dope he
was carrying, and a fight inside a public building was not the
smartest move to make. "I'm standing here with business to
do."

"Yeah," Victoria agreed quickly, "let's do it."

Charlie One-Thumb produced a plastic bag and offered it to
her. "Straight from the factory to you," he said.

"You mean it's local?" she wondered out loud.

"Hell's that to you?" Charlie One-Thumb's reaction was instant, his suspicions aroused.

"Nothing," Victoria said.

"Goddamn right, nothing. Exactly fucking nothing." Charlie
One-Thumb stared, unblinking, into Victoria's eyes.

"Sorry I asked," she said earnestly, wondering how she could
cover her gaffe.

But he was not appeased. He took back the plastic bag from
Victoria's hands and replaced it in his pocket. "I don't like this.
No good. Let's go."

Mowery did not move to step aside. "Hey, man, don't cut me
loose. She don't know the rules yet."

"I don't know the lady," Charlie One-Thumb spat.

"You know me. I look like a cop to you?" Mowery insisted.

Charlie One-Thumb considered the logic of this for a moment. "Well . . . You got twenty-two yards?"

"I have," Victoria said quickly. "I'm the bank."

"Price should be two large. Discount, how I figure it," Mowery said.

Charlie One-Thumb nodded his head. "Guess that's right. Okay."

The exchange was made, money for powdered methamphetamine.

Two city cops sat in a black-and-white on the opposite side of Lincoln Boulevard. What they saw was a patrol officer's red flag. Mowery was of the ilk that offended the establishment: rugged, long hair, tattooed, riding a chopper with a woman on the back. If there was a pretext to pull him over, the police would find one. They would then have a reason to run him on radio. A computerized record check would be made for outstanding warrants, for example. Unpaid parking tickets would give them an excuse to book him, to search him. A man and a woman of their type almost certainly had something to hide. The officers waited, engine running, their eyes never leaving the chopper.

Mowery and Victoria had pockets full of enough dope to make page two of most newspapers and two Hell's Angels watching them from the store. If they were arrested with the methamphetamine they had just bought from Charlie One-Thumb, then released, the game would be up.

The engine of the chopped-down Harley thrummed, eager to blast, its rider equally anxious to cut loose, to be free of what would become a face-off between him and the fuzz. Mowery waited for the police to make a move. They waited for him.

Mowery gunned the chopper's engine. It snarled, snapped.

"Don't," Victoria warned. As she spoke into his ear she saw Carlander and Nease parked on the opposite side of the boulevard hardly twenty yards from the city cops. She also understood that Carlander was powerless to intervene lest he be seen by Charlie One-Thumb and Easy Gene.

As Carlander watched events about to explode, it was one of the many times that he wished that his unit had access to radios. But the risk was too great. Hell's Angels, indeed many bikers, were known to monitor police frequencies with scanners. The two Narcotics officers could only slide deeper into their own car seats and watch.

Traffic was flowing between Mowery and the waiting police car. The busy four-way light changed, giving north-south traffic a green light. Cars arriving at the intersection slowed, braked, and began to form a barrier eight lanes deep between chopper and cop car. Mowery began to crank hard on the Harley's handlebar gas feed until the engine jumped to six thousand revs.

Instinctively, Victoria put her arms around his waist and locked them in place. As though it were a signal, Mowery popped the clutch, leaned the bike over hard, and burned rubber for ten feet, kicking the transmission into increasingly higher-ratio gears as they sped down Lincoln Boulevard in an easterly direction.

The city cops had anticipated a sudden dash. Their car was stepped up with a law enforcement "intercept package" designed for high-speed pursuit. The police officer giving chase to Mowery ripped a long trail of rubber and aimed his vehicle over a median divider, then around six lanes of cars, all beginning to move as the light changed again.

Carlander made no attempt to keep up with the chase. It would give him away. He could only wait.

Mowery and Victoria tore down Lincoln Boulevard, hitting eighty miles per hour, cutting in and out of cars and trucks. The police car wailed its siren, blinked its lights, and parted the sea of cars in front. The police officer in the passenger seat used his radio to call for help from all available units. Within minutes more police cars joined up.

What was providing Mowery and Victoria with their best chance of escape was heavy traffic. No matter how effective the siren and red light, the car continually had to slow for people to clear a path.

Mowery would have had little trouble outrunning a single police car, but the accepted method of running down a fleeing suspect was for three or more units to travel in the same direction, using radios to coordinate turns that would block off numbers of streets with at least one car for each street. The pursued vehicle would thus sooner or later turn into a converging police unit.

Mowery was unpredictable, though, and he had guts. He blasted down alleys at flat-out speeds and launched from them into cross streets with no thought to oncoming or crossing traffic. He rode on sidewalks and under freeway overpasses. He looked constantly for an entrance to a freeway where he could use the cutting characteristic of the bike to best advantage and at the same time limit those following to a single line astern.

Clinging to Mowery for dear life, Victoria was certain that she would never see Bill again, or swim in warm Pacific waters, or visit with her parents and siblings. She would be found by her fellow officers, a bleeding, unrecognizably broken body slammed up against a concrete bridge abutment. Mowery made a left onto Rembrandt in Villa Park. Police units took up chase positions on four nearby streets. They used two cars to block off the entrance to the 55 freeway on Van Owen and chased Mowery and Victoria back north.

Mowery had a dire need for that freeway. Realizing that his escape to the north had been cut off, he slowed the bike slightly, leaned it deep, and opened the throttle, cutting a clean U in the middle of Rembrandt. He accelerated hard and passed through two oncoming police cars that had spun sideways attempting to create a roadblock. He wheeled down an incline that bordered the storm drain of Santiago Creek. He considered alternatives with police units closing in, gunned the engine, and half slid, half rolled down the concrete ditch.

On the back of the saddle Victoria had an unbreakable lock around Mowery's midsection.

Near a cloverleaf for highways 55 and 91, Mowery gunned the engine of the Harley, scaled the paved walls, and emerged at the top on a vacant lot. He kicked the chopper into second gear and wound it as tight as the machine would go. The transmission would either rip itself apart or would propel its riders up yet another hill, this one covered with ice-plant.

A police helicopter was ascending near the throat of the cloverleaf when Mowery and Victoria arrived at ramp level. Mowery gunned the chopper again, belted it into low gear, and took on another heavy section of freeway shoulder vegetation. The chopper's rear wheel began to spin without traction over the moist and slippery surface.

Cars along the freeway were screeching to smoky stops as police cars gave hard pursuit. When Mowery and Victoria arrived at the top of the elevated roadway, he lurched the bike into the tail end of the traffic headed north and, ultimately, to the 91 freeway interchange. He zoomed in and out of lanes, mostly in the emergency lane—and he believed this was an emergency—then wove through four other lines of cars and trucks, while running at seventy-plus miles per hour.

Having doubled back from his starting point, Mowery seemed to be outdistancing the chase cars. At the Olive off-ramp he dropped through two lines of cars, speeding first up, then down streets lacing Peralta Hills. Finally, he plunged the bike into foliage near Imperial Park.

And they sat. Victoria gasped for air. Mowery had no surplus of oxygen, either, his chest heaving as they listened for pursuit, the quiet of late day pulsing with cracking sounds of hot engine metal cooling fast, causing bits of moisture in the grass to hiss as they were turned into steam.

Mowery removed his leather jacket and stowed it under the chopper. Victoria took off her navy blue windbreaker as well as her dark glasses. After a time they left the bike and walked, leisurely, along the park's golf course, appearing no different from other young people who had adopted Orange County's laid-back lifestyle of flowing hair and denim. Several times police units flashed by but paid them no mind. Coming across a restaurant, they went inside and took a seat.

Mowery looked across the table at Victoria. She was shaking, her face red. "Scared?"

She nodded her head vigorously. Then shook it. "Not scared. Excited. Scared, too, I guess."

"Me, too. Kick-ass, wasn't it? Huh? See them babies in the ditch?" Mowery's eyes were bright, shining.

"You mean the river?" Victoria asked, adrenaline still coursing through her body.

"Yeah. The river. Bet the cars that went down there are still there. Hope the fucking tide comes in and washes 'em out."

They both laughed.

"God, I mean . . . What a rush!" she said, wiping matted hair from her face.

"How about a drink?" he asked her.

"What'll it be?" a waitress asked.

"Ahhhhh. Quart of whiskey, two glasses," Mowery said.

The middle-aged waitress was not amused. "We don't have that here, sir," she said, lips pursed.

"Could you run next door and get it for us?"

"I can't believe you said that," Victoria said. "Bring me a Coke. Big one."

"Okay. And pie. Got boysenberry pie? No? Apple. À la mode. Make it two." Mowery was still laughing at himself. "This is what meth does for you," he said after the waitress had gone. "That's why they call it speed. You don't pour alcohol on top of speed. Not when you have the real thing. You know that."

"I'll call the store. Carlander's going to shit," Victoria said and rose to call from a pay phone in the restaurant.

Carlander was not in the office when she called, and she left a message about where they were located. She returned to the table. She could not help but notice the looks she got from other customers. Some were flirtatious, some jealous, others condemning.

"See that hummer cross Hoover?" Mowery's eyes were still bright. "Had his foot stomped down flat on the brake but he was going ass-backward."

"He was spinning!" Victoria found her excitement rising again. "Down into the ditch. . . . I didn't think we'd make it. I honest to God thought we were going to die. How fast did we go?"

"Guess," Mowery challenged.

"I don't know. I bet you don't, either," she dared. She could not imagine that he would have taken the time to look. "A hundred? Think we did a hundred?"

"I don't know. Naw, that'd be against the law," he said.

"I thought they had us in the park," she said, shaking her head at the memory.

"Hell," he scoffed.

"Really, I thought they had us," she insisted.

Color gradually drained from Victoria's flushed face. "God, here I am raving about . . . we ran away from the police. High-speed chase on a motorcycle and I'm . . . I'm a cop, and I'm ready to buy drinks because we beat 'em."

She regarded Mowery for a long moment, and he her.

"Still got your gun?" he said.

She sobered, became alert. "Yes. Why?"

Mowery lowered his voice, shifted his eyes around the room. "Let's take this place off."

"What?"

"You stick your iron up that fat bastard's nose and hold everybody while I clean out the cash," he said, his voice just above an urgent whisper.

"What do you mean?" she said, her mouth parted in alarm.

"Easy money. I fire up the Hog, you run out the door, maybe fire a couple rounds past the asshole's ears, just to keep 'em standing awhile, then hop on behind me. We're fucking gone." He nodded his head for emphasis.

Victoria continued to stare at him. Then she dropped her head onto her folded arms and began to shake all over. She was unable to stop her convulsive laughter. She understood that all of this was the product of hysteria. Post–nervous system shock or something.

The two of them were still laughing when Carlander, in ill humor, arrived at their table.

"The hell's so funny?" the detective demanded.

"We're going to hold the place up," Victoria informed her colleague.

"What're you talking about?" Carlander looked from one to the other.

"I'm going to put my gun on the manager," Victoria said. "Mowery's going to grab the cash and we split on the bike."

"What's so funny about that?" Carlander insisted.

Victoria and Mowery began laughing all the harder.

"I don't have to ask whose stupid fucking idea that was," Carlander grumbled. "Mowery would do it, no problem there. You know what you left behind you on the streets out there? Still looking for you. Doubt if I could have called it off if I wanted to.

Anyway, I'm not going to tell 'em and don't you, either. We'd all go to jail," Carlander grumbled.

The waitress arrived, pencil poised.

"Bring me some pie, will you?" Carlander said. "And a hamburger. Make it a couple."

He looked at Victoria. "Give me the evidence. You still have the evidence, don't you? Give it to me and I'll mark it." He put a hand into his jacket pocket and came forth with a plastic evidence bag. "We'll do the paperwork and get the hell out of here before they start a house-to-house search."

Mowery rose from the table. "I'll get the bike," he said.

"I don't see how you can," Victoria said, frowning.

"Can't leave it out there too long. Sombody'll steal it." They grinned at each other. "All right. I'll wait'll it gets dark," Mowery added.

"Yeah," said Carlander, still in ill humor, "they pick your ass up, do me a favor and go to jail. Don't fucking call me."

"Did you see him ride that bike?" Victoria asked after Mowery had gone. "Fantastic. I never saw anything like that in my life. No wonder . . . I was scared, Wayne. Really. But hell, I always am, anyway, on that thing. But something happened today, I couldn't, didn't have time to think about it. I just hung on. What would have happened if they caught him? I mean us?"

"Somebody would've got hurt, his butt woulda been cooling off upstate in Soledad. We'd be looking for jobs, you and me," he said without hesitation.

"After what he was trying to do for us? You think so?" It was clear to Victoria that they had turned the corner. Certainly Mowery had become a productive citizen. He had risked his life today, for the team.

"What's he trying to do for us? You thinking Mowery is gonna coach Little League next season?" Carlander challenged. "Figure he's going to open a savings account and then buy a house, plant flowers? C'mon. He's a biker. He's the kind of guy we're trying to put away. Thief. And if he gets a chance he'll deal drugs, do holdups. Killing wouldn't cost him thirteen minutes' sleep."

"Maybe."

"Maybe?" Carlander said, incredulous that she could doubt what he was saying.

"People aren't always . . ." she began, then trailed off. Carlander didn't understand. He couldn't. He wasn't in a position to experience what she had gone through.

"Mowery isn't people," Carlander interrupted.

No response.

"How's Bill doin'?" he asked.

"Fine." Victoria felt suddenly deflated.

"What's 'fine' mean?"

She had to live with him and Mowery and Nease for fourteen hours every day, but her private business was her own. "Means he's just fine, I guess. Don't see him much," Victoria said to close off the conversation, but having said as much, she realized it was true. She saw precious little of her husband and it was a constant ache.

"Take tomorrow morning off and get reacquainted," Carlander said, biting into his sandwich.

"Sunday," she said simply.

"Am I eating this hamburger here by myself? I know tomorrow is Sunday. I'm saying relax. Have some fun." He had noticed lately the obvious strain on Victoria. He wanted her to emerge from the program with everything intact, including her marriage.

"The Angels are having a picnic," Victoria said, knowing that Carlander would understand its meaning.

He hesitated. He regarded the last bite of his second hamburger as he considered. "Hmmm. Lot of heavies'll be there. Bet on that. Where're they going?"

"Mulholland somewhere." Victoria was almost looking forward to the ride. The scenery was beautiful, and Malibu rides were typically done at low cruising speeds.

"Malibu," he mused to himself. The Malibu mountains were a maze of paved roads that wound through a hundred miles of beautiful countryside just above some of the most expensive real estate in southern California. It was a biker's paradise.

"Yeah, I think so," Victoria said.

Carlander had determined to spend time with his children.

The team was working too many hours. "Ah, shine the picnic," he said to Victoria. "Take the day off."

"Dandy," she said dryly. She knew that a day off would be the smart thing for everyone to do, but she also knew that the operation would not move forward while they were at home.

"Testy today. Minute ago you were a happy little cop broad. Now you're testy." Carlander took a large bite out of his hamburger.

"Sorry." Postexcitement depression had set in. She was suddenly exhausted.

"Don't be sorry and don't be testy. Let me tell you something, Vicky." Carlander turned to look her in the eyes. "You're doing a hell of a job. I mean not a pretty good one, but a hell of a big-time job. Gates is going quietly bugshit over that stuff you picked up at the Roaring 20's. Dope about Butch and the rest of it. We're running the guy and we think he's the shooter last year at the Capri, just like you said. And the shit on Dago Paul. He's got a warrant, all right, a one-eighty-seven in Connecticut. Gates thinks you're very special. Everybody else does, too. Won't be long you'll be moving up fast. You'll be a captain or a chief someday and I'll be calling you ma'am."

"Come on, Wayne . . ." Although Victoria felt embarrassed, she was certain he was right. She realized fully that she was unique not only because she was a woman but because she was effective in the field.

"I don't have a college education. That's part of what it takes and you got it. Plus a feel for this business. You got that, too. You're paying the price . . . we all do, but there are some prices aren't worth it. Like Bill. He's not worth nailing all these bastards. All of 'em."

It was past midnight, as usual, when she arrived home. Bill had gone to bed. There was a note on the kitchen counter: *Call home.* The terseness of the note alarmed Victoria. It sounded ominous. It was too early in the morning to wake her family— she would wait a few hours—but her concern caused her to shake Bill from deep sleep.

"What's wrong with my mother?" Victoria asked.

"Your mother?" Bill rubbed his eyes, his nose, tried to rise up through the dark pool of comfort he had suddenly left. "Nothing."

"Then who called? Is my father all right? The kids?" she demanded to know.

"Relax. Your father called. Your mother's coming out for a visit. She and, ah, Lucille and Maxine," Bill recalled with effort. "They're going to see your Aunt Pauline in Wichita first."

"Oh, God, no. She can't do that." Victoria's mother and sisters had traveled several times to southern California to visit with her, and Victoria looked forward to the visits immensely. But now she was alarmed. "She can't come," she repeated.

"Want me to meet 'em at the airport in the morning and tell 'em to get on the next plane back?" Bill offered facetiously.

"Of course not but . . . but they can't see me like . . ." She stopped herself in midsentence.

"Why not? Anything wrong with the way you are?" Bill sat up in bed, pulling another pillow behind him.

Victoria looked at her husband for an ulterior meaning in his question. "No," she said. "It's just that I don't think they'd have much fun if they came now. I . . . I couldn't spend time with them and . . ."

"And someone might see you with them? Somebody on a motorcycle?" he offered.

It was true. Bikes were everywhere. She saw them in her dreams. Victoria had become so paranoid about people who rode motorcycles that it didn't make any difference to her that the majority of them were law-abiding citizens. In her fearful fantasies they were all interconnected, a network of cop-hating crooks and killers. Plus, to receive her mother and sisters while she was rising in the morning, dragging in after midnight after a day spent roaring from town to town on the back of a chopper, was in her mind out of the question. She said as much to Bill.

"Your mother knows you're a deputy sheriff," Bill said. "So do your sisters. Tell them you're working on a case. They'll understand."

He spoke without conviction, as though he were presenting her with another barricade to knock down. "It isn't that," she said in frustration.

"Then what? Tell me so I can go back to sleep," he said, looking at a bedside clock.

Victoria knew what the problem was. She could feel the changes that she had undergone living with the bikers and she couldn't bear the thought of her family seeing them, too.

# CHAPTER 11

Supersonic Chuck, a.k.a. Charles Morgan Frey, was a wannabe Hell's Angel. They thought he was "lame," however, with no "value." They had no room for trainees, Mowery had explained to Victoria. Like so many bikers, though, Supersonic Chuck was a dealer of all kinds of drugs, including meth. Making a case against him was worth the time and trouble because the suspect was part of a larger whole. Victoria had to pursue every lead available.

"Prob'ly won't like this one," Mowery said to her as he slowed for a STOP sign in Anaheim.

"I don't like any of them. What makes this different?" They were approaching a mobile home park and she noticed its profusion of palm trees made sickly from heavy concentrations of poison particulate spewed by automobiles into the air. There were no new trailers parked among homes that seemed better called shanties on wheels. Nor was there anything mobile about the trailers that Victoria could see as Mowery wove among the narrow "streets." They were wheelless, blocked up, or had flat tires, with bare dirt yards fronting aluminum doors, junk cars, children's broken toys, and broken people.

"Supersonic Chuck. He's different," Mowery said over his shoulder as he pulled up in front of a small trailer made of aluminum and shaped like a large bathtub turned upside down. It had been manufactured by an aircraft company that intended to diversify its product line back in the late forties when peace briefly threatened American enterprise. The trailer bore lines of rivets and had been left unpainted like the fuselage of an ill-fated bomber.

Victoria thought Mowery had made a mistake. Surely nobody could live here. Flies swarmed around trash piled up in over-flowing barrels, cans, and cartons. Weeds struggled valiantly in baked clay soil so hard only ants could dig through it.

"Supersonic Chuck's inside," Mowery said.

Victoria followed him reluctantly to the threshold of the trailer. It was necessary for Mowery to bend his knees and turn slightly sideways to maneuver his wide shoulders into the opening. "You here, Chuck?" he said into the gloom.

"Yeah. That you, Shane? Come on in, man." The voice from inside sounded more distant than Victoria thought possible. She stopped short inside the door and was almost repelled backward by a sickening stench that grabbed at her vitals.

"God. Oh, God, I have to get out of here," she mumbled. Her flight was checked by Mowery's hand on her arm.

"Not too spiffy, is it?" He laughed easily. "Supersonic Chuck's saving money he'd spend on a maid and keeping it hisself. That right, Chuck?"

"What's that?" A man's voice became more audible as he emerged from a tiny stall that contained, Victoria could now see, a bathroom.

"You don't need a maid, I was telling Lady Sam here." Mowery laughed again in genuine amusement. He was clearly enjoying Victoria's discomfort, a unique blow struck against law enforcement.

Victoria groped in her jeans pockets for a handkerchief to put over her nose. She remembered her bandanna, rolled and tied around her head to control her flowing locks on the bike. She snatched it from her blonde hair and placed it squarely over mouth and nose. If Supersonic Pig was offended, so be it. Mowery guided her toward one of two chairs in the trailer. They were placed around a linoleum-topped table supported by metal legs. The tabletop was piled with overflowing ashtrays, food cans, some with spoons stuck to their solidified contents, empty beer bottles, scraps of food, and plastic cups. On the floor parts of motorcycles were lying askew, still greasy after their removal; pornographic magazines lay wherever tossed, tools, plastic milk bottles containing water, a broken coffeepot, cardboard boxes full of toilet paper rolls, a filthy first-aid kit, a bed with a cover—Victoria judged it once was a sheet—so black from dirt it was unrecognizable at first look, and a quilt equally filthy balled atop the bed.

"Wanna beer?" Supersonic Chuck asked his guests. He wedged open the lid of a plastic picnic cooler and withdrew a bottle of Budweiser beer, still dripping from warm water that long ago was ice.

"Hell, yeah, I'll have one," Mowery said, enjoying himself hugely.

"How about you, Sam?" Supersonic Chuck asked.

Victoria was now able to breathe through her nose without gagging, but she was not prepared to touch anything to her mouth until she was safely outside this garbage dump. Supersonic Chuck was about thirty years old, she guessed. He was a bit shorter than average and tended toward paunchiness brought about by, according to the evidence around her, vast quantities of beer. His clothes were filthy and he had not shaved in more weeks than Victoria could estimate. He wore the uniform of the biker: jeans, wide belt from which a chain was attached. He seemed to be wearing a T-shirt underneath his biker's vest, but it might have been just dirt. "No," she croaked. "Nothing."

Supersonic Chuck smiled. "Well, breakfast of champions," he said, tipping the Bud bottle in her direction before swallowing half its contents in a single gulp. He belched and smiled again in her direction. "Place needs a little work here and there," he admitted.

Mowery turned toward Victoria. "See, Supersonic Chuck here is gonna win a bet . . ."

"Won it. Yesterday," said Supersonic Chuck, interrupting.

Mowery nodded vigorously, pleased to be corrected. "Okay. Right on. So he won it," Mowery resumed explaining to Victoria. "Bet Mexican Kenny and Shifter that he could go a year without taking a bath. Stinks a little, hell, stinks a lot, but you won," Mowery finished, hoisting his Bud toward the filthy biker.

"How much?" Victoria gasped, incredulous, removing the bandanna from her nose once again to speak.

"Hundred dollars," said Supersonic Chuck proudly.

"A hun . . ." She could not finish the words. "Not a million dollars?"

"Huh? Million. Hell, no. Hey, lookit this." Supersonic Chuck put toe to heel and pushed a motorcycle boot from his foot. Underneath was a blackened foot with shreds hanging from ankles and toes.

"God," Victoria breathed. "What happened to your foot?"

"Part of the bet," Supersonic Chuck beamed. "Couldn't change socks, neither."

Mowery howled with laughter and Supersonic Chuck howled with him. Victoria could find nothing humorous in this macabre setting. She was aware that she was observing herself to see if her mind had slipped as far as her new colleagues'. She looked toward Mowery with imploring eyes. "Let's buy the whites," she said, referring to the Benzedrine deal promised.

"Sure thing, Sam," Mowery responded. He accepted a second bottle of beer offered by his host. "We came for the crank. Buffalo call you about it? Is it meth? We could use some of that."

"Naw, all I got's whites, but they're righteous. Shit you not, man, real good product." Supersonic Chuck retrieved a tattered shoe box from under his bed, hidden among rags that once might have been articles of clothing. From inside the box he withdrew one of several small plastic bags full of white tablets. He handed the bag to Mowery, who glanced at them briefly before passing them on to Victoria. She took more time to examine the pills but decided against opening the bag to look closer. She was desperate to be out of the tin hovel. "How much?" she said.

"There's five hundred in there . . . I'll take seventy-five bucks." Supersonic Chuck nodded his head in agreement with his own price.

Mowery contradicted him with an opposite movement of his head. "That don't come to a dime apiece," he said, not willing to attempt to calculate the amount of overcharge. "Price we're paying for whites."

"Then I don't make shit," Supersonic Chuck complained.

"Hey, man, then get off your ass into different work. Like steal fuckin' televisions or something." Mowery was confident, enjoying Supersonic Chuck's discomfort.

"Aw, hell. Okay. Fifty. I'm giving the shit away, but you can have 'em at fifty. How about sixty so I can make a dime?"

The deal was struck at fifty dollars, but a small commission was paid to Supersonic Chuck in the form of thirty tabs returned from the bag of five hundred. Victoria peeled off cash taken from the Orange County Sheriff's Department drug procurement budget and handed it over to the biker.

"Hear you're an Angel now," Supersonic Chuck said to Mowery with obvious envy. "Like, shit, man, that's real good. They should take me. Know what I mean? I mean, I told 'em I'd join. Don't know what the hell's the problem."

"I don't either, Chuckie," Mowery said encouragingly. "Hell, man, you got it all. And you can ride."

"Hey, can I ride or what?" He looked again to Mowery for confirmation that he was a stellar bike rider. Then he looked toward Victoria. "I mean I'm dynamite on wheels," he explained to her. "Know how I got my name? Supersonic Chuck? Because I can ride. Nobody better than me on two wheels. Like Shane just said."

Mowery was quick to support him. "Chuck was on his Harley doing about eighty miles an hour going down Euclid over at Garden Grove . . ."

"Hundred miles an hour," Supersonic Chuck interrupted.

"You couldn't get a hundred out of that pig you were herding . . ."

"Cops said I was going over a hundred," the biker insisted.

Mowery nodded in mock agreement. "Cops never lie, so it must have been over a hundred. Chuckie boy here gets to the Lincoln intersection about the same time a whole bunch of other cars did, too, and he drives through a Toyota . . ."

"Clean the hell through it." Supersonic Chuck nodded vigorously as he twisted the cap from another Budweiser.

"Not clear through," Mowery corrected.

"No, by God, clear through," Supersonic Chuck argued.

"Bad enough." Mowery regarded Victoria as he spoke. "Did go through the passenger-side door. Stuck right in the middle of the Toyota. Chuckie here went over the top of the car and just kept on going till he floated down on top of another car or two and then a pickup truck. Climbed down off the truck and kept on keeping on." Mowery broke into a grin and waited for Victoria to join him.

Despite herself Victoria was impressed with the story. "You mean you got away?"

Supersonic Chuck laughed, nodded his head. "Yeah. Whipping one foot down in front of another, cut through enough streets to stop in Stanton. Got home before light."

"How bad were you hurt?" Victoria asked. "Didn't you have to go to a hospital?"

"Scratched up a little, is all. Wearing leathers, you know." Supersonic Chuck beamed as he looked back and forth between his guests, delighted with the attention.

"Anybody hurt in the car you hit?" Victoria wanted to know.

"Nope," he said with pride.

Mowery's eyes caught Victoria's. A smile tugged at the corners of his mouth. Then he said evenly, "Two women in the front seat. One of 'em died."

"A Jap," Supersonic Chuck said, as though the victim's ethnicity explained his lack of remorse.

Victoria looked at Supersonic Chuck. The bike rider pulled heavily on his beer, face still beaming, unchanged by Mowery's revelation. Victoria did not have an appropriate response for the role of biker's girl that she was playing. So she said nothing.

Outside, inhaling the comparatively fresh air of Orange County's smog-filled ozone, Victoria willingly took her place on the chopper behind Mowery. "He's a bottom-feeder," Mowery observed, still in good spirits. "Angels wouldn't touch him."

Victoria shook her head, not really caring about his club affiliation. She only wanted to get onto the chopper and ride away.

\* \* \*

Victoria and Carlander were charged not only with putting as many drug-dealing bikers out of business as possible, but also with knowing at all times where Mowery was. But it wasn't easy.

Mowery was not only a high-impact presence envied by other bikers for his quick, easy entry into the Hell's Angels, but his reputation for raw guts was enhanced by a trip he had made with Dwayne Earl "Shifter" Warner to the town of Redlands in San Bernardino County. Shifter drove one of two stolen cars, the second driven by Mowery. The cars were to be sold to a man by the name of Johnny Sklar, a Chicago-based crook who made regular runs to the West Coast to pick up stolen autos for resale in the Midwest. The cars in question were a BMW and a Mercedes sedan. These cars had license plates and registrations supplied to them by Trudy Morse, who worked at the California Department of Motor Vehicles in Santa Ana. Neither Victoria nor Carlander was with Mowery on this trip, which later raised the question of whether or not he was "working" in his capacity of confidential informer for the Orange County Sheriff's Office or in fact committing a crime for his own gain.

The meeting with Sklar was to take place at one o'clock in the afternoon at a drinking spot called Haleys. Shifter and Mowery arrived early by design and went inside to have a drink and wait. By 2:30 P.M. Sklar still had not arrived. The waiting put Shifter in a bad mood. He and Mowery worked their way steadily through one long-necked bottle of beer after another, eventually drifting to the rear of the barroom where there was a pool table. Neither player was much good at the game, and the winner was a matter of indifference to both men. By five o'clock Shifter had had more pool than he cared for. He suggested they give up. The deal was likely blown, anyway.

The room had by then filled with workers from surrounding industrial sites, including the Fontana steel mill, and construction people working on the fabrication of an industrial park near I-10. Two men who appeared to be steelworkers strolled to the rear of the room and for a moment watched Shifter and Mowery as they played. Then one of the steelworkers placed a quarter on the table. He said, "We challenge the winner."

Shifter was lining up a shot as he said, "Pick up your quarter. We're not through."

The man took a drink from his beer mug while he measured Shifter. The biker stood several inches under six feet. He wore a tank top with "HARLEY-DAVIDSON" across the front. Shifter was not stocky, but his arms were sinewy muscle. Unlike Mowery's, Shifter's long black hair was tied in a ponytail. His wide belt theatrically sported stainless-steel studs. A person unfamiliar with the species might assume that his getup was the affectation of a small man trying to appear tough. If that was what the steelworkers thought, they were incorrect.

"Only one table in the house," the man said evenly. "You gotta take challenges."

Again, Shifter did not meet the steelworker's eyes but picked up the quarter and threw it across the room. Having missed his shot, he stepped to one side for Mowery to take his turn. The insulting message could not have been more clear.

Mowery watched from the corner of his eye while the construction workers returned to the front of the bar; one of them used a telephone as another took up station at the door, his eyes fixed on the bikers at the pool table.

"The dude ain't callin' out for pizza," Mowery said out of the side of his mouth to Shifter.

"Don't expect he is," Shifter agreed.

The arrival of reinforcements took less than ten minutes. Mowery and Shifter heard car doors slam outside. The spurned steelworker met his newly arrived colleagues as their numbers filled the door. Their conversation was not audible to Mowery and Shifter from across the room, but it did not have to be heard to be understood. And it was brief. Mowery and Shifter saw about a dozen men starting to move toward them across the room.

"I see two knives," Mowery said calmly. "Skinny guy in the middle, bald prick on the left."

Shifter laughed. "Wait'll they see my sword." He smashed his cue stick violently on the edge of the pool table. When the stick snapped it broke along the grain, creating a long, very sharp point. The sudden crack briefly caught the approaching steelworkers by surprise and their steps faltered for a moment. Mowery picked up three pool balls in his immense hand. He threw them with all of his strength into the oncoming battlers, striking two men, one painfully. More important, the initiative was now with Mowery and Shifter.

The pool table occupied a place near a corner of two walls and offered a defensible position on either protected side. Since the steelworkers had the advantage of bringing the fight, they also were able to choose their tools. Each carried a weapon in the form of bats, chains, bottles, or chairs. Mowery could see one man carrying a length of re-bar steel, a weapon that could be found in quantity lying about any construction project. That was the man who worried him most and with whom he aimed to deal decisively at all costs.

Mowery swung his own cue stick in a horizontal, sweeping motion to distract attention from the first two men before him. As they rocked slightly away, he delivered a kick to the first man's knee. It reversed in the socket with a crunch that told Mowery that the man was out of this fight and probably into a wheelchair. He felt several blows to his upper body, but they did not register consciously. He caught another steelworker on the head with his swinging cue, but the heavy end of the stick found a hard hat. The hat went flying and Mowery quickly delivered two more chopping blows with the cue stick to the same target area, both times feeling dull thuds as the strikes landed against neck and head. The man gurgled in pain and went down. Mowery could see that the man wielding the steel re-bar was now in position to strike.

Shifter had lunged with his improvised sword at the bald man carrying a knife. Shifter aimed for the man's chest, but the man jumped up and backward, causing Shifter's thrust to fall low. The broken cue stick entered the man's abdomen, penetrating deep. The man screamed as he dropped to his knees and clutched his bloody wound, his knife clattering to the floor. Shifter took a chair on his shoulder which, contrary to movie scenarios, did not shatter but delivered a withering, hurting blow. His left side went temporarily numb and he could feel bones broken in his shoulder. But he was able to use the heavy end of the pool cue against the temple of his attacker's head. The first blow stunned his assailant; the second split his scalp, perhaps his skull. Shifter took another blow with a heavy object he thought was a jack handle, on the same numb side but closer to his neck. This time the pain was sharp and severe. He was effectively fighting with only one hand now, and he was losing his grip on the cue stick from sweat or perhaps blood that had made it slick.

Mowery saw the steelworker bring the re-bar whipping down with a clearly audible rush of parting air. He ducked to his right and forward into the arms of another steelworker. Quick though he was in his sidestep, he took a hit from the re-bar and bones broke in his hand. In response Mowery lunged. With his right hand he grabbed at the re-bar man's face. His huge thumb slid into the man's mouth between cheek and gum. He clenched his grip tightly and pulled viciously down. One side of the man's face was torn open in a jagged, bloody line from ear to lower jaw. The man tried to scream, but the sound he made was a vomitus gagging noise. He dropped the re-bar and did not stop roaring and holding his face until long after Mowery had turned him loose.

Mowery whirled in another direction, snatching up the re-bar as he moved. He felt a red-hot pain in his side but did not slacken his assault with the re-bar now firmly in his giant paw. He flailed mightily at waist-high targets, hearing bones crunch and men bellow. It was all over in minutes. Nobody could avoid the steel re-bar or stop Mowery short of using a gun. The bar rapidly cleared of steelworkers, leaving only the two bikers and the proprietor.

Mowery looked at the bartender, who was in turn staring, horrified, at him. "Relax, asshole," Mowery growled. But the bartender could only point. Protruding from his side was the hilt of a knife. Mowery pulled it out and blood began pouring at a steady rate from the wound. "God," the bartender gasped.

"You call the cops?" Mowery asked the man. He shook his head.

"Hell," Shifter said, "you know somebody did. Let's get the fuck outta here. You okay?"

"Yeah, I'll live," Mowery responded.

"How bad is it?" Shifter nodded toward the knife wound.

"Didn't hit anything real bad or it'd be pumping out. This is just oozing," he said, clamping his hand over the gash.

The two were walking out when Shifter stopped, turned, and

walked back to the bartender. "Here," he said to the bartender, "I'm paying for the damage." He reached inside his pocket and pulled out all of the money he had: six dollars. He dropped it on the bar and followed Mowery out the door.

Neither Mowery nor Shifter had their wounds tended by a doctor. There was considerable blood on the Mercedes' genuine leather seats by the time Mowery parked the stolen car back in Yorba Linda. He spent the night at Shifter's while the telephone at his motel room rang insistently through the evening and into the early morning hours. Carlander made a notation on an official report form concerning Mowery's absence but decided to hold on to the document until he talked to Mowery in person.

Carlander was not the only person trying to reach Mowery by telephone. Ray Glore called the next day. Laughing softly, Glore said that he had heard about the disagreement with some folks out at Redlands and he asked Mowery how he felt. Mowery said he was fine. Good, Glore said, because he was having some dudes and their ladies to his house the next night, and Mowery and Victoria were invited.

Victoria was aware that invitations to Glore's parties were passports to the inner circle of the Hell's Angels and were given to only their most trusted associates. She did not deceive herself that the party would mean relaxation for her. On the contrary, she knew that business would be discussed and names would be divulged. It was deeper into the group, Carlander confided to her, than he had hoped they would get when they started.

# CHAPTER 12

Virtually all of the bikers Victoria associated with as a law enforcement officer could have been labeled bad people. They were, after all, people who engaged in a wide assortment of criminal enterprises on a continuing basis. She thought Ray Glore was different. He went beyond bad to what she believed was evil.

January 30, 1977. Since the location of Ray Glore's house was known to only a few, Mowery's and Victoria's invitation included arrangements for them to be escorted there by someone else. Carlander was excited about the dinner. Victoria was excited, too, but for different reasons. She could think only of Glore's cold black eyes and his cutting girlfriend. Toni's matter-of-fact reference to pornographic films chilled Victoria for reasons that she did not herself understand. Through her reading she learned that many of the most grisly crimes were committed by people with aberrant sexual proclivities. What was cause and what was effect she did not know, nor did she care. But she did know that both Toni and her massage-parlor-owner and pornofilm-director boyfriend, Ray Glore, had sexual appetites that were anything but normal.

"Hell, Victoria, me and Nease'll be right there," Carlander soothed. "You'll be wearing a wire. We'll hear everything that's happening around you. What I can't handle, what Nease can't help me with, we'll get backup. Relax. It's gonna work out." Carlander chewed listlessly on a hamburger, ignoring his French fries. A sure sign, Victoria thought, that even Carlander was off stride.

"The guy is weird, Wayne," Victoria said, nervously sipping her third cup of coffee. Her mouth tasted like battery acid. She was afraid and did not care who knew. "And the girl, Toni. She's weird and she's dangerous, too. She wanted to know if I was in the phone book. I'll bet she checked."

"So?" he shrugged. "Tell her that Cook is your maiden name. How's she gonna know the difference? She brings it up, we'll know she checked."

"Wish we knew where the place is," Nease offered.

"Well, we don't know," Carlander said. "So we follow 'em. Like we always do. Eat your fajitas."

"I don't want a full stomach in case I get shot in the gut," Nease said with a straight face.

"You know what I should do? I should get that rookie girl, Karen, out here, back me up. I'd do it, too, but you'd fucking love it and you'd go home. What is it, after seven o'clock? Quittin' time for you." Carlander was only half-kidding Nease.

"What do you think, Mowery?" Nease asked the biker. "You think this Glore guy is puttin' on a big dinner just to get Victoria here into a place where he can kill her?"

Mowery seldom spoke during these pre-op meetings except when asked. "Possible," he said. He drummed his fingers absently on the tabletop and finished his coffee in a single gulp.

"Bullshit. He wouldn't go to the trouble of takin' you to his place. He'd do it somewhere else," Carlander reasoned.

"We don't know where we're going," Mowery reminded Carlander.

Listening to her possible murder being discussed in detached, even clinical terms made Victoria want to throw up.

Carlander could see her face become ashen. "Come on," he said to Victoria, "let's get you wired up."

The foursome left Love's Restaurant near Santa Ana and stepped into a Dodge van. Borrowed from the police impound, the van was painted solid black and its mag wheels gleamed under lights from a nearby billboard. After drawing curtains across the front of the van, Carlander helped Victoria into her wire. The listening device consisted of a metal box an inch thick, three inches wide, and four inches long. Running from one end of the box were two wires approximately four inches long that served as an antenna. The box itself contained small batteries and a voice-activated microphone. The device could be placed on almost any location on the body, and Victoria tried them all before settling on an armpit. The small of her back was dangerous at a party, where hands often wandered. Besides, she already carried a 9-mm semiautomatic pistol there. It was not impossible to conceal both there, but it was not easy.

Carlander and Nease had a receiver inside their truck that was contained inside a briefcase. The incoming message activated a magnetic recording tape, and either Carlander or Nease could listen concurrently through an earplug. Effective range was approximately two blocks under reasonable conditions. Hilly terrain tended to interfere with the signal, but as long as contact was maintained, the wire would be effective.

The night was cool enough that Victoria could wear a stylish black leather jacket over the transmitter. As a precaution, however, she wore a powder blue velour shirt on the outside of her jeans. There would be no bulge to attract attention. There was one more thing to do.

Carlander stepped out of the van and approached the chopper. He reached into his shoulder holster for his gun and, using the barrel as a tool, smartly struck the bike's red taillight. The glass lens punctured neatly into a round hole as small pieces of plastic fell to the pavement.

"Hey, man . . . the fuck are you doing?" Mowery demanded.

Carlander returned Mowery's look and, instead of answering, merely smiled.

\* \* \*

Victoria and Mowery waited together in Room 121 of the Six-pence Motel. She was already feeling the irritation of wearing the wire, tape pulling against her skin. She considered removing the tape and changing the box's location just slightly. But it meant she would have to go for fresh tape outside, out in the van. There was always a chance that their escort to Glore's place would arrive at that inopportune moment. Besides, she felt that any other location on her body would become irritated as well over time.

She looked at Mowery. He was slumped in a frayed easy chair, clicking his way through television channels, apparently uncon-cerned with coming events. She could not understand his cour-age. Her hands were shaking, her body trembling, and she felt sick to her stomach. On reflection over past months she admit-ted to herself that she had been constantly afraid, and she dis-liked the part of herself that yielded to numbing terror when coolness was called for. She tried to convince herself that she was afraid because her imagination was superior to those of the bikers she was attempting to put in jail. But in moments of hon-esty she knew that she had no corner on brainpower, even among Hell's Angels.

More than anything at this moment, she wanted Bill. She wanted to talk with him, to be comforted by him, to laugh at something he might say. He always chose the right words for any occasion.

She became aware that Mowery had spoken to her. "What?" she said.

"You don't look so good," he repeated.

"Thanks." She was not interested in Mowery's opinion. She felt powerless to change her frame of mind, and if that showed in her appearance, then she couldn't do anything about that, ei-ther.

"You sick?" he asked.

"No, I'm fine," she insisted. But she was not fine. Secretly she was afraid that her nerve would break and she would give herself away in a house full of Hell's Angels.

Mowery pulled himself up to his full height of six feet four inches and moved toward her. Instinctively Victoria backed up a step. He reached out a hand and rubbed the tips of his fingers over her forehead. The touch was immediately comforting, and she almost sagged as her nerves relaxed.

"You're sweating," Mowery said simply.

Victoria reached for her purse and cigarettes, then remembered that she was trying to quit. Hearing the sound of a motorcycle, she nervously parted the window blinds to see outside. The parking area of the motel was entirely visible, but the motorcycle had merely passed by on the street.

"Maybe you got all you're gonna get," the biker said.

"What do you mean?" Victoria responded.

"How many buys we made? Fifty? Sixty? Not bad. Maybe you can't get shit on Glore. He's smart," he said reasonably.

"We'll get him," Victoria said without fervor.

"For what? Runnin' a massage parlor?" He pressed her for another answer. "Besides, what do you care?"

"What kind of question is that? I'm a cop. It's my job . . ."

"You're no cop," Mowery interrupted, sure of himself. "You're a lady. Hell's Angels can smell cops five minutes after they take a shower. How come you're bustin' that dynamite ass of yours . . . ?"

Victoria interrupted him vehemently. "What I do and how I do it is none of your business. And I don't like the way you're talking."

"And you got all the rest of it, too," he said, smiling.

Victoria's shaking had not stopped, but her voice was measured. "You've gone right to the wall. One more step, one more word, and I walk out that door. The operation stops and you go back inside."

Mowery regarded her for a long moment, then smiled again. "You're no cop. Cop would do whatever it takes to nail somebody like Glore. You'd walk out the door on a bust just because somebody likes your ass. That ain't a hell of a lot of dedication."

Victoria turned away, pretending to look out the window again. In fact, she was trying to support herself against the wall. She had ambition, she reminded herself. She wanted a career. She was an achiever and had been one for as long as she could remember. And she had determination. Now a hardheaded crook was telling her that she was nothing more than a wilting flower. She had postponed having a family and worked long hours because she believed that her work for society was important. Was she kidding herself?

"Isn't true," she said to Mowery without looking over her shoulder at him. "Walking out the door is drawing the line where you're concerned. You're one of them. I've got lines drawn inside my head: what I'll do, how far I'll go, what I'll let other people do. I'm just telling you where your line is."

He was trying to get to her, control her, she was certain. He hated the idea that he, the tough macho dude, was at the mercy of a woman. Yet knowing his motives did not comfort her. Her fear was that he had seen something in her that she had not accounted for. And if Mowery could see it, then others could, too.

This time the sound of motorcycle engines was loud. She peered through the slats in the blinds and saw three choppers. She easily recognized Buffalo and Fat Mike. She did not recognize the third rider but would meet him later. He was Lenny Erickson, an officer in what would become the Ventura chapter of the Hell's Angels.

Mowery strode to the door and stood grinning at the Hell's Angels before him. It was a crisp January 1977 night. "About fucking time you assholes got here. I'm starving."

"You ready to get down, big guy?" Buffalo said to Mowery, but his eyes were on Victoria. "Hi, there, Lady Sam. Damn, you are certainly beautiful." He gunned the engine of his Harley chopper several times. Victoria thought he was probably speeding on meth.

"Hell, I'm hungry, too. I'm with you, Shane," Fat Mike called.

Buffalo introduced the third member of Mowery's and Victoria's escort. "This here is Lenny Erickson. Lenny's from Ventura." While Mowery stepped over to Lenny's bike to shake his hand, Victoria appraised the man from up the coast. He was in his early thirties, with sandy hair and light skin with a trace of freckles that were not unpleasant in appearance. He wore a T-shirt with a leather vest against night air that caused others, including Mowery and Victoria, to wear full jackets. He might have been handsome were it not for his lifeless eyes and pouting, unsmiling mouth. She had seen eyes like Erickson's before in a state hospital holding cell for emotionally disturbed violent offenders. In fact, Lenny Erickson would die a violent death.

"Ready, man?" Buffalo asked. Mowery swung aboard his chopper as Victoria settled behind him, placing her feet on the elevated rests bolted onto the side of the machine. They now felt natural to her.

Carlander waited until the motorcycles were leaving the parking lot before he started the engine of his van. He turned on his headlights and followed. The formation of motorcycles turned north on State College Boulevard. Almost immediately the Angels began to speed past automobile traffic, to keep up. Nor did he believe that the Hell's Angels in front of him had any cause to believe that they were being followed.

They continued north past East Anaheim Center, and at Placentia Avenue Carlander suspected the four bikers might turn onto the Riverside Freeway, but they did not. If Victoria's motorcycle escorts had far to travel, they would use the first on-ramp they could find. When they did not, Carlander assumed Glore's residence would not be far away. He was wrong.

At Bastanchury Road in Fullerton, the bikers suddenly turned west and accelerated. Carlander punched his van hard while turning out his headlights, using the street lamps to drive by. In a matter of seconds he was doing eighty miles per hour and a Fullerton PD cruiser appeared on his tail with red light flashing. "Watch the bikes, Bud," he instructed Nease. Carlander stood on his brakes, thrusting Nease and himself smartly against their seat-belt restraints. Carlander held in one hand his Orange County Sheriff's Office gold investigator's badge and his business card in the other. When the two Fullerton cops hurried to the side of his van, their hands near their holsters, Carlander thrust the card into their midst. "Sergeant Wayne Carlander, Orange County Sheriff's Office. I'm on an undercover assignment, call my office and check," he blurted in a single breath and, without waiting for permission, jammed the van into gear and peeled rubber, getting rapidly back onto the trail.

"Goddamnit . . ." he heard one of the frustrated officers yelling after them. Carlander could easily put himself in their places. It was considered minimum etiquette to notify other jurisdictions when an undercover assignment was being conducted on their turf. It saved frayed nerves and often prevented injury, sometimes even death.

"They hung a right at Harbor," Nease said, never taking his eyes off Mowery's distant taillight. The white light was as good as a beacon for anyone following.

"Got 'em?" Nease barked out of the corner of his mouth.

"Yeah. I got 'em." Carlander kept up a brisk pace until the motorcycles turned on Lambert Road in La Habra. The bikers raced along, then abruptly turned north again on Euclid. Carlander had almost reached a position behind the motorcycles where he could reduce speed slightly when a blinking red light appeared in his rearview mirror. "Shit. Another one," he said to Nease. There was nothing to do but again stop as quickly as possible so that the chase could be resumed. He was beginning to wonder about how safe Victoria would be if he was going to lose contact with her within the first fifteen miles. His words with the La Habra Police Department were not as easily handled as the last traffic stop, but Carlander managed to blast away from the roadside soon enough to catch the bikers at Puente and Whittier. Only now they were headed east.

"They got us made," Nease groaned.

"I don't know. Maybe not," Carlander said, eyes glued to the white taillight.

"Then why the hell they going east, man? They're shaking us." Nease began to rub his thigh as though to remove sweat from his palms.

"So they're not going direct. Figures they're gonna be careful," Carlander said, thinking out loud.

"We oughta call for help," Nease said, looking through both sides of the van's windows.

"Keep your eyes on the light. We call for other cars, then they know they're made and we blow our op," Carlander said evenly, as though explaining simple addition.

The Hell's Angels were out of Orange County, now moving fast through the city traffic of West Covina. They made a right turn on a red light, and Carlander, more than a dozen cars behind, could not wait for the signal to change. He turned the wheel and fired the van down a delivery alley scarcely ten feet wide. Nease watched in morbid fascination while the speedometer rose quickly up to sixty miles per hour. He pressed his foot against the floorboard, subconsciously braking the vehicle as it plunged headlong out of the alley and slid sideways onto Hollenbeck Avenue. Carlander careened around streets in San Dimas still convinced that he and Nease were undetected, at least by the Hell's Angels on their bikes.

The bikers got onto the 210 Freeway, arriving in the foothills of the San Gabriel Mountains. They passed through Glendora, Azusa, and Monrovia. Carlander was sweating despite open windows and high speeds. He flicked a glance at Nease, who was likewise mopping moisture from his forehead. Carlander felt his confidence returning as the pace became even on the freeway. He occupied the far right lane as much as possible. The bikes had just transited Pasedena en route to Altadena when he found himself behind a group of trucks and cars moving at about the same speed covering the width of the six-lane freeway. He attempted to break through the logjam, but the harder he tried the less cooperation he received from other drivers, who, by unspoken communication, contrived to keep him blocked out as long as possible.

Nease's attention had become distracted from the white taillight by Carlander's maneuvering. In an effort to make up for lost ground, Carlander crossed four lanes into the inside lane and stepped hard on the gas pedal. A driver in the second lane also stepped on the gas, in order to frustrate him. Carlander cursed at the driver through Nease's open window. The driver responded with his upraised middle finger. While this was happening, the Hell's Angels, who had been weaving in and out of traffic freely, unchallenged by motorists only too glad to give way, took the Marengo Street off-ramp. Carlander bellowed curses as he caught sight of the motorcycles disappearing down the ramp onto a street below. He bulled the van suicidally through five lanes of traffic and skidded to a full stop on the shoulder of the road. He and Nease could see the Angels passing underneath a freeway overpass, then turning west again on Foothill Boulevard.

Without hesitation Carlander released his foot from the brake pedal, spun the steering wheel to the right, and, with Bud Nease grinding his jaws together with enough pressure to make diamonds, plunged the van down a forty-five-degree embankment toward the pavement below. Though Carlander attempted to slow their descent by using his brakes, the tires of the van slid over ice plant with no discernible decrease in speed. The wheels of the van slammed onto a street with a terrific crash without, amazingly, blowing out the two front tires. Oncoming traffic swerved to avoid them.

When Carlander made his turn west on Foothill Boulevard, the bikes were no longer in sight. With no other course open, he hurtled down the street, running a red light at almost ninety miles per hour. Another blinking red light filled his rearview mirror. For several moments Carlander had no intention of slowing his vehicle. To hell with them. He had to find Victoria. Better judgment prevailed, however, and he slowed to a stop. As a county sheriff's deputy began to tell him that he did not enjoy making speeding stops, Carlander showed him his own badge, flicked his business card in the deputy's direction, and assured him that he didn't much enjoy being stopped, either, and that he had to go. The van screeched off into the night.

Carlander and Nease flew through Tujunga and the smaller town of Sunland, and there Foothill Boulevard stretched across sparsely populated terrain that included Tujunga Canyon. Carlander thought he caught sight of a white light where a taillight should have been. He stepped harder on the gas, trying to close the gap. When they had crossed Big Canyon Wash, a jumble of huge boulders tossed about by heavy floods in ages past, the white light had disappeared again. This time he believed the motorcycles had stopped.

"They're around here," he said to Nease.

"Where?" his partner asked.

"Don't know," Carlander said simply. He quickly pulled to the side of the road and switched off the van engine. He listened. The night was still save for occasional cars. "Turn on your receiver," he said to Nease.

"It's on." Nease listened intently. The receiver was as quiet as the night. "Jesus, where do we look?"

Suddenly they heard a burst of motorcycle engines at a distance of several hundred yards. Carlander stabbed the van's starter button, jerked the van into gear, and kicked up a blanket of dirt, rocks, and dust until he hit the pavement and kept pace with the bikes, one of which showed a white taillight. The two investigators were led down San Fernando Road near the 118 Freeway that transited the entire massive valley. Off Fox Street the motorcycles hung a hard left and traveled up a long, unlit canyon road that became Omelveny Avenue, a dead end.

Ray Glore's house, 8516 Omelveny Avenue, was virtually hidden from view of the road and from other neighbors. It was located two miles up one of the many canyons that snaked through the San Gabriel Mountains among the Angeles National Forests. Behind a cyclone fence topped with barbed wire dogs barked and snarled from the dark. As Victoria and Mowery followed their escort into the Glore compound, two German shepherds and two Dobermans charged at them howling, their heads snapping sharply back when they reached the end of their chains. The house was ranch style, about thirty years old, and probably set a tone for this part of the valley when it was built. Two doors to the unattached garage, Victoria could see, were reinforced with steel frames and were bolted and double-locked.

As she approached the open door to the house, she noticed that where a lawn had once grown weeds had taken over. Brick trim around the house was stained, damaged, and an occasional brick was missing. It reminded Victoria of a case of schizophrenia she had once studied in college. The victim of the disease was incapable of personal cleanliness, and everything that came in contact with him eventually fell into a condition of living death.

The inside of the house, she was surprised to see, was reasonably well kept. The living room had a very large fireplace, and though the floor was concrete slab painted forest green it was softened by several rugs. A very large window occupied the central wall opposite the fireplace. Victoria could see that the house was built in an L shape, with the picture window affording a view of a patio. She stared through the window at the patio, the centerpiece of which was a single large eucalyptus that fire had reduced to a blackened snag. While the scorched trunk was not dead, it bore deep scars put there by thrown knives.

Victoria recognized most of those present from numberless encounters in bars. Among them LACO Paul sat in his wheelchair, occupying a prominent position near the unlit fireplace.

Victoria knew that the man always carried a gun. He had black hair, thinning at the top, and a heavy black beard. He had a particularly foul mouth among a group that took second place to no one in vulgarity.

LACO Paul had broken his spine in a biking accident on Highway 2, which wound down from Mount Wilson above Pasadena. Now a paraplegic, he still seemed to possess considerable influence among his brethren. He also had the constant company of an attractive woman in her middle thirties who, so Victoria was told, performed a variety of sex acts with friends and associates of LACO Paul's at his request, an appeasement to his inability to participate in a more conventional fashion. Victoria had been around the man enough to know that his mood swings were extreme, and she therefore treaded carefully in his presence. What interested her was the fragmented information that he had divulged about his source of income. Unless she had misunderstood, it seemed that LACO Paul was supported by a "medical pension" from the Hell's Angels organization, made available to brothers who were injured on bikes. Tonight might be an opportunity to learn more.

Nearby, Whitey Parsons swilled beer from a large glass vessel that Victoria thought was an ivy planter. Parsons was muscular and might have been a handsome man had not the years brought about so many blows from fights, pavement meeting flesh in bike wrecks and dental indifference. Parsons had a reputation as a courageous fighter, a willingness to trade pain for pain until the opponent could stand no more. It was rumored that Parsons had once shot to death two people who welshed on a deal. Afterward, the apocryphal story went, Parsons sat in a living room chair watching a daytime movie on television while his second victim bled to death before him.

Parsons had on his arm a woman Victoria recognized as an ex-wife of a popular television series star. Among other tattoos on the lady's arms and breasts were ornate spider webs under her armpits and at the ankles of both feet. The woman seemed slow to respond to Parsons as he absently amused himself under her tank top, and Victoria figured she was strung out on something.

The president of the Hell's Angels' Fontana chapter, Gary

Robles, emerged from the kitchen. Robles was unsteady on his legs, but he immediately recognized Mowery and made his way toward him. "Shane, my man," Robles said, offering his palm. "Seems like a long time, maybe two, three days since I seen you last." Robles laughed at his own humor and Mowery joined him. Robles smiled hugely at Victoria. "Lady Sam. Shane here's a lucky fucker having a righteous lady like you back his bike."

Victoria could see that the party was not especially large. Across the room, standing by a stereo, was Toni, Ray Glore's girl. Toni had been watching her. She said something to the girl with her, then beckoned for Victoria to join them. As she arrived at the far side of the spacious living room she could see that Toni and the other girl were snorting a line of powder.

"Wanna fluff some speed?" Toni asked.

Victoria shook her head. "I've been drinking vodka. Can't mix 'em or I get sick," she said.

Toni regarded her for a long moment, and Victoria intensely resented the fact that such a small girl, years younger than herself, could create within her such strong feelings of fear.

"This is Rita." Toni nodded toward her female companion. "She's my girlfriend."

Victoria was almost shocked at the casual mention of another sexual partner. Rita was not beautiful, yet Victoria could understand that she was appealing in a masculine way. She was slightly barrel-chested, giving her breasts the appearance of being larger than they were. She wore a short-sleeved purple blouse tucked into tight black trousers. Her hair was short and combed rather than brushed. The pupils of her eyes, Victoria could see, were dilated.

"Hi, Rita, glad to meet you," Victoria said.

Rita smirked rather than smiled. Her eyelids fell and rose in acknowledgment of their introduction while no pretense was made of warmth.

"You look nice, Sam." Toni's eyes flicked past Victoria toward Mowery, then around the room, then back to Victoria, then off again. Speed.

"Where's Ray?" Victoria heard herself say. In fact, she was not eager to see him but felt compelled to ask.

"Out in the kitchen. Not cooking," Toni added. "He's

bullshitting with Butch. She got dynamite tits?" Toni said to Rita. "Told you she won the wet T-shirt contest." It was a moment before Victoria realized Toni was talking about her. Rita forced herself to appraise Victoria's breasts and commented, "They look great. Really."

"Butch?" Victoria asked. "He here?"

"Butch. Yeah. Bugger Butch." But Toni's attention was wandering again.

"Don't nobody go outside. Dogs are loose," Ray Glore announced. *The dogs are loose.* It meant the dogs would keep people away. It also meant the dogs would keep everyone else inside. Victoria shuddered.

She walked in the direction of the kitchen. En route she passed an oak-paneled recreation room that featured an expensive pool table and comfortable chairs surrounding a large-screen TV. What arrested her progress were the gun cases that lined the walls. There were nine in all, each containing several rifles, few of which could be said to be hunting guns, unless a human being was the intended game. There were semiautomatic pieces such as M16's, AR-15's, AK assault rifles with banana clips, a Thompson submachine gun, and many others. The collection also included handguns such as Colt Army .45's, a Walther P-38, revolvers like a .357 Magnum, Diamondbacks, even a Walther 9-mm PPK like the one Victoria carried under her shirt. She also noted that as far as she could tell, all of the guns were loaded, ready for instant use. It struck her that Ray Glore was a man who would want a gun at hand. She would remember to tell this to Carlander. She knew, too, that the Federal Bureau of Alcohol, Tobacco, and Firearms would salivate over the cache of weapons in Glore's house. There was no question in her mind that if these guns were visible there would be more stashed around the house. There were likely to be explosives on the grounds as well.

She found Mowery hanging out in the kitchen drinking beer. It was warm inside the house, and the tape holding the wire transmitter to her body was irritating her considerably. She tried to shut the thought out of her mind.

"Beer?" Mowery asked, holding out a long-necked bottle. Victoria was surprised at his consideration. "Sure," she said.

Others were there in the kitchen. "Hi, Bruno," she said, finding herself almost pleased to see him. Although Bruno was dangerous, he was pleasant enough with Victoria. Mexican Kenny was cooking while his girlfriend, Buffy, sporadically helped between drinks of gin and gulps of pills. The menu was spaghetti. The aroma wafting from a large pan seemed promising, Victoria thought. She sniffed the room for garlic bread and found it at once, not yet toasted but buttered and waiting for the oven. Denny Decker, president of the San Bernardino Hell's Angels, known as the "San Berdoo" chapter, was leaning against a doorway describing Mowery's and Shifter Warner's recent fight in Redlands. Victoria was aware that Hell's Angels did less exaggerating about their individual and collective battles than most bikers, or so it appeared to her. She realized as she listened that Mowery had been involved in a criminal enterprise only yesterday and had not reported that fact to either her or Carlander. She caught Mowery's eyes more than once during Decker's rendition. The biker's face revealed nothing of what he was thinking, but Victoria believed she saw a twitch of a smile at either side of his square jaw.

Ray Glore was present in the kitchen, and he was watching Victoria.

"Hi," she said.

Glore smiled and Victoria felt a chill run through her. Glore turned to speak softly into the ear of Lenny Erickson. Was it her imagination, or did Erickson start to turn his head toward her, then check his motion? Glore finished the one-sided, whispered conversation, then looked slowly around the kitchen in a reptilian gaze that reminded Victoria of a giant lizard surveying his tropical kingdom. As Victoria took a chair at the kitchen table, Glore shuffled to Mowery's side.

"Cliff, how are ya?" Glore asked, a thin smile across his bloodless lips.

"Good. You, Ray?" Mowery responded.

"Real good, Cliff. Having a good time? How about something to go with the beer? Meth? Anything you want, Cliff, 'cept horse. You know that. We don't do that dirty shit here."

"I'm good right now, Ray." Mowery nodded in thanks.

"Makin' enough money for yourself?" Glore asked Mowery. "You're one of us now. Want to take care of you, man. It's what the Hell's Angels are all about. Taking care of friends. Enemies, too." Glore smiled enough to show crooked yellow teeth. "I run a string of massage parlors, Cliff. Always looking for girls. You bring girls to work for me and I'll pay you half of what they bring in. How's that? They'll massage you, too. They'll take your pants off any time you come in, suck your cock down to the root, man." Glore chuckled softly as he watched for a reaction. He had purposely allowed his filth to reach Victoria's ears, clearly enjoying his perverted game, whatever it was. "I got one working for me can't be more than fourteen. Tight little pussy. She'll take it in the ass, too. Bring me some more like her, and you'll make serious dough, Cliff. Got to think about yourself, man." He continued to describe acts that the teenager was willing to do, explicitly pointing out that when business was slow, Mowery might like to drop by and watch while Glore put some of the girls through their paces. Then Glore squeezed Mowery's arm affectionately before moving to another part of the kitchen, ignoring Victoria entirely.

Victoria knew she was seeing evil in the flesh. That Glore was a loathsome human being was obvious. What was frightening were the complexities of his diseased mind. She was certain that his obscene offer to Mowery was intended as a message to her. He wanted to humiliate her, to intimidate her. He wanted to show his power over her as well as over Mowery. He wanted Victoria to know that Mowery could not protect her if Glore decided otherwise.

Victoria did not look at Mowery. She felt that people in the kitchen were staring at her, waiting for a reaction. She was too embarrassed to meet anyone's eyes.

For a minute she sat at the kitchen table gazing at her bottle of beer. She was barely conscious of conversation and laughter going on around her. She knew that she had to function, shake off the grip of Glore's psychological jolt. Like a dreamer swimming to the surface from the depths of sleep, she became aware of another voice in the room with which she was familiar. She strained to concentrate on what the voice was saying.

". . . 'cause I don't like them smartass motherfuckers any fucking way. Hearing what I'm saying? Damn sure ain't letting one of 'em put his hands on my ass."

Laughter. The kitchen had attracted a crowd of people. "He put his hands on you?" Victoria recognized Mowery's voice. She looked up to see him leaning on a kitchen counter, speaking to Bugger Butch. "You let him do that?"

"Shit, no, I didn't let him do that." Bugger Butch laughed in good-natured irritation at Mowery's suggestion. "Fucking planted that college-ass little prick." With his head tilted back he tipped up his beer bottle and drained it.

Victoria's heart began to race. Could this really be the Capri Bar killer? Officers from every jurisdiction of southern California would give a great deal to nail the killer of the young man who had died in his father's arms on his birthday. It was almost too much to hope for.

Mowery pulled another bottle from a nearby refrigerator, twisted off the cap, and handed the full bottle to Bugger Butch. As he did so he flicked a knowing glance toward Victoria.

"College jerkoff, huh?" Mowery asked, egging him on.

"Yep. All tanned up real good, hanging out with them fucking surf thrashers. Kissing each other's dick, probably."

Victoria hoped that Carlander was in position outside to pick up Bugger Butch's voice. She moved in her chair so that her microphone would be unimpeded. She was bursting with questions, but she had learned not to ask. It would be a mistake to appear to be too interested. Mowery, on the other hand, felt no such qualms, and it seemed to her that he had now taken the side of justice, at least against this psychopath.

There had been two men, Victoria clearly recalled from police investigation reports. Her skin was burning from the tape, but in her excitement she ignored the discomfort. She had just heard a confession of cold-blooded murder by the killer himself. She could only hope that Carlander had not missed it.

"How come you and Prisoner Joe weren't riding your scooters?" Mowery asked.

"Joe? Never even knew that fuckhead then. Little Dee was with me." Bugger Butch began to laugh. "Hell, we was too fucked up to ride a sled, man."

Mowery joined Butch in hearty laughter. Victoria caught Mowery's eye and he looked at her fully, the source of his persisting smile, she knew, not for a murderer. It was for her. Perhaps for himself, too.

"Wanta see the studio?" Toni leaned against the kitchen table and against Victoria's shoulder as she extended her invitation. Victoria knew without being reminded that Ray Glore and Toni made pornographic movies. Until now she had not known where. Her police training overrode her instinct to recoil. And though she was Mowery's old lady, there were limits to those things she could avoid without inviting suspicion.

"Sure," she said, "let's see it."

Toni led the way out of the kitchen, past the rec room, into a hallway. Toni turned the knob of one of the doors, pushed it open, and stepped inside. What first struck Victoria was that the bedroom, about four hundred square feet, indeed contained film equipment. There was a 35-mm motion picture camera mounted on a tripod, a small camera dolly nearby. The camera was equipped with a zoom lens. Also in the room were two sets of lights and light reflectors of the kind Victoria had once seen at Laguna Beach when a Hollywood film company was shooting a scene for television.

As in the rest of the house, the bedroom floor was slab concrete. There were no rugs, however. Victoria judged that the camera would dolly about the room easier without them. The walls were painted dull white to minimize glare. Upon them were pornographic "art" pictures, some painted, some drawn, some photographed. All included explicit details of male and female reproductive organs, often exaggerated in size. Women were depicted in positions of fellatio or sodomy, seldom in "straight" sexual postures. There were depictions of whips and chains, but they were mild, and Victoria thought they were meant more to amuse than to stimulate. If not for the setting, Victoria would have thought some of the erotica was actually well done.

Furniture was scarce in the room and on all four walls there were mirrors, reflecting back toward a huge bed. It seemed to Victoria that the bed might be two king-size beds bound together into one. The sheets and covers, including a quilt, must have been specially made.

Occupying a space on the bed was Rita. Toni's self-proclaimed girlfriend had ingested more alcohol or more drugs or a combination of both since Victoria had met her upon arrival. Rita's eyes were fully dilated, as were Toni's, for that matter, and she moved quite slowly, paying no attention to Victoria, her eyes focusing instead on an object distant in space. Toni sat on the edge of the bed near Rita. "Sit down," the young girl invited Victoria.

"I'm okay," Victoria said, wishing fervently that she had a cigarette and match to keep her hands occupied.

Toni laughed at Victoria's discomfort. "Christ, c'mon. Relax."

Victoria had no intention of joining Toni and Rita on the bed and did not care if either of them were offended. She stepped over to the lone chair and carried it around to where she could join her hostess. She placed the chair as far from them as possible but close enough to avoid being obviously unfriendly.

Toni allowed her hand to find its way under Rita's blouse and to fondle her breasts. Victoria was certain that she was being tested. Toni's sensual fondling of Rita was a direct challenge to where Victoria's head was at.

Victoria decided that it was somewhere else. "I'll leave you two alone," she said, starting to rise from the chair.

"Sit down." Toni's command caused Victoria to hesitate. "We're all friends, Sam. Isn't that right?"

"Yeah. Sure, we're friends," Victoria heard herself saying. She did not like the defensive tone of her own voice. She had nothing to apologize for.

"So don't be so tightass," Toni said, not removing her active hand from Rita, who was beginning to respond.

Victoria rose from the chair, determined not to be controlled. "Hey, your party, you do what you want. I'm not bi."

A smile spread across Toni's face. Victoria had no way of knowing what it meant: an affirmation of Toni's suspicions or an admission that Victoria was within her rights to act as she pleased. As she turned away, Victoria was brought up short by the sight of Glore.

Occupying the doorway, he stood motionless, light from the hall behind him casting deep shadows across his face. He said nothing. It was impossible for Victoria to know what he was looking at as he inhabited the bedroom like a cold, evil fog that would not go away.

Victoria had to force herself to continue on her way toward the door. Glore made no move to allow her to pass, but his stare was now clearly fixed on the monolithic bed. Victoria glanced over her shoulder in reflex. Toni had unzipped Rita's black outer pants and was slowly working them down over her hips. Disgusted, Victoria pushed her way past Glore and almost ran down the hallway to the kitchen.

"Let's get out of here," she said.

"Aw, hell . . ." Mowery started to resist.

"Right now." There was no mistaking the determination in her voice.

Mowery nodded. "Okay. Let's haul ass, then."

Neither Glore nor Toni were on hand to control the four dogs left outside to guard the compound. Buffy, Mexican Kenny's woman, said she'd hold them.

As they approached the front door Mowery nudged Victoria to get her attention. "Hey, Lenny," he said to Erickson, who occupied an overstuffed chair, his eyes gazing at the ceiling. The eyes did not move to regard Mowery as the biker spoke. "Toni's lookin' to make a picture, man. They need you in there."

"Not interested, man." Erickson blew cigarette smoke softly upward.

Outside, Mowery chuckled softly. "Done too much time in the slam."

Carlander and Nease had found Glore's house, but not before a lengthy search that consumed precious time. And not without inviting the attention of people in the neighborhood. Carlander was less concerned that someone would call the cops and report a prowler than that they might call Glore. The van cruised one street after another within a one-mile radius of where they had last seen Mowery's white taillight disappear. As Nease strained to pick up Victoria's wire signal, Carlander racked his brain to locate the house in the foothills that Glore occupied. After retracing his route several times, he could see house lights switched off, better to see out, harder to see in. He knew they were being observed.

He drove the van for two miles east on Omelveny Avenue, a long, dark country road, passing a few houses, none of which suggested Hell's Angels. He was about to turn the van around when he heard dogs barking. Dogs were ubiquitous in this part of the valley, but this chorus of barks arrested his attention. They were the snarling, angry kinds of noises made by aggressive, possibly trained attack animals. It occurred to Carlander that a man like Ray Glore would likely keep fierce dogs. In the end it was a cinch to follow the noise made by the barking animals to the tree-shrouded, secluded compound with heavy cyclone fencing surrounding it. Carlander did not have to be told that he had found the right place. He left his lights out and backed the van into heavy brush that obscured the van midway to the windows. He and Nease would not be seen unless looked for.

"I got her," Nease whispered. The corners of his mouth began to curl underneath his full mustache.

"What's happening?" Carlander asked.

Nease concentrated, pressing his earphones hard to his head. "Another girl. Wants to show her . . . something . . . she says sure, let's see it. . . ."

"What?" Carlander asked. "See what?"

Nease did not respond but shrugged his shoulders as he continued to listen. Carlander slumped down into the seat of the van and reached for a bag of roasted and salted sunflower seeds. He began to study the compound, making mental notes about Glore's house that he believed might be useful at a later time when they raided the place. He was particularly interested in the garage, which he thought would be a formidable defensive position if . . .

"They're leaving."

"What?" It was too soon.

"Mowery says okay, they're gonna haul ass." Nease relayed the pertinent information to his partner. "I think something's wrong," he added, straining to hear.

"What's wrong?" Carlander waited. "Damn it, Nease, tell me what the hell is wrong."

"I don't . . ." Nease strained to hear.

The two detectives saw the front door of the house open,

background light illuminating the form of a woman who stepped outside. At their distance Carlander could not be sure, but he did not think it was Victoria. The barking of the dogs grew louder. Then another form was framed in the light of the door. There was no mistaking Clifford Mowery. Behind him was yet another woman. Carlander still could not make a positive identification, but he was satisfied that the figure behind Mowery was Victoria. He relaxed slightly when it became apparent that neither was being assaulted or chased in any way. He waited until he heard the sound of Mowery's chopper roaring into life before hitting the start switch on his van. Forty minutes later, traveling at moderate speeds, Carlander's van followed Mowery and Victoria to Sambo's Restaurant on 7th Street in Long Beach.

It was five minutes to one o'clock in the morning, but Sambo's had a fair number of customers. Near Carlander's table a man vigorously mopped the floor with a pungent disinfectant while a sleepy young waitress kept one eye on a wall clock and another eye on her order pad. "Four hamburgers, fries, three coffees and a large Coke," Carlander told the waitress, ordering for all of them.

"I don't want coffee," Nease said. "You have to go to that place again, we got to get one of them tranquilizer guns for the fucking dogs. If we gotta get in there quick, we won't have time to make friends with those bozos, give 'em a steak and shit like that."

"What do you want? Iced tea?" Carlander asked while the waitress waited. "We have to go in quick, we're not going to put the nice doggies down with tranquilizer. We blow 'em up. Bring him iced tea."

"I don't want coffee, neither," Mowery said as he swiveled his head around toward the entrance of the restaurant.

"Shit. Hell, bring the stuff I ordered, kid," he said to the waitress, "and we'll sort it out when you get back. We'll vote." Carlander pushed the movable table closer to Mowery and Victoria to make more room for his wider girth. "Hey," he said, rubbing his hands together in anticipation of a day's work well done, "who was the guy you were talking to on the way out the door? Who was making a picture? You mean a movie picture?"

Mowery nodded, smiling. "Glore's snatch. Toni. She's a weird bitch, so's her friends."

"So what's Glore? Class president in high school?" Carlander laughed at his own joke and was joined by Nease.

"They get some freaky guys to be president of classes, you know," Nease observed. "Guys that can't do nothing else."

Carlander fixed his partner with a mock withering stare. "We had a guy, class president in our school once, had a crippled foot. You making fun of cripples?"

Victoria slowly turned her head away and allowed her eyes to settle on a distant object outside the window's darkness.

"Anyway, what's the scoop on the guy you talked to?" Carlander returned to business once more.

Mowery glanced back toward Victoria. She did not acknowledge his look but was aware that he was watching her. "Dude by the name of Erickson. Lenny. He's an Angel. Lives up the coast near Ventura."

Carlander became interested. "I didn't know they had a chapter up there."

Mowery shook his head. "They don't. Lot of 'em live up there, though. Grow a shitload of pot around there, too."

"Yeah? You know where?" Carlander lowered his voice and leaned toward Mowery.

"Yeah, we're out down at the station," Nease said. The three men broke into laughter. Victoria did not laugh but continued to look detached.

"Anyway," Mowery went on, "I guess Toni was getting it on with her girlfriend, maybe doing a show for Glore, so I tell Erickson he oughta haul back there and maybe jump into a starring role." Mowery beamed, looking for support from Victoria. She continued to be distant.

Carlander was slightly disappointed. "What else?"

Mowery nodded his head toward Victoria. "Ask the lady dick here. She got the whole rap on the guy who iced the kid in Huntington Beach couple years back."

Carlander's face lit up like a Christmas tree as he turned toward Victoria. "That right, Vicky? You saw the guy? For Chrissake, tell me. Go."

"Little Dee. He pulled the trigger," Victoria said in a monotone.

"Little Dee?" Carlander asked, confused. "Who's he?"

"Ah," Mowery interjected, "Bugger Butch's running buddy."

Carlander looked first at Mowery, then back to Victoria. "Little Dee, huh? He did the shooting? Not Bugger Butch?"

"Little Dee," Victoria repeated, not realizing she had inverted the roles of Bugger Butch and Little Dee in Butch's narration.

Carlander looked again at Mowery. The biker was watching Victoria closely. It seemed to Carlander that Mowery had more to say but was holding it back. "Victoria, Huntington Beach PD reports say that a guy wearin' a black cowboy hat with Butch on the side of it shot the kid. But, hell, witnesses don't always see what they think they see. We know that. Butch says Little Dee shot the surfer?"

Victoria did not answer but nodded her head absently.

"Okay," the investigator said. He turned to Nease. "Get that on the wire?"

Nease shook his head in the negative. "Not that."

Carlander groaned. "We're paddling around in the fucking swamps while you guys are in the house. Lost you for a while," he explained to no one in particular.

Victoria suddenly came alert, focused on Carlander. "You what? Did you say you lost us?"

"Yeah, for a few minutes, but . . ." Carlander began.

"A few minutes? We were in that goddamn place longer than a few minutes. It took that murdering son of a bitch longer than a few minutes to tell that story and you say you didn't get it?" Her voice increased in volume, and a few people turned in their booths.

Carlander was soothing as he spoke slightly above a whisper to her. "We weren't far away, just got hung up when we lost your white light."

Victoria's face turned cold with anger. "Just got hung up," she bit off her words. "Hung up. You promised me you would always be there. But you weren't. You lied to me."

"Hey, come on . . ." Carlander began.

"Liar!" she seethed, her voice hoarse.

"Victoria." Carlander reached across the table for her hand. She jerked it back sharply.

"Let me out of here," she said to Mowery.

Without getting Carlander's approval, Mowery rose so that Victoria could slide out of the booth. She did not make for the ladies' room but walked with long, purposeful strides toward the front door, passing their waitress en route with their order.

"Take her home, Bud," Carlander said to Nease.

Nease followed after Victoria but snatched a hamburger from the plate as he departed.

Carlander regarded Mowery for a long moment. "What was it like in there?"

"Party. Kickass fun, you know, man." Mowery did not reach for food but drank the coffee instead.

Carlander breathed deeply. "Don't give me your smart bull-shit. It's late and I'm tired."

Mowery was not visibly affected by Carlander's serious mien. "Hey, big tough cop, if you don't like my smartass bullshit, why don't you pull on your motorcycle boots and go to the next party yourself?"

Carlander's temper began to escalate. He restrained an impulse to grab Mowery by the throat by leaning as far back in the booth as possible. "That mean you want out?" he asked.

"Maybe."

"What does 'maybe' mean?" Carlander wanted to know. He waited, but Mowery only drank his coffee. Carlander took the first bite out of his hamburger. He decided on a different approach. "I'll tell you something, Shane." Carlander's use of Mowery's street name was rare. "You're doing good. Better than I thought. Damn sight better than Keith Taylor figured you'd do. I think you could, ah, if things would've been different, you and me could've . . ."

"You like your rat, huh?"

"Huh?" Carlander stopped chewing.

"I said, you like your rat. Big rat. I'm six-four. I could eat more cheese than you could buy, I'll bet."

"Huh? Fuck are you talking about? I'm trying to tell you I

think you're doing really good and you're insulting me."
Carlander was perplexed.

"We're all insulting each other, man. You insult me. I insult
your ass. Nease, too. You insult him. But we all insult Victoria.
We're playing grab-ass, yanking each other's dork, you, me,
Nease. She's stuck with slobs like you and me, bad enough. But
back there . . ." Mowery motioned rhythmically with his thumb
in the general direction whence they came.

Carlander's eyes closed for a moment, then opened. He let
his breath out very slowly. "Bad, huh?"

Mowery did not move a muscle. Carlander now understood.
He was suddenly no longer hungry.

# CHAPTER 13

During the past five months Victoria had lived in fear of being seen on the street with Bill. Bikers go to record shops, beaches, movies, and ice cream parlors, just like everyone else. Once while they were shopping at a local supermarket, the Hell's Angel Buffalo entered the same store. Victoria thought she spotted him first and separated herself from Bill. She dodged around aisles until the biker reached a checkout counter and then he left the store. But being so close to him without Carlander and Nease nearby, at a moment when her guard was down, left her shaking.

She quickly became paranoid of motorcycles and felt safe only inside their home. On her third night away from her undercover role while Mowery was in jail from the doughnut shop fight, she and Bill decided to invite some friends over for a drink. Robin and Jean Eindorf had long been Victoria's and Bill's pals from their carefree beach days. It sounded like fun to share a jug of white wine, eat casadilla, and play cards.

That night, however, Bill and Victoria moved about their kitchen with a hint of formality. Casual bumps brought "S'cuse me," and "Ill get it . . . No, that's all right, I'll get it . . ." There was stiffness between them, each trying hard to please the other. From the moment the Eindorfs arrived, tension between the couple affected them. As the four sat in the living room, the Eindorfs led the conversation by bringing the Deckers up to speed on their activities. Jean had tried to get pregnant for the past eight months without success, and they were going to a specialist for tests; Robin was studying for a real estate license. His engineering job with McDonnell Douglas was secure, but real estate was skyrocketing out of sight. Besides, Jean was bored with her accounting job and was anxious to help him fix up houses.

"You won't get rich working on commissions," Jean said, "but you have to do it for a while. Work for somebody else. A broker. But not for long."

"Yeah. I'll make the deals," Robin teased, "and Jean can fix up the houses. You know, clean 'em, paint 'em inside and out, plant gardens, repair anything that's wrong. I'll collect the money."

Jean droned on about condos, Robin supplying support for details until Victoria abruptly stood up.

"Where're you going, Vicky?" Jean asked.

"I . . . I'm going to get something in the kitchen," Victoria said, anxious to leave the room.

"I'll help." Jean rose to follow.

"No. I can do it. Stay there and visit with Bill," Victoria said.

"Oh, I want to talk to you. We never see you guys since you joined the police department. What do you do there? Give out parking tickets or something?"

"Investigations," Victoria said with forced patience.

"Oh, that must be fun. How can you stand the starvation wages, though? Not that I'm doing any better myself. God, I can't wait to get out of that office. You know we only have one window in our office? And the boss gets that. Larry Nerse. He lives in Westchester. That's where property is going through the roof. West side of Sepulveda . . ."

"I don't give a fuck."

"What?"

Victoria turned toward her friend. "I said I don't give a fuck. Anything ever go through that empty goddamn head of yours besides condos and interest rates?" Victoria's voice was matter-of-fact. Her friend's mouth opened, then closed again without emitting a sound.

Hors d'oeuvres were half-eaten and a second bottle of chilled wine left unopened in the wake of the Eindorfs' early departure.

"Glass of wine before I put the bottle away?" Bill asked.

Victoria shook her head, preferring to drink a beer as she sat in an overstuffed chair.

"Well," he said, "you saved us a buck and a quarter we would have spent on their Christmas card this year. That's a plus."

Victoria did not respond, continuing to sip her beer.

"Hey, how about I whip down to Sands Realty tomorrow and see if they can use another husband-and-wife team? Why swim upstream? We can start by selling our own house. I think that's how everybody starts." Bill was determined to cheer her up, to let his wife know that he was with her.

"That's not funny." Victoria clicked on the television as though to redirect her thoughts as well as his.

"I think it is," Bill said.

"I'm really sorry," Victoria said but without enthusiasm. In truth, Jean had bugged her for years, and in a perverse way she was satisfied that she had managed to insult one of her closest friends.

"Forget it. We can always buy new friends. Good ones next time," Bill suggested.

"It's just that I couldn't stand to hear about condominiums anymore. One more fucking condo would have done me in," she said.

Five months ago Victoria had used foul language sparingly. Now she swore like a trucker. "Me, too," Bill said, aiming for another try at cheer. "We should be talking about unimproved property. Makes more sense. Appraisals are easier. Less subjective. And we can build our own house if we get a lot we really like . . ."

This time it worked. Victoria began to laugh. She continued until she was breathless.

"Feel better?" he asked.

"Yeah." She nodded vigorously.

But Bill was not sure that he felt better. He was worried about her.

When Mowery was arrested, nobody believed Carlander was going to get him out. Victoria was almost happy about the prospect for a different assignment. She felt like she was out of school for the summer. She was relieved, too, that people on the street would stop looking at her like she was scum. Hanging out with Cliff and his motorcycle buddies was not only scary but demeaning. They were a subculture of sociopaths. Being with them constantly eroded her feeling of self-worth.

One time she remembered vividly. She and Mowery had been waiting to meet Carlander at the Huntington Beach pier. They were eating chili dogs, watching people fish from the pier. A child smiled at them and approached. Victoria smiled back, kneeling to speak with the toddler. The child's mother quickly took him by the hand. "Don't go near people like that," she said.

Victoria was pierced by the remark. She wanted to confront the woman, tell her that she had a respectable home and husband, but then her eyes dropped to view herself. She was bronzed from the sun, her clothes covered with road dust, her boots scuffed and soiled with oil and dirt. She thought, "If it waddles like a duck, quacks like a duck . . ." She didn't know whether to laugh or cry at the irony.

Nor was her feeling of anomie infrequent. Southern California drivers are notorious for rude, even dangerous habits on the road. Everyone is in a hurry. Shouting, horn-blowing, fist-shaking, even shootings are the norm. Victoria had once prided herself on not becoming emotionally involved with others on highways, but she began to return a middle-finger salute to people who honked their horn at her and Mowery. Once she even felt like reaching for her 9-mm semiautomatic when they were cut off at an intersection. She checked that motion but instead bellowed "motherfuckers" as she and Mowery drove by. This aggressiveness had her feeling off-balance when added to the way Mowery drove a motorcycle and the casual way in which bikers carried guns and talked about using them. With that added to the absence from Bill, she had found the assignment far more difficult than she could have imagined. The pressure was getting to her.

Days telescoped together in a frenzy of rapid trips on the chopper across towns, across the county, fast buys of drugs, late hours, later meetings, crime reports, wire setups. Victoria could not remember the last time she had had a full night's sleep, at least a few hours devoid of troublesome dreams. In her dreams a shotgun smashed through her bedroom window, both barrels exploded, and Bill was torn in half. In another recurring dream the house was on fire. She and Bill would run outside to find their home surrounded by Hell's Angels, all carrying torches, all laughing and making obscene gestures.

On February 1, 1977, Victoria bought Percodan and Quaaludes from biker Frank Earl Chance in Fullerton. Frank's street name was Pharmaceutical Frank, an obvious reference to the merchandise he sold. He represented a cabal of licensed physicians in Orange County, one of whom, Dr. Freeze of Cypress, provided him with hundreds of prescriptions for Atromid, Meprobamate, Stelazine, Seritrate, Tuinal, Ionamin, and Priscoline. The next day she and Mowery made a buy from Robert "Red" Carl Benjamine of Huntington Beach, who sold five "pieces" of cocaine. In making the deal, Benjamine measured and bagged the drugs on the same kitchen table where his fourteen-year-old son was doing his homework, and two younger children played in the same room. Victoria paid him $750 and vowed to herself that she would make it her personal business to see that the man was convicted for every rap they could lay on him.

Deputy District Attorney Ron Kreber, ex-Marine, ex–police officer, was now in charge of collating the river of evidence rolling in every day. Anticipating his prosecution of the cases, Kreber began to make suggestions to Carlander about selected cases that needed special attention: a second buy here, clarification of identity there. Kreber could find only one drug buy from Michael Lee Mason, a.k.a. Bruno. They needed at least one more, he said, to prove an unmistakable pattern of criminal drug dealing.

Victoria dutifully called Bruno on the telephone at his Harley-Davidson Sportster Shop and asked for an ounce of crank. The price, he told her over the telephone, was normally

$600, but he would let her have it for $550. They agreed to meet at the Backdoor Bar in Anaheim.

Victoria called Mowery at the Sixpence Motel, but there was no answer. She called a page number for Carlander and waited a few minutes until he called her back. She asked if he knew where Mowery was. He did not. Their strict rules for Mowery's confinement to his motel room when not in their company had been relaxed of late, not by spoken consent but by nonenforcement. At the moment Victoria was irritated, even angry at having to move among the gang without him, but she told herself that Bruno was practically a buddy and therefore no danger. She felt more than a little hypocritical that she was on her way to gather the hard evidence a man she almost considered a friend. She had always imagined, though not with conviction, that Bruno could be counted on to protect her in Mowery's absence. It was a small but real part of what had become her schizo-phrenic existence.

The Backdoor Bar was, literally, in back of everybody's door. Apartments and business locations rose on four sides of the bar, with only an alley for a way out of the parking lot. Victoria was early in arriving and was therefore surprised to see Bruno, a man given to casual regard for time, already there. With him was Vic Mena. Victoria knew Mena only slightly but was familiar with his police dossier. He had a long record of violent crime, and had several warrants out for his arrest that were not being acted upon until Carlander's operation was complete. Mena was a sus-pect in more than one murder, and it was rumored that he was the Hell's Angels' premier hit man.

She greeted Bruno cordially and was pleasant in saying hello to Mena. She had last seen him at the wet T-shirt contest at the Roaring 20's but did not want to bring that up. "So," she said to Bruno, "I brought the money."

Bruno nodded his head slightly in her reference to business but made no move to effect his end of the deal. Instead he said, "Where's Mowery?"

"I don't know," she said truthfully. It struck her as odd that Bruno did not refer to Mowery as Shane, as was his habit. Nor did he seem particularly warm.

"No idea at all?" Mena asked with studied casualness.

"No, I, uh, called his place, thought he might like to party to-night, but nobody home. He'll show up," she responded.

"I bet he will." Mena's smile showed his lower teeth.

Victoria suppressed a shudder. "Yes, he always does," she said. Either these Hell's Angels were making no attempt to be friendly, or her imagination was deceiving her. She didn't know Mena well enough to have a firm opinion, but Bruno seemed definitely out of sorts.

Mena's head swung slowly toward Bruno, the phony smile revealing itself again. "Maybe he got busted," he said.

"Yeah, possible." Bruno regarded Victoria with a penetrating look. "Ever think he might get took off by the cops?" he said to her.

Victoria's knees were weakening. She felt she could not stand if she had to. When she heard herself speak, it sounded like another woman's voice. "Wouldn't be surprised. One thing he knows is jails." She felt herself smile and was almost surprised when Bruno and Mena joined her.

Mena said matter-of-factly, "Gotta be careful. We got a rat with us."

Her mouth went dry. She could not trust herself to speak, so she made no attempt. She had no recollection of how long she sat silent before managing to croak, "Rat?"

"Yeah. Ain't that a bitch?" Mena said.

"Sure you don't know where Mowery is?" Bruno asked. Victoria shook her head from side to side. "Too bad," Bruno said. "See, we figure Mowery is just the dude to help us with the motherfucker we're after. No idea, huh? Where he is?"

Victoria shook her head again. She found her voice and hoped it would not fail completely. "Who, ah, who is it?"

"A bitch." Mena leaned back in his chair and smiled hugely. "Can you fucking believe it?" Mena and Bruno both laughed.

They were toying with her, Victoria realized. She began thinking about the 9-mm gun under her jacket. "She, ah, get an Angel?" she said, maneuvering for position.

"Naw," Mena said, leaning toward Victoria. "She isn't gonna get a fucking Angel, neither. I mean, she might be trying but all bikers probably look alike to her. Boyfriend has shit for brains, too. We'll handle 'em. Catch the broad, we're gonna pour lye down her throat. Him, too. Won't even kill 'em. They can get food out of tubes," Mena explained. "Eats their guts out. For sure they won't collect Social Security, not gonna live that long. Meantime they get basic fucking nourishment outta plastic straws."

Victoria moved slightly sideways in her chair, increasing her chance of getting the gun clear of her waistline. She was debating whether to pull the trigger immediately or to wait for their reaction as she came up with the gun. She would take out Mena first if she could. To stall for more precious seconds she continued the conversation. "What does she look like?"

"Dog, I guess. I mean, she couldn't be what she is and look like you," Bruno said. Then, "I'm gonna put something on your chair." Bruno leaned closer toward Victoria, his hand moving under the table.

Victoria became aware that there was an object touching her leg. "What's that?" she said.

"What'd you call me for?" he asked innocently, his eyes widening in question.

Victoria touched the object without looking at it. It felt like a small paper bag with a rubber band around to keep it closed. She did not look but kept her eyes on the two men at the table.

"Ah, tell you what, Sam, you give me five and a half yards and I'll count it later. Okay?" Bruno said, still grinning.

Victoria reached behind her. Her hand was inches away from the 9-mm auto as well as near her pocket containing cash. She hesitated. Which should she come up with? She grabbed the precounted bills and slipped them under the table to Bruno.

"Want a beer?" he said to her.

She glanced at Vic Mena. The out-of-town Angel was watching her intently. "No, thanks," she said. "I have to get rid of this stuff."

Bruno turned toward Mena. "Sam here sells the shit to her rich friends. Hey," he said turning back to her, "know a lady looks like you wants to ride my bike?"

She rose to her feet, expecting her legs not to support her, and pasted on a smile. She knew the smile looked forced, and she hoped they would think she was only tired. "I'll call you if I do." Victoria moved in measured steps toward the door, reached the parking lot outside, and began walking toward her car. She used all of her willpower not to break into a full run. She opened the door and got inside. She next expected the muzzle of a gun, perhaps fitted with a silencer, to appear next to her head. She refused to look. She started the car, backed out of its parking place, drove onto Manchester, and accelerated away.

Victoria monitored her rearview mirror, expecting to be followed. They might be trying to locate Mowery by tailing her, she reasoned. She drove straight toward the Orange County Sheriff's Office in Santa Ana. There was no longer any need for caution, since they knew about her and Mowery. She ran a red metering light to gain access to the southbound I-5 freeway, ignoring irate drivers honking their horns at her illegal maneuver. She continued weaving in and out of traffic until she reached the Euclid off-ramp. She took it and raced down that boulevard to Flower Street and the safety of the Sheriff's administration buildings.

She took the stairs to Carlander's office two at a time. Bursting through the squad room door, she saw the investigator working his way through a stack of paperwork. "Hi, Vicky, how's it going?" His attention returned immediately to the papers before him.

"How's it going?" she gasped. "They know. We're blown. They made Mowery and me, too. Where the hell have you been? Sitting here when I could have been killed?"

"Huh? Who knows what? Sit down." Carlander moved a chair over for her, but Victoria was too excited to sit.

"They're looking for Mowery. They know about him and me, too. Bruno told me, and that animal Vic Mena," she said. She rummaged in her jacket pocket and came up with a mashed package of stale cigarettes. She tore the pack almost in half trying to wedge one out. After she had lit up she looked up to see Carlander smiling.

"Talking about the CI that got burned in Fullerton?" Carlander said, cool and amused. "She wasn't a cop, you know. She was working with a Fullerton dick and two Feds. They got made last night. That what you mean?"

"No ... no, that isn't it," Victoria insisted, yet she was confused. She vividly remembered the nuances of Bruno and Mena.

"Well, what, then? What'd Bruno say? You make the buy?"

Carlander stopped what he was doing to listen. Victoria related the conversation, including the double entendres, their implied threats.

"I doubt they were talking about you or Mowery, or you wouldn't be here. This confidential informer Fullerton PD was working with made a buy last night, cocaine. They had maybe forty, fifty cops up at Craig Park, staked out for the deal to go down. Chinese fire drill. Druggies had to fight their way through narcs to deliver the shit and collect the money." Carlander laughed. "Federal operation, you know. Couldn't be helped."

"A CI?" Victoria asked, bewildered.

"Yeah, CI. Not a cop. She was running with the Outlaws," Carlander confirmed.

"How about her contact?" Victoria asked as she sank slowly into the chair.

Carlander shrugged. "A cop. But he didn't ride a bike. Drove a car and worked in an auto body shop, way I hear it. I don't know how much they got and I don't give a shit. Want somethin' to eat?"

Victoria shook her head.

"We got to stay on Mowery's ass better," Carlander said as he scooped up the paperwork, hated by all policemen. "I finally get him on the phone and he's juiced. Drinking beer is okay if you or me are with him, but him going off to get sloshed is not gonna be okay. Right? Gotta restore a little order."

The next day Victoria called in sick. More accurately, Bill called on her behalf to say that Victoria was ill, and she made no objection. She had already locked the windows of the house and closed the blinds and drapes. Bill took the day off from a commercial wiring job, intending to make up the time by working Saturday or Sunday. He had suggested that they go to a supermarket for groceries and, while at the shopping center, have lunch. Victoria agreed at once but became increasingly nervous as she showered and dressed. By the time she had run a brush through her hair—allowing it to dry naturally, as was her habit—she could not face the thought of leaving the protection of her house.

"I know," she said to Bill, attempting to sound enthused, "let's have lunch here. We both eat out too much."

Bill thought for a moment, then smiled. "Sounds good to me. If we went out to eat, we'd have pasta or salad and wine, maybe some cheese. That sound okay with you?"

Victoria nodded, relieved. "Garlic bread, too."

"Yeah," Bill agreed.

They had everything in the house. There was less than half a loaf of French bread and only two heels of wheat bread to make garlic toast, but neither suggested going to a store for more. They constructed a chef's salad, cut up two apples to go with sharp cheddar cheese, and used plenty of celery salt on the cheese to make a gourmet snack. Dry red Merlot from Trader Joe's tasted delicious. Bill thought Victoria's nervousness had eased considerably as their conversation developed by recalling names of friends not seen for months, even laughing over Victoria's insult of Jean and Robin Eindorf.

"Oh, God, someday I have to call Jean. Have to call her and tell her. Aaaggghhhh," Victoria stuck a finger theatrically down her throat. She poured the last bit of wine from the bottle into her glass without realizing that Bill had not finished his first.

"Sure. She'll understand," Bill said.

"Understand what?" Victoria said.

"What happened," he said gently and with good humor.

Victoria studied his face. "Fuck her."

"Are you giving me permission?" Bill asked, trying to keep their promising lunch interlude light.

"That what you want? Jean Eindorf?" Victoria's mouth sagged from the sapping effects of the wine. She had consumed a good deal of alcohol in a short period of time. She saw Bill laugh with real humor. "I'm not jealous," she said, and meant it.

Her eyes fell and tears appeared on her cheeks. Bill moved to her side and put his arms around her as her shoulders gently shook.

"Oh hell, Bill . . ." Victoria said, her arms tight around him. "I don't like myself anymore." She began to cry full, heaving sobs. "I can hear myself talk and I hate it . . . hate what I look like . . . sound like, like somebody else . . . and the things I say." The floodgates were open now and Bill encouraged her to let it go. She was saying things that they had both known for some time but never discussed. He knew that her biker-hard veneer was just that, a shell that she had adopted to protect herself.

"I like you," he contradicted gently, stroking her hair.

"No, you don't. How can you? I'm . . . I'm different now," she said.

"Maybe the wrapper," Bill soothed, "not what's inside. Why don't you take a nap? We can do something later. Go to a show, maybe, or just hang out if you want."

Victoria nodded, then returned Bill's kiss on the lips. It was not a passionate kiss, but a reassuring one. She did indeed feel tired. She entered their bedroom and lay down for what she thought would be a few minutes of rest. She slept for fourteen hours, awakened long enough to use the bathroom, then returned to bed and slept for another twelve.

By eleven o'clock the next morning Bill had made all of the telephone calls to his boss and to his suppliers and contractors that he would normally have made from the office before going into the field. As he stuffed papers into his briefcase he heard a motorcycle pulling into their driveway. He glanced out of the window to confirm the source of the noise, then walked outside.

Bill recognized Mowery at first sight, as though he had known the man for years. Victoria had not described him in detail, nor, for that matter, had she talked about any of the bikers with whom she interacted. It didn't matter. The man who dwarfed the chopper, flowing hair touching wide shoulders, could be no one else. "Hi," Mowery said, arrogantly pulling fingerless gloves from his hands.

"Hi," Bill responded. He thought Mowery resembled a liquor advertisement on the back cover of a slick magazine.

"Sam around?" the biker asked, still seated upon the chopper.

Bill was of course familiar with Victoria's undercover name, but was grudging in its use by the man who was spending more time with his wife than he was. "Who?"

Mowery smiled broadly at Bill's refusal to acknowledge an intimate name Mowery could use but that was effectively denied Bill. "Victoria. Your wife."

Bill kicked himself in minor reproach for seeming petty. And for keeping himself outside of his wife's professional loop. "She's sleeping. Doesn't feel too well."

For long moments Mowery regarded Victoria's husband, saying nothing. He could see why a woman could go for Bill Decker, but only for a while. He'd be bored to shit if he was a woman hanging around with Bill. Eight to five. Big change in his life would be eight-thirty to five-thirty. Mowery knew that he was a war hero, not the kind that people would write a book about, but one who had fought in Vietnam and had the medals to prove it. He guessed he could see it in Bill's steady eyes. Like the Hell's Angels, Mowery was patriotic, was envious of other people's military service, and would have gone himself but had been frustrated, like most Angels, by a police record that kept him out. Bill's trouble, Mowery thought, was that he stopped fighting when the war was over.

"Want to come in? We've got coffee made," Bill offered. He was aware that several of his neighbors had become interested in the visitor standing in his driveway. Not that he was trying to remove Mowery from the scene out of embarrassment, but he thought he should exercise some discretion out of consideration for his wife's, and Mowery's, work.

Inside, Mowery declined the offer of a chair but accepted black coffee. He leaned backward, his buttocks easily reaching the top of the counter that made a horseshoe around the kitchen. Bill marveled at the outlaw's total ease in any surroundings, the certainty that all situations were within his power to handle. Mowery seemed to define his own space, his own presence. He was the big cat.

"Anything I can do for you?" Bill asked, interested.

"Like what?"

Bill at once realized that Mowery did not like him. And he knew why. With relief, Bill was suddenly certain that Mowery had not had sex with Victoria, an unwanted thought that surfaced from time to time. If Mowery had been sexually involved with his wife he would have not been resentful, challenging. As for the antagonism, it was Mowery's problem, not his. He merely waited for the biker to take the next step.

"She okay?" Mowery asked.

"I'm fine." Victoria, still sleepy, entered the kitchen and

reached for the coffeepot. After pouring a cup, she turned to Bill, put an arm around him, and kissed him on the cheek. He kissed her back.

"Carlander said you were pretty messed up," Mowery said to her. "Told me about Bruno and you and Vic Mena, and that bust over at Fullerton. You thought it was our ass, huh?" He sounded concerned.

"Looked that way for a while," Victoria responded, still looking at Bill.

"Nothing you need?" Mowery asked. "You're cool, now?" The smile remained. Bill felt like an outsider but did not excuse himself. Nor would he ask questions yet. He would do that later, when Victoria felt like confiding in him.

"Sure. Fine. Ready to go to work." Victoria turned back to Bill. She kissed him again, squeezed his arm. "Sleep helped a lot. I feel good now."

Bill delayed his own departure from the house while his wife sped off to work on the back of a Harley chopper.

Victoria enjoyed the knowledge that necks around the neighborhood were craning to the breaking point as eyeballs followed her rapid motion along the street. Her pleasure, while perverse, was great.

# CHAPTER 14

Mowery had met a man by the name of Ed Diodati in the Huddle Bar in Reseda. The two drank beer and swapped stories of cross-country rides, residences in mutual jails, and women unknowingly shared. Very quickly Diodati revealed that he and his old lady, Carol, dealt drugs in case Mowery needed a source. Mowery allowed that he was always looking for new connections. Diodati gave Mowery his address in Anaheim and directions about how to get there. He also provided Mowery with a telephone number to call to make sure he or Carol was home.

Mowery explained to Victoria and Carlander that Diodati was not a Hell's Angel but was connected with the Fugitives motorcycle club. He was at least forty and, because of substance abuse along with a life of crime, looked older. He was no longer soaring with the eagles, Mowery suggested, but even aging bike warriors maintained connections. Carlander decided that they would make a buy from him and if possible from his woman, Carol.

The location was in another of the countless canyons buried

away in a foothill arroyo. It reminded Victoria of Glore's location for accessibility but did not approach the security of Glore's property, nor did it have the same ominous quality of pure menace. Diodati's place was secluded and dark but was rickety and ill-kempt. *No self-respecting guard dog would live here,* she thought as Mowery guided the chopper down a rutted driveway into a neglected yard.

Nease had the night off, but Carlander had no trouble following Mowery, now absent a fast-moving escort of Hell's Angels, into Anaheim's sparsely populated hill area. He had to park his car a quarter-mile from the house and walk among brush and rocks to gain a vantage point of the house that satisfied his surveillance requirements. Carlander was aware that he was in rattlesnake country. He made himself believe that all snakes were asleep after sundown and concentrated his attention on the house.

Victoria and Mowery knocked on the back door of the house per instructions. It was opened by Ed Diodati, who greeted them in a state that Victoria recognized as under the influence. In the living room Victoria noticed a flat board about five inches wide and six feet in length that was suspended by wires from the ceiling. She thought the object was a little strange, but the word strange could be used to describe most of the people she had met during the past six months. Gestured to by her host to sit, she took the most obvious seat, a place on the sofa. Mowery took a chair across from her while Ed Diodati left an overstuffed chair empty in favor of a cane straight-back with a broken wicker seat. They were in the process of getting small talk out of the way in order to get down to business when an object appeared inches in front of Victoria's face. She let out a scream and did a backward flip over the sofa, where she landed hard on the floor. She heard Ed laugh. She was angered to hear Mowery join him. From her knees, still on the floor, Victoria looked up at the apparition that had just caused her involuntary gymnastics. It was a python snake, several feet long, and thick. She thought she was too large for the snake to swallow, but she had no way of knowing whether the snake realized that.

Carol Mann appeared in the living room before Victoria had recovered. The sight of her made Victoria the narcotics agent want to do another backward flip. She immediately recognized the woman as a former OCJ inmate when Victoria had been doing duty in the women's county jail. Carol Mann was older than Victoria, much harder, streetwise, and had been carrying a gun at the time of her arrest. She had seldom smiled then and not at all tonight as she watched Victoria circling on her hands and knees away from the python.

The purchase of three plastic envelopes of white powder—crank—took place shortly after the snake withdrew to its elevated sleeping platform. It seemed inconceivable to Victoria that Carol Mann had failed to recognize her. The taciturn woman was difficult to read in any event, and as closely as Victoria watched Carol, to know for sure. Nor could she communicate her apprehension to Mowery while they were in the presence of Ed Diodati. She was especially alarmed when Carol Mann called Ed into the kitchen for a hushed conversation. Surely they were talking about her and Mowery.

There was no reason to extend social amenities after the business of buying dope was finished. Victoria moved toward the front door without thinking that their hosts might want them to exit whence they came, by the rear of the house. She resisted momentary panic when the door did not immediately open after unlocking it. In fact, there were four locks keeping the door closed. By the time she had freed the last she felt foolish. Going through the back door would indeed have been easier. Mowery was amused, Diodati said nothing. Carol Mann did not speak, but Victoria could feel the woman's stare even after she and Mowery were outside preparing to mount the chopper.

Mowery punched the bike into life and waved a careless hand in their direction as he let in the clutch.

"She made me," Victoria announced that night to Carlander and Mowery. In place of their usual late-night restaurant rendezvous, they sat inside the van that Carlander had used before. "She had six months left to do on a one-year sentence for assault with a deadly weapon when I was assigned to the jail."

"What'd she say?" Carlander wanted to know.

"Nothing," Victoria said. She waited for Carlander to come up with a solution to a problem that they had all feared would happen sooner or later.

"He's not an Angel," Mowery offered, as though that some-how put everything into perspective.

Victoria was aware that she was jumpy, aware that she had cried wolf when buying from Bruno and Vic Mena. But her re-action then, as now, was reasonable given the circumstances. She ignored Mowery's observation and spoke again to Carlander. "I can't believe she didn't recognize me. I think she did. Hell, I know she did. She never blinked. Like her fucking snake. They're probably inseparable."

"Okay." Carlander finished making entries in his report and diary in neat, deliberate script. "Anybody think to bring some pop? Coffee or something?"

"Okay, what?" Victoria asked Carlander.

"Who does she know? Nobody. No Angels, for sure," Mowery said, as casual about Victoria's fears as Carlander.

"I don't know yet," Carlander said without looking up.

Victoria leaned heavily against the side of the van. Carlander and Mowery occupied the two front seats. Their excuse to have her sit in the back was that she was smaller than the men. Of course she was smaller; what the hell did that have to do with anything? she wondered.

"Okay, I'll take care of it," Carlander said. "We'll use that other girl . . ."

"Karen?" Victoria prompted.

"Yeah," Carlander assented. "Her."

Mowery momentarily looked up. "What for?"

"Yeah. What for?" Victoria echoed.

Carlander explained patiently. "We keep you out of sight for a few days. Karen can do a couple buys for us, and we keep our eyeballs and ears open for anybody asking about you. Won't take any time at all to figure out if this Carol Mann made you."

Mowery asked the obvious question. At least it was obvious to him. "Why don't you keep me out of sight, couple, three days? Couple, three weeks, maybe."

"We'll do some bikers in other clubs," Carlander said, ignor-ing Mowery. "Meet you at Love's tomorrow," the detective said, referring to an oft-used restaurant not far from the Sixpence Motel. "We'll start early, around ten."

\* \* \*

There were other officers from the Orange County Sheriff's Office Narcotics Division working contacts provided by Carlander who occasionally assisted him when the pecularities of a given operation needed added manpower. When Karen Higgins was again contacted by Carlander and asked to work in the field, a change from her assignment at the women's jail, she responded with alacrity. Also working the periphery of several cases were Investigators Grams and Horton, veteran Narcotics men.

Jerry Wayne Davis, a.k.a. Jerry Pickens, sold two balloons of heroin to Karen Higgins in the company of Clifford Mowery. Dwayne Kent Neuberger also sold heroin to Karen. The sale was witnessed by Mowery while Carlander, Nease, and Horton were staked out at Fazio's Bar in Garden Grove. Neuberger suggested to Mowery that he could supply guns of any kind. Mowery said he was always interested in guns and would get back to him. This information was turned over to agents of the Bureau of Alcohol, Tobacco, and Firearms.

Karen Higgins and Mowery, operating from astride the chopper, made several more buys, including heroin from Ruben Ballesteros, a young Mexican. Ballesteros fancied himself a gang leader despite his five-foot three-inch stature and one hundred and ten pounds. He was a streetwise youth whose orders to his Latino *amigos* were carried out without question. Ruben Ballesteros was proud of the fact that he could supply virtually any illegal drug asked for.

Mowery made an appointment to meet Ballesteros in the parking lot of the California Department of Motor Vehicles in Fullerton. In addition to Carlander, Detectives Hunt, Dogue, Dickerson, and Hernandez were staked out in the parking lot.

Ballesteros had an entourage of Mexican bodyguards who traveled with him in a 1966 Oldsmobile 98. Mowery thought the car had been fitted with the hydraulic "lifters" that were popular among young Latino men in southern California, but he realized when Ballesteros arrived in the DMV parking lot that the car simply had broken shock absorbers.

Narcotics detective Hernandez was still talking with Mowery and Karen, who were leaning against the chopper, when Ballesteros arrived. The Mexican stepped out of his heavy car, followed by four of his implacable gang members. There was no time for Hernandez to dissolve into the street scene, so he remained as though he belonged there. "Why did you bring those fucking narcs with you?" Ballesteros said.

"We didn't bring no fucking narcs, man," the narc responded.

"Yeah?" went the exchange. "You dindn't see 'em, man? Right behind you was two narcs."

"We didn't see 'em," Herandez said and looked toward Mowery for supporting confirmation.

"Yeah. That's right." Mowery was cool but amazed.

"Shit," the Mexican spat. "What'choo you want?"

"Ah, balloons," Hernandez said, not knowing what else to say. "Four."

"Give me the money," Ballesteros said.

Karen handed Ballesteros two hundred dollars in marked twenty-dollar bills. The Mexican counted the money and duly handed over four balloons of what later tested to be heroin. Ballesteros and his "gang" stepped back into their Oldsmobile but paused while the passenger side electric window creaked and jerked its way down. Ballesteros fixed them with what he believed was his intimidating stare and said, "Next time don't bring no fucking narcs wit'choo."

When the officers later made out their crime activities reports, one of them wrote a physical description of Ballesteros and added the notation "No discernable I.Q."

Victoria had not taken time off during the period that Karen Higgins rode the chopper. She was most often with Carlander or Nease in an automobile following the buys.

Following the Ballesteros buy Victoria went home early, as did Carlander and Mowery, for the simple reason that the chopper was down again, this time with a broken timing chain. While Carlander occasionally authorized the motorcycle to be repaired at Bruno's shop, many of the repairs were accomplished by Mowery. So on February 22, 1977, while the chopper was down, everybody should have been in bed getting some rest for the following day. Carlander decided to make sure.

Carlander and Victoria had lightened their grip on Mowery,

surveilling him only three or four times per week. Carlander was following no particular pattern when, rather than go to bed around midnight, he decided to check on Mowery.

He drove to the Sixpence Motel, parked his police undercover car in an inconspicuous location where he could see Mowery's door, and took up a sack of sunflower seeds.

At 2:30 A.M. the door of Mowery's unit opened and a woman appeared from within. Anyone who knew the biker would hardly raise an eyebrow at the sight of a woman coming out of his room. Certainly not Carlander. Except in this case he knew the woman.

She was a cop.

He watched while Karen Higgins kissed Mowery passionately on the lips before walking away. Carlander experienced a sense of betrayal, frustration, and dark rage. For several minutes he sat in the dark of his car, staring at nothing at all. He could only imagine the damage that these two people had done to a six-month-long criminal investigation that had expended thousands of man-hours and involved scores of specialized police officers, forensic experts, and legal prosecutors, not to mention the waste of tens of thousands of taxpayers' dollars. The ramifications of what defense attorneys could do with this information boggled Carlander's mind.

The Orange County Sheriff's Office had to be above reproach. Its sworn officers had to be meticulous in the way they conducted their private as well as professional lives. Sexual relations between a female officer and a convicted criminal out on probation would guarantee banner newspaper headlines. The Sheriff's Office would have lost its moral as well as legal position of a dispassionate enforcer of law. The greenest defense lawyer could petition the court to have a case that had been investigated under these circumstances thrown out.

Carlander would have to lay it all out for Sheriff Brad Gates the next day. In the meantime, he had to find out for himself what had happened. He started the engine of his car, drove six blocks to a pay telephone, and dialed Victoria's home telephone number.

It seemed to her that she was reaching for the telephone before it had actually rung. "Hello?"

"Get dressed and meet me at the office," a voice said.

"You mean the station?" she asked.

"You know about an office somewhere I don't know about?" Carlander barked sarcastically. "Hell, yes, the station." *Not cool,* he thought to himself, but he had a suspicion about Victoria and it was beginning to show.

"Mowery?" Victoria asked.

"Who the hell else?" Carlander growled over the wire.

Mowery, indeed. Out of consideration for Bill she did not turn on a light while she quickly dressed. He could not help waking from sleep, but chose not to ask about the problem. Hell, he thought, if he was married to a pediatrician the result from a late-night call would be the same.

As Victoria entered the Narcotics squad room, she found Carlander pacing. The room was obscenely well lit for the lateness of the hour. At the far end of the office was another officer at a desk using a telephone. Carlander jerked his head toward the other investigator and said to her, "Come on, let's go where we can talk."

Victoria remained one step behind Carlander as he opened four doors on the second floor before finding an unused room. She felt as though she were a student ordered into the principal's office. Despite the absurdity of the notion, she could not quell her shaky knees and increased pulse. She became annoyed at herself and quickly turned that anger toward Carlander. "Okay, Wayne, if the turkey killed somebody, we could handle it in the morning. I could have used the sleep . . ."

"Karen Higgins was wrapped around Mowery this morning. I saw her come out of his place."

Victoria's anger melted like an ice cube dropped into hot water. Her focus shifted from Carlander onto a place on the ceiling. She tried to find words. The first to come out were, "I don't believe it."

"She walked out of his room less than an hour ago. Kissed him good-bye before she left," Carlander said, watching Victoria's eyes.

"She wouldn't do that," Victoria heard herself say. Karen Higgins might be unseasoned in police work, but she was thoroughly professional in her approach to the job. And she was not stupid. She would not jeopardize her career for a toss in the sack with ... with a ...

"Did you know about this?" he asked, biting off his words.

"What the hell do you mean? What makes you think I know about this? You better think about what you're saying before you start accusing me of a damn thing," she said, her original anger at Carlander returning.

"I'm not accusing you, Vicky, I want to know what you know, that's all," he said.

"Then change the way you ask."

"All right, let's get at it," Carlander said. "What did she tell you? You're friends, aren't you?"

It was true. Victoria felt a kind of big-sister instinct toward Karen, who was about three years younger. After Karen worked those first few buys, Victoria had made a point of having lunch with her whenever possible. Karen often called Victoria on weekends, and the two would sometimes talk for more than an hour. Karen had few women in her profession to talk with, and she thirsted for Victoria's company. Victoria liked Karen's sense of humor and thought she would be great fun to socialize with in the future when Victoria was no longer living like a gangster's moll. She had not met Karen's husband, Paul, but he sounded like a good guy, someone Bill would like to know.

Karen had been eager to receive advice. Victoria remembered once describing the dangers of being flirtatious with fellow officers as well as the public while on the job. The younger policewoman agreed, and not once had Victoria heard rumors that Karen was anything but straight-arrow. She said as much to Carlander.

Carlander's face was florid. "How long has she been making it with the guy?"

"Aren't you taking a lot for granted?" she asked. "She leaves his room and kisses him good-bye. Not smart, maybe, but that isn't a case for carnal liaison."

"I've got enough right now to have her ass booted out of the department," Carlander countered.

She knew he was correct. Not necessarily right, but able to accomplish that very event. "That what you want? To get rid of her?"

"Stop it, goddamnit, Vicky. I've got important cases ready to fall apart because your friend has hot pants. Think about it. Tell me what you know."

Victoria settled slowly onto a chair. She absently opened a drawer and found a pack of cigarettes. Without hesitation she helped herself. "There's nothing to tell. Nothing I know, anyway. We're friends but we're not down to swapping fantasies yet."

Carlander's smile was grim. "Too bad. Be great to just hang her and get it over with."

Victoria said, "What do we do if you're right?"

Carlander thought for a moment. "We find out first. You're right about that. No doubt in my mind, but we gotta know before we do anything. Then, if she did what I think happened between them, we go to Mitch, and Tom, and Gates. No way around that."

Victoria shuddered at the thought of facing Brad Gates's legendary fury. He never accepted a reason for conduct less than moral. She hoped for Karen's sake that the kiss was impulsive and that her visit to Mowery's room was strictly business. The more she thought about it, however, the less likely it seemed.

"Come on," Carlander said.

Victoria did not have to ask Carlander where they were going.

It was 5:30 A.M. when they arrived at the Sixpence. Victoria would not have pounded on anyone's door at this tranquil hour of the day, but Carlander slammed a huge balled fist into it. "Open the door, Mowery. Right now. Move it."

Mowery never moved fast unless he chose to do so. Victoria was surprised when the door opened before Carlander finished pounding on it the second time. The biker was barefoot, bare chested, and his denim jeans were not fully fastened. Victoria felt a wave of understanding for Karen's taste in flesh, however ill-advised. *Every woman's fantasy outlaw,* she thought to herself once again. Mowery's hair was mussed, and he rubbed his eyes.

Victoria followed Carlander inside. She had never seen him in such a rage. Carlander was capable of doing damage. She was therefore nervous, unable to sit while he shoved his face as near as possible into Mowery's.

Mowery avoided Carlander's challenge by collapsing onto the

bed from which he had just risen and interlacing his fingers behind his head. Carlander stopped short of sitting on the bed near Mowery, but he instead pulled up a straight-backed chair as near as possible.

"Karen Higgins came out of here after two in the morning. How come?" he demanded.

"Come in, Wayne," Mowery said. "You too, Sam," he said, smiling.

Carlander dismissed Mowery's diversion. "Answer me, goddamnit."

"Why she left? 'Cause she had to get home. Couldn't stay here all night," the biker responded flippantly.

"There's nothing funny about what I asked you, Mowery. And you're not funny. Don't bullshit me. Did you and Karen Higgins have sex?" Carlander's voice was uncharacteristically low.

The unexpected change in his tone might have affected Mowery the same way it affected Victoria. The confidence dropped out of his voice. "Naw. Hell, naw. I'm not that dumb, man."

Carlander's teeth shone through stretched lips. "Dumb. We know you're dumb. Dumb is what you do best. Only had one human being in the whole fucking world ever tried to keep you out of jail, and now you're sitting there on your ass lying to him. I call that dumb."

"Carlander, no way would . . ." the biker began.

Carlander stopped Mowery with an upraised hand. "Don't do it again. Think real hard."

"Hey, hold it, man. You come knocking my fucking door down and you get in my face about what's happening with my sex life and you're telling me to think about it. Well, fuck you. What I do with my dick is none of your . . ."

Victoria recoiled as she saw Carlander leap off the edge of his chair. She literally did not register that Carlander was assaulting Mowery until the policeman had delivered three powerful blows with his foreman to Mowery's face. Victoria heard herself cry out from reflex. It seemed that Mowery's facial bones would shatter. Another blow would kill him, she thought. But Mowery fought back. Though groggy and still on his back on the bed, he tried to kick Carlander. He had no leverage and no angle, though, and the kicks failed to damage the detective. Mowery then swung a hooking punch to the side of Carlander's head, but the detective felt it coming, ducked slightly, and let the blow bounce harmlessly off the back of his head.

Victoria flinched when she saw Carlander use the edge of his flattened hand in a chopping motion on Mowery's face. The biker tried to turn away, but Carlander's judo punch caught Mowery above the eye. Before Mowery could retaliate, Carlander put an armlock around the convict's neck and applied pressure to the carotid artery. With blood supply cut off to his brain, Mowery ceased struggling almost immediately. Before he could wake, Carlander rolled Mowery onto his stomach, put his hand behind his back, and cuffed him.

"What now?" Victoria asked her partner. Carlander did not answer. He resumed his place in the chair near Mowery's bed. The biker regained consciousness within a few seconds, tried to turn over, and discovered that he was handcuffed. He managed to prop himself up to a near-sitting position with his back to the wall behind the bed.

Carlander said nothing for several minutes while Victoria paced the room. She was so relieved that this was not happening to her that she had forgotten to pity Karen. She now understood what soldiers meant when their friends were killed in combat: It was numbing and the loss they suffered grevious, but there was a deep feeling of relief that the bullet hit someone else.

"Thanks a lot, Cliff," Victoria said. "You really know how to treat your friends." She looked Mowery straight in the eye until he lowered his own. Then she turned toward Carlander and jerked her head in a silent signal to go outside.

As the two were walking out of Mowery's door the big convict called after Carlander, "Hey, how about taking off the cuffs?"

Carlander could see that the handcuffs were very uncomfortable, especially when they were placed behind the man's back. "Maybe later. I got a busy day."

Victoria waited for Carlander to close the motel door behind him and to join her outside. "We need to talk to Karen."

"Disagree," the detective said. "Let her tell her story to the sheriff. That's the man who calls the next shot."

Carlander went to his superior, Lieutenant Sim Middleton,

and reported the recent developments between Mowery and Deputy Higgins. Middleton received the oral report, then instructed Carlander, and Victoria through him, to say nothing about the matter and to make no other report until instructed by him or Sheriff Gates.

If Carlander thought there was such a thing as victim or perpetrator, he did not volunteer as much to Victoria. Nor did she ask. She was certain that he was not emotional about either person but was concerned only with how his prize investigation would be affected in the eyes of first the sheriff and then the district attorney.

Late that same afternoon Sheriff Brad Gates wasted no time in calling a meeting of the parties involved, save Mowery and Karen Higgins. He needed all of the facts laid out before him before confronting Deputy Higgins with misconduct charges serious enough to cause her dismissal. Prosecution even for criminal misdemeanor was not out of the question. Placed around Gates's large desk were two semicircles. In the second row of chairs was the command staff, including three chiefs: Raul Ramos, Bill Wallace, and Thad Dwyer. Seated in front of them were the officers directly involved in the undercover operation: Mitchell, Middleton, Victoria, and Carlander.

The atmosphere in the room was tense. Brad Gates slowly panned the room before him. It occurred to Victoria that he might be using the time and silence to gain control of his obvious feelings of anger. His flaming red hair was now a perfect match for his livid face.

"This Mowery," he spat at Carlander, "you believe what he told you?"

"No, sir," Carlander responded.

"What the hell does that mean?" Gates demanded.

"I haven't had a chance to check it out much. Haven't had a chance to really interrogate the guy, try to pin him down. He just said they've been seeing each other." Carlander was in a roomful of professionals who understood that a thorough report was a time-consuming process.

Gates turned toward Victoria. She felt like a butterfly about to be skewered. "I'll ask you straight out. I'll appreciate your answer the same way. Did you sleep with Clifford Mowery?"

"No, sir," Victoria said evenly.

"Never did?" he repeated, wanting to be sure, watching her intently for body language that might contradict her denial.

"No, sir. Never did, never will." She was not offended by Brad Gates's forceful probe. She understood the need.

"Ever kiss him?" Gates said, digging deeper. "Like kids might do in the backseat of a car, or maybe a kiss good night?"

Victoria remembered the wet T-shirt contest and Mowery's kiss on her lips while they danced, but she decided that the contact was of no consequence. "No, sir."

Gates turned his attention back toward Carlander. For a long moment the sheriff locked eyes with one of his most able investigators. After a long pause while, Victoria later thought, Gates was framing his next remark, Carlander said, chuckling, "Don't look at me. I didn't sleep with him."

The room remained deadly silent. The smile lingering on Carlander's face waned.

"How many cases has she worked on?" Gates asked Carlander.

"I don't know, sir," Carlander said. "I'd have to go through all of our reports to find out."

"Do it. Your operation is suspended as of right now and until further notice. Got it? Mowery stays in his room. He even blinks an eye, put him right there in a cell." Gates pointed through his window and across at the Orange County Jail. "I want you four, and Bud Nease, to work on nothing else until you find out exactly what cases she worked on, who she's had contact with on your bust list, and anything else about her involvement in your program since you started. If I had to make a judgment about where we're at now, I'd say she blew the whole goddamn operation out of the water."

For her own safety, Victoria had been forbidden to come near the Sheriff's Office since going undercover. This was not the time to make an exception. So for the next two weeks, Carlander met Victoria in out-of-the-way locations, including parked cars, restaurants, and libraries. He would bring her a stack of crime reports to study and take back those that he had given her the day before. Then they would discuss cases that either officer thought needed particular attention. Of special issue was separating out any of her connections from those who might have crossed paths with any of Karen Higgins's connections. Those cases were sometimes tainted, and unless an independent source could be used to verify that a criminal act had been committed by the suspect, he or she was removed from the growing arrest list. Time was of the essence because if the program were to be continued, Victoria and Mowery could not be gone long from the Hell's Angel's social scene.

The day after Gates's meeting, Higgins was relieved of duties pending the outcome of an internal investigation. She was at first incensed, demanded to know what she was being investigated for, and, when told, vehemently denied the charges.

For most of the next two weeks Sheriff Gates reviewed all personnel involved and participated in the interrogation of Clifford Mowery. He spent as many hours as any of the team familiarizing himself with the details of every investigator's activities in the nearly seven-month-long investigation. At the end of two weeks, Karen Higgins was called before Sheriff Gates for a meeting that would be "off the record." She requested that her lawyer be present, and Gates agreed.

As Gates considered his pending confrontation with Higgins, his primary objective was to preserve the massive investigative assignment almost completed by his unique undercover team. The evidence gathered had already exceeded his initial hopes and promised to inflict sweeping damage on criminal biker gangs in this as well as adjacent counties in southern California. His second purpose was to preserve the reputation of the Orange County Sheriff's Office from scandal. No doubt he did consider protecting himself, but the larger issue was the credibility of the Department's ethical stature in a criminal courtroom. Less measurable but no less certain was that public disrespect for law enforcement agencies would be reflected by an increase in crime activities. Damage of this kind could take years to repair, possibly at considerable cost to the taxpayer. When Higgins was summoned into his office, Gates informed her that she had been seen coming out of Mowery's room at the Sixpence Motel and that she had been observed kissing him on one of those visits. Gates related in full detail the description of her alleged activities Mowery had supplied during his interrogation. Higgins stubbornly maintained that if she had been seen in the Sixpence Motel, it was only in connection with her duties, not a romantic tryst.

Brad Gates was angry that one of his employees, a sworn officer of the county, would lie to him. He gave her an ultimatum. She had twenty-four hours to tender her resignation to the Orange County Sheriff's Office. He was offering her a quiet way out for the obvious reason that he wanted to save the other narcotics cases. If she refused to resign, he would launch a full-scale investigation of the facts, which he would then use against her in a formal hearing.

The following afternoon a letter containing Deputy Karen Higgins's resignation was delivered to Sheriff Brad Gates.

All echelons of the sheriff's department who were connected with the undercover operation breathed a collective sigh of relief when, on the night of March 2, 1977, the right lady cop was once again on the back of Mowery's Harley-Davidson. They were headed for the Alpine Inn, a drinking house and eatery in Silverado Canyon, Yorba Linda. The Hell's Angels were planning a large dinner party. Jack Forbes, alias Dago Paul, was expected to be in attendance and the Boston police had urged the Orange County Sheriff's Office to bring in Forbes at any cost. He was a known killer, and Boston PD did not want to take the chance of waiting until Carlander's undercover operation arrived at its orderly termination before putting handcuffs on their man. Neither Carlander nor Sim Middleton wanted to make a move that they felt could compromise their entire subrosa program, but interdepartmental cooperation was important to maintain. Therefore, a plan was devised whereby Jack Forbes would be surveilled by four additional officers and isolated from the other Angels when he emerged from the dinner. Whatever direction Forbes took, he would be followed by one of the officers. When his route was ascertained, a radio signal would be sent to a waiting police cruiser, backed up by two motorcycle policemen, in case Forbes was riding his chopper instead of a car. He would be pulled over to the side of the road and asked to take a Breathalyzer test. No matter how Forbes checked out, he would be put under arrest. At the station house he would be told that a homicide warrant had been issued for him in Boston, a fact he well knew, and that he would be held for delivery to that jurisdiction.

Mowery was briefed on his status. He was still in violation of his parole contract and subject to return to the penitentiary without notice. Sheriff Gates had not yet given his approval to resume operations that included Mowery. However, it was decided that he would be allowed to attend dinner with the Hell's Angels since he would be expected to be there and not to do so would put him under suspicion. Mowery was not told about the plan to take Jack Forbes into custody, but that was a strong reason to have Victoria present at the dinner—to have help from the inside.

Victoria and Mowery were among the first to arrive at that dinner party. Dago Paul was not on hand, nor did he arrive by midnight. By 1:00 A.M. the party had heated up to the usual level of Hell's Angel noise and debauchery, still with no Dago Paul. While waiting, one of the officers staking out the Alpine Inn, Sergeant Art Johnson, spent his idle time taking down the numbers of all vehicles parked around or near the inn. By 4:30 A.M. all the Angels had left the restaurant, and Jack Forbes had not appeared. The stakeout was called off. The exercise might have been a huge waste of time save for a remark made by Fat Mike when Mowery wondered aloud, casually, where the hell Forbes had gone to. Fat Mike looked at Mowery, surprised. "Why don't you ask your sister? She's living with him."

# CHAPTER 15

While it was never an objective of the undercover operation to rehabilitate Mowery, there nevertheless were some changes in him that did not escape Carlander's attention. Contrary to his initial assertions that Victoria would at all times have to defend herself from bikers, Mowery had more than once protected her. And he was clearly more productive in targeting important members of the biker gangs than in the beginning of the operation. These gains notwithstanding, Mowery remained a ticking time bomb.

On March 10, 1977, the telephone rang in Carlander's house. He had been up most of the night on a stakeout and had spent less than three hours in bed. It was Mowery. Specific orders from Sheriff Brad Gates to Carlander and Victoria involved a directive to watch Mowery like hawks. The sheriff had considered putting a tap on Mowery's telephone line, but in the end he decided to get on with wrapping up Carlander's investigations with as few added aggravations as possible. Everyone agreed, however, that Mowery was as larcenous in his heart as ever and was not to be trusted. "I want this guy watched from the time he puts his boots on in the morning, all day, and then tucked into bed at night." Even Gates had smiled at his own imagery. "Carlander, you do the tucking."

"I want out of this fucking room, man," Mowery drawled over the telephone.

Carlander was neither solicitous nor angry. "Better than some places you could be sitting on your ass."

"I want to go to a swap meet," Mowery said, ignoring Carlander's facetious comment.

"Swap meets are trouble," Carlander said, bored. "You don't need any more of that in your life."

"Somebody's selling guns at this one," Mowery said, sure he would get Carlander's sharp attention. Gun trafficking was a heavy rap.

"They sell guns at every swap meet. Stay home," the detective said.

"You're a hard case, man," Mowery breathed, but he continued doggedly with his justification for leaving the Sixpence Motel. "Mad Dog Fero's in town. Him and Denny Decker are expecting me to go."

"Quit conning me, Mowery. You trying to help the sheriff's department? Come on," Carlander said sarcastically.

"Hey, suit your fucking self, Carlander," Mowery pressed. "But you can't do your wonderful work without me and I wanta go outside, kick back."

Carlander was aware that Mowery had a point. The biker, Carlander grudgingly admitted, was showing no signs of paralysis at the prospect of going back inside the slammer as a parole violator following the Higgins departmental embarrassment. It was even possible that he was trying to make amends for his blunder with Karen Higgins. "Yeah, well, you're dangerous when you're out kicking back," Carlander said.

"So, a few of the brothers are headed out to L.A. County to the Expo. Swap meet out there," Mowery repeated. "That so bad?"

Carlander began to reason with himself. Maybe it wasn't such a bad idea after all. If Mowery really wanted to he would get out anyway. Probably wreck the whole undercover operation if he got desperate enough. "Think you might set up a gun buy out there, huh?"

"Anything's possible," Mowery suggested.

The big detective thought for several moments before making up his mind. "It's not okay, but I'm not going to come by or call your place today. Like, maybe you don't feel good, want to lay around your bed, take it easy."

"Gotcha," Mowery responded.

"I hope to hell not," Carlander said into a dead line as he replaced the telephone. He did not waste a moment wondering if he had made the right or wrong decision. Instead, he grabbed a jacket from behind his chair and headed for the door. He would trail Mowery to the Exhibition Center. He might be stupid, but he wasn't naive.

A motorcycle swap meet of large proportions had been planned for March 11, 1977. The place was the Exhibition Center on the grounds of Exhibition Park near the University of Southern California campus. A few short miles east and south was the snakelike complex of the I-10, 710, 101, and I-5 freeway interchanges near the heart of Los Angeles. It was a highway maze ideal for planning a getaway, if one were needed, and especially accommodating for eluding pursuit on a motorcycle. The Hell's Angels were well known for devising group activities with such things in mind, including road conditions, where they led, and how accessible they were. Some law enforcement agencies later attributed the location of the Exhibition Center fight to typical Hell's Angels clever planning. In fact, the Angels had no idea that a battle was going to take place, much less who they would meet. What made the battle an epic one was the ferocity with which it was fought.

This swap meet catered to motorcycle owners and riders, though everything was sold there from used automobile transmissions, engines, and tires to counterfeit articles of clothing to new music tapes to neckties to Indian blankets to jewelry, guns, and everything in between. Everything was for sale, anything could be traded. Some of the guns would be illegally bought and sold without the required legal waiting time being observed, some music tapes would be pirate versions, some hot jewelry would be well mixed with clean merchandise. Every swap meet in southern California attracted a few police officers, always personnel from Burglary who strolled through the booths and displays looking for the more expensive, conspicuous merchandise that might have been carelessly offered for sale after a theft. But police coverage of a swap meet was pro forma and usually conducted with low visibility. This particular swap meet would be no different.

Two cops from LAPD Burglary detail made a point to schedule a half-day at the swap meet because they heard the Mongols would be there, along with the Outlaws, Renegades, and Satan's Slaves motorcycle clubs. With these groups in attendance, the odds went sharply up that some weighty deals for hot merchandise would happen.

At the time, the police did not know that the Hell's Angels would be there. Crowds began to arrive at the Exhibition Center on the morning of a day unseasonably warm even for Los Angeles. The building was about the size of three football fields. Portable toilet facilities were added outside in the parking area, where more space for sales booths had been staked out on the tarmac. Fast-food kiosks were plentiful, offering Mexican dishes as well as traditional American hot dogs and hamburgers, bakery goods, and liquids of all kinds except alcohol. While consumption of alcoholic beverages on the grounds of the swap meet was against the law, the practice was largely ignored by security personnel unless drinkers became unruly.

By two o'clock there were as many as three thousand people milling about inside the Exhibition Center and several hundred outside. In addition to cars parked in orderly rows, there were hundreds of motorcycles. The owners of those bikes were "flying" their colors. Hell's Angels wore their infamous white-horned death's head with a pair of wings sweeping upward behind the skull. Each jacket was a battle flag, and a Hell's Angel would fight literally to the death before he would take off his colors. To do otherwise was an act of cowardice.

Months and even years later people who witnessed the Exhibition Center fight would argue about how many bikers were involved, how many were Hell's Angels, and how many other clubs were present and participated in the battle. Some exaggerated estimates put the number of Hell's Angels at nearly one hundred, Mongols at three hundred.

In fact, the Angels had twelve club members present along with two prospects, or members on probation. One of them was Mowery.

The Mongols in attendance that day numbered about sixty. In absolute numbers, including other clubs friendly with the Mongols, there were about three dozen more. These included members of the Renegades and Outlaws. Adding mightily to the confusion of numbers was the fact that a substantial number of unaffiliated shoppers at the swap meet became carried away and joined in the melee.

Among the Hell's Angels were Michael Lee Mason, a.k.a. "Bruno," Lenny Erickson, Whitey Parsons, Mad Dog Fero, Denny Decker, Buffalo, Mowery, and Gary Robles from Fontana. With Robles was one of the youngest, most violent of all the Hell's Angels, Greg Davit, a Fontana chapter officer, along with six others from the Los Angeles and San Bernardino chapters. Greg Davit was six feet three inches tall, two hundred and thirty pounds, very quick and strong. Several years before, he had been an exceptionally young Hell's Angel when he was admitted for membership at the age of eighteen, and he was one of the few Hell's Angels ever allowed to resign from active membership.

The Hell's Angels did not arrive prepared for a fight at the swap meet. It was later said that the dispute began over a woman. Whitey Parsons had had a relationship with Rene Rice, a dancer at a Los Angeles disco. Rene was concurrently the girlfriend of Martin "Cargo" Hobart, a Mongol. Hobart had talked around town about how he would someday kill Parsons. To make matters worse, Rene told any of her girlfriends who would listen that life with the Angels, compared with the Mongols, was like being with men in the fast lane instead of dogs in a junkyard.

Cargo Hobart saw Parsons standing among the dense crowd, talking with another biker. An exposed, unprotected back was more than Hobart could have hoped for. Snatching from his waist a heavy-duty chain that doubled as an ornamental belt around his jeans and a tie-down for his motorcycle, Hobart hefted the chain, then slipped through the crowds to get as near to Parsons as possible without detection. The last few people around Parsons quickly melted aside as the Mongol swung his doubled length of chain over his head and brought it singing downward onto Parsons's with all of his strength. The Angel talking with Parsons, Gary Robles, caught sight of Hobart from the corner of his eye and yelled a warning: "Behind you!"

Parsons did not bother to look. Out of reflex he spun. The hurled chain missed his head but did not miss his body completely. The chain caught him on the right shoulder, breaking Parsons's collarbone. Although the broken shoulder must have been excruciatingly painful, Parsons shook it off and immediately reached for a weapon. There was an automobile racing engine display nearby with an assortment of spare parts. Parsons grasped a piston by its attached connecting rod and used this as a mace. He feinted once before cutting loose with a blow aimed at Hobart's head. Hobart took the piston shot to the side of his skull and went down like a felled wapiti. Parsons did not aim another shot to Hobart's head because he knew that it would finish him, and Parsons wanted his attacker to suffer more injury before dying. So Parsons began to administer deliberate, measured blows to the semiconscious man's body prostrate on the floor. Hobart's ribs broke, his arms were shattered, and his legs were smashed. Parsons might easily have killed Hobart then and there but for the fact that other Mongols came to the aid of their fallen comrade.

For several long moments Parsons and Gary Robles fought with ten Mongols. In the time following Hobart's initial attack, everyone had a chance to lay hands on a weapon of some kind. Baseball bats appeared, along with knives, wrenches, brass knuckles. Mowery wielded a kickstand. As he used it, the kickstand was a devastating weapon. He swung the long, heavy metal object with abandon at anybody wearing a Mongols jacket and, in fact, at anybody who was not wearing Hell's Angels colors. There was panic among those customers of the swap meet who were not participants in the fight. Gang members in combat organized without much effort, accustomed as they were to street warfare. Innocents or noncombatants were horrified to see blood flowing so freely, and there was a mad rush to get to the exits. But the accent was on mad. Many exits were locked as thousands of people clambered in vain to escape the violence inside. Shouts for police were repeated constantly, but until reinforcements could arrive the numbers of police were too few. Those who were on location could do little to influence the riot.

Carlander had no intention of going inside the Exhibition Center. He wanted to avoid being seen with Mowery, so when the fight broke out, he merely watched through one of the open doors. There was nothing he could do. By now the Los Angeles Police Department would have been called and units dispatched, although they would probably not bust their humps getting there. Cops commonly feel that when bad guys are fighting each other, let them keep at it as long as the mayhem is limited.

As Carlander looked on, the battle inside the Exhibition Center continued to rage. All fourteen Angels were fully engaged against more than fifty Mongols and their supporters. Danny Decker was using an aluminum softball bat with devastating results. Skulls could be heard cracking, bones snapping. Hell's Angels allowed themselves to be pushed against the walls of the building not because they were retreating, but because then their backs were protected. Mad Dog Fero used his favorite weapons, brass knuckles on each hand. Not brass, in fact, but stainless steel, the metal knuckles had slots to place four fingers inside, and atop the knuckles were studs. Any kind of blow to the face or body resulted in serious, disabling injury: a broken face, shattered rib, mangled nose, lacerations. Among all the Hell's Angels, Mad Dog Fero had an enormous capacity to sustain damage and continue fighting. Whatever his threshold of pain was, it would not be found by the Mongols on this day.

Lenny Erickson and Bruno did not make it to a wall but stood back to back holding off several Mongols and a number of Renegades. Bruno had picked up the prostrate Hobart's heavy chain and was using it with overwhelming effect. Each time he swung the doubled chain, something would break: flesh, bones, another weapon.

From behind him he heard laughter. It was Erickson. "Hey, man, you're hitting me with that fucking thing on your backswing."

For his part, Erickson had a razor-sharp knife in his right hand while using a leather jacket wrapped around his left arm as a shield against incoming stabs and blows. If Erickson did not kill somebody, it wasn't for lack of trying. It was even possible that one of the more severely wounded of those he dispatched might have later died. Hospitals and doctors' offices within a twenty-mile radius of the Exhibition Center dispensed treatment in the form of setting broken bones and stitching lacerations on an extraordinary number of bikers within hours of the end of the fight.

Mowery, meanwhile, kept lashing out with his kickstand. Two weeks after the fight had taken place, Victoria was wearing a wire while talking a drug deal. While she and suspected drug dealer Howie Plum sat in a car waiting for Mowery to return from inside an apartment, Plum could talk of nothing else but Mowery and the damage he had done with the kickstand. Every biker in the city had heard of his feats. He dispatched foes with each powerful swing of the kickstand, delivering jarring blows to the head and body that caused split skulls and torn flesh.

It was, however, the fighting skills of Greg Davit that assured that the Hell's Angels would have not just a victory but a rout. Davit was trained in karate, and he was blindingly quick with his hands and feet. He seemed to be everywhere at once, delivering stunning blows with a seven-foot pole on which a nearby merchant had hung rugs. While there were more of these sticks to go around, no one but Davit could manipulate them effectively. The Japanese had perfected the use of the bokken hundreds of years before, and in the hands of an expert it had a devastating effect on the Angels' foes.

Still watching with great interest, Carlander spoke to a lieutenant from the Los Angeles Police Department. "You gonna bust these guys?" he asked.

"Who're you?" the officer wanted to know.

"Name's Carlander, Orange County Sheriff's Office, but I really don't want to show you a badge."

The lieutenant nodded in understanding. "Okay. Yeah, pretty soon we'll bust it up. We'll let 'em thin out a bit before we go in." It made good sense to let the combatants exhaust themselves before sending in police who, after all, wanted to make arrests, not fight with the antagonists.

Carlander looked around the parking lot. A formidable array of ambulances, police cruisers, paddy wagons, and motorcycles was assembling. Medics were deliberate in readying their stretchers, taking up medical bags, and carrying out portable IVs and oxygen bottles.

"I got somebody in there I don't want to have go to jail, if you don't mind," Carlander said to the lieutenant.

"Which one?" the LAPD officer asked.

"That guy with the kickstand in his hand," Carlander responded. For a minute the two cops watched Mowery do his work with the kickstand.

The lieutenant shook his head in wonder. "My God. That guy should be the first to go."

Carlander winced as he watched Mowery swing his weapon like a scythe and hit a biker behind the ears. The detective almost felt guilty of abetting a criminal activity as he watched Mowery dispatch one Mongol after another. On the other hand, none of the Mongols were informants. Even if some were, he was not so sure he cared to save any of them anyway.

"What's he to you?" the LAPD man asked.

"CI," Carlander snapped, hoping to discourage further queries.

"One in a million, huh? That what that fucker is? Why, he's a damn Hell's Angel. Ought to electrocute the bastard."

"Might do that someday, Lieutenant," Carlander agreed. "Might pull the switch myself."

The Outlaws were the first group to break and run. Their absence was hardly noticed by the Angels, who were still outnumbered and could only see rank after rank of Mongols and Renegades in their faces.

Mowery saw a blade coming at him but could not avoid its thrust. He had faced many knives in the several minutes of the fight but had been able to strike first with his kickstand. This knife thrust, however, came from his left just as he was turning. By the time he could make any kind of defensive move, the long blade had penetrated completely through his hand, continued into his chest, struck a bone, deflected, and continued another dozen millimeters into the chest cavity until the knife reached its hilt. With his left hand effectively pinned against his chest, Mowery swung the kickstand in a backstroke with his right arm. The kickstand caught the exposed Mongol on the side of his face. Mowery felt a dull crunch and knew instinctively that the knifer would do no more damage. The many attackers arrayed against him all stopped, as though on signal, to eye the ghastly chest wound. The injury looked more damaging than it was, though. The fact that the blade traveled through his hand doubtless saved his life, as it passed a fraction of an inch from his heart. The momentary cessation of attack by his enemies allowed Mowery to pull the long blade back through his left hand. It was as though the wound had never existed. He appeared to gain strength and, rather than defend himself from attackers, began to charge after them.

By the time police units and medical teams were in place to stop it all, the Mongols and their colleagues had fled.

In their retreat, the leader of the Mongols shouted, "Mongols to the doors, Mongols to the doors." To the doors they went, climbing over, through, and around other people to escape. To a man, the Mongols tore off their jackets and left them on the floor of the Exhibition Center.

It should be noted that most of the Renegades, of whom there were far fewer than Mongols, seemed willing to slug it out with the Hell's Angels and would have but for the personal intervention of a single Los Angeles deputy sheriff. He moved from the sidelines of the brawl and thrust himself into the very center. As he shouted at both sides to cease immediately, he pulled his service revolver and thumbed back the hammer of the weapon.

The cocking of a pistol is unmistakable, and everyone calmed down immediately. One of the Hell's Angels who was in the middle of the fight later said, "That fucking cop had guts, man. Anybody could've taken him out. I mean, he didn't have eyes in the back of his head. But hell, we already won. Know what I mean?"

Mowery was taken to a nearby hospital by Carlander, where his wounds were treated. He left with Carlander immediately afterward.

# CHAPTER 16

In the seventh month of the undercover operation Victoria thought she was getting a second wind. She was beginning to feed on the wildness of the rides, the danger of dark places and unexpected night meetings. Yet this was only delusion, part of the fatigue and mental strain that never gave her rest.

On Friday, April 1, 1977, Victoria and Mowery had a meeting in Anaheim at Dan Wilson's Auto Body Shop. A blond man in his late twenties stepped forward as they arrived in Victoria's car. The chopper was down again for repairs. The man introduced himself as John Hahne. Victoria thought the formality was odd, since Mowery knew the guy, although later he said that he did not know him well. There was no handshake. Mowery made no secret of the fact that he disliked Hahne, but would not tell her his reasons.

When Mowery and Victoria confirmed to Hahne that they were indeed there to buy cocaine, a van pulled up alongside her car. The driver remained behind the wheel while Hahne introduced him as Gerard. Victoria was unable to get an accurate description of Gerard, but he had lifeless eyes. Victoria had become highly interested in eyes since the beginning of her tenure as a police officer. She could not make out if Gerard was under the influence of drugs, but she could see cold black eyes that moved with the deliberate, unblinking character of a basking crocodile.

After Gerard had fully surveyed Victoria and Mowery, he pulled his car to the far end of the small parking lot near a Tastee-Freez. Hahne followed him there and for several minutes they spoke to each other, overheard by no one.

Hahne returned and got into Victoria's car, sitting directly behind Mowery's seat. Victoria was uneasy. It would have been more natural for Hahne to sit in a position roughly between the two of them so that communication would be easier. As it was now, Mowery could not see Hahne without turning around uncomfortably. And Hahne could keep an eye on Victoria while covering Mowery with hardly the flick of an eye. Victoria could tell that Mowery was uneasy as well. The biker turned, in the passenger's seat, meaning to drape his arm carelessly over the back of his seat, but was frustrated by the head support on the seat that was becoming standard on all new automobiles. If Hahne noticed the unsettling effect he was having, he never let on.

"Follow the van," he said, smiling, as though they were all going to have fun.

"Where to?" Victoria asked as she stepped on the gas.

"South," Hahne said, his pasted-on smile never wavering.

"Okay. How far south?" Victoria hoped that Carlander would be close on her tail. What would happen if they changed from her car to the van? Who would Carlander follow?

Hahne did not respond to her question. It was as though she had not uttered a word. They drove through the industrial area of Downey, down isolated avenues among warehouses and chemical holding tanks that cast long, menacing shadows. Victoria looked in her rearview mirror, hoping to pick up Carlander's headlights.

"What are you looking for?"' Hahne asked in an unctuous voice.

"Cops," Victoria said honestly.

She kept pace with the Chevy van in front of her. It never went more than five miles per hour over the posted speed limit.

"Did you bring the money?" Hahne asked Victoria.

"Sure. We've got it," she said. For the first time she wished that Mowery was carrying a gun. He was a force to be reckoned with against fists, feet, and knives, but the man wasn't born who could outpunch a bullet. At least she had . . .

Victoria did not feel her gun. She pressed against the back of the seat but could not feel the hardness of the .380 auto that should have been in her waistband. She touched her elbows against her jacket, but it was not in those pockets, either. Mowery leaned toward her, extending a hand. "What's wrong, honey?" he said. "That kink in your back bothering you again?" He gently but firmly did a frisk where he knew she normally carried her semiautomatic. She looked at him out of the corner of her eye and saw the same expression on his face that she had.

"It's okay now," she said. "Thanks."

"Let's have it," Hahne said.

"Let's wait till we have the stuff," Mowery said to Hahne. Victoria preferred that he take a minimal part in a drug buy for several reasons, and Carlander agreed. First, she was the sworn police officer, and it was she who would carry the most weight in court testimony. It was her name, not Mowery's, that would go on the bottom of a crime report that she would write. Second, it had become a part of their m.o. that everyone who knew them as a couple knew that Victoria controlled the cash. She didn't trust him with money, she would say lightly but certainly. He would smile and shrug. It was widely known and made perfect sense to anyone who knew him. But this night things were different. They had never been ripped off for their cash, though Victoria routinely carried a good deal of it, because Mowery was a formidable deterrent. Also, whereas the biker community was lethal to outsiders, Lady Sam and Shane Mowery were on the inside and as such enjoyed near-total immunity among those who feared retribution from the Angels. But Hahne was not a biker. He was a referral. Nor did Victoria know anything about him. And she felt that whatever Mowery knew about him wasn't enough.

On a long stretch of straight road in Santa Fe Springs, Victoria glanced again into the rearview mirror. She suddenly felt a familiar chill deep inside her gut. Carlander's headlights were not there. For a moment her thoughts whirled. She asked herself what would happen if Carlander were ten yards behind. The answer was, probably nothing. There was no reason why Hahne couldn't put a bullet into Mowery's brain, then turn on her. It was not comforting to imagine that Hahne would be arrested while she and Mowery were stretched out on the highway in rubber bags.

Minutes later they were traveling on Whittier Boulevard toward La Habra. The Chevy van ahead of Victoria made several turns, including U-turns, which were clearly evasive maneuvers to detect or foil following vehicles. Victoria looked in vain for Carlander. She was about to give him up for lost when they emerged from a four-way stop sign in a lower-middle-class neighborhood as he arrived at one of the cross-streets. She almost gasped with relief but had the presence of mind to step on the gas pedal to follow the van. Hahne chuckled at the fact that she had cut off the car that Carlander was driving.

They were in La Habra, at the border of Orange and Los Angeles counties, when Hahne leaned back in his seat and said, "Pull over right here and shut off the engine."

Houses were sparse, ideal for murder. Victoria sensed that Mowery was gathering himself, disguised as a languid stretch, one arm flopping backward into the rear seat area. Victoria and Mowery had encountered enough paranoid drug dealers to know that the distance they had traveled and the precautions taken by Hahne on this trip far exceeded those needed to buy an ounce of cocaine. Or an ounce of anything.

"How about the van?" Victoria asked. The vehicle they had been following continued down the street, then turned a corner a block ahead.

"He'll be back." Hahne was not looking toward the van but glanced at an ill-kept house behind them. "Give me the cash."

Victoria hesitated. Maybe Mowery was waiting for the exchange to divert Hahne's eyes to the money. Victoria held it in her hand. Hahne took the cash. Mowery did nothing. "Be right back," Hahne said and got out of the car.

As they watched, Hahne walked briskly to the rundown

house. He navigated a half-dozen steps, then knocked on a door. Heavy curtains covered the windows, and when the door was opened Victoria could see that the lights in the house were dimmed. Hahne went inside.

"Where's Gerard?" Victoria asked aloud.

"I don't know," Mowery responded, preoccupied.

"What do you think?" she asked, as much to quiet her jumpy nerves as to learn what Mowery thought. She glanced nervously out of the windows of her car, up then down the street, for a sign of Carlander. She saw none. "Shit," she said.

"I think we should haul ass," Mowery said, watching the house intently.

Victoria thought that was a good idea but did not turn on the ignition. She would give herself another minute to see what happened. There was no one behind her and they were both watching the house. Carlander had to be nearby. No reason to run yet.

Victoria was reaching to turn the key in the ignition when Hahne returned to Victoria's car. He stood next to her window. "Got another thou?" he asked.

"What for?" she responded.

"Man's got some meth inside. I can get you two jars for a grand," Hahne explained glibly.

From the corner of her eye she could see Mowery slowly shaking his head. She considered for a moment, then arched her back as she reached into a front pocket of her tight jeans. She could feel Hahne eyeing her body. She came up with the necessary amount of money, prepacked with paper clips into $500 bundles, making counting at night unnecessary. "I've always got a place to unload crank." She hoped her voice sounded steadier than she felt. Hahne took the money and walked back toward the house.

"The hell did you do that for?" an irked Mowery wanted to know.

"If they were going to hold us up, they wouldn't try to make another sale. I think we'll be all right." Victoria was operating on logic, not the gut-knotting fear that had pervaded her emotions from the moment they left downtown Anaheim. Victoria saw a movement in her rearview mirror. She peered into it and could see the front part of Carlander's car parked behind her on an intersecting street a block away. She felt a surge of confidence, though not enough to stop the tremors in her hands and legs. Mowery stepped out of the car and sat in the backseat.

When Hahne returned with two plastic bags of white powder he sat in the passenger seat, Mowery now behind him. The move was not lost on the dope dealer. He smiled but said nothing while Victoria performed a field test on the powder and noted a positive reaction. The expertise of field-testing drugs did not in any way connote a trained police or narc officer. Every drug dealer who needs to turn a profit must be able to check the quality of drugs he or she buys. Hahne smoked a cigarette and waited confidently for Victoria to respond.

"Okay," she said. "Looks good."

"Want something else?" Hahne asked.

Instinctively Victoria glanced around the car. She saw nothing untoward and Carlander still waited inconspicuously down the block. "Like what?" she said.

Hahne reached into his pocket and came up with a ring. "Like it?" he asked.

Victoria was not an expert but was aware that she was looking at a very large diamond in a gold setting. "Sure," she said.

"We cut it off a hand." Hahne said.

Victoria controlled a gagging reaction. "Oh, no," she said. She used the pretext of showing the ring to Mowery in order to avert her eyes from Hahne's.

"It's for sale," Hahne said, a pleasant smile on his face.

"I, uh, well, how much of this kind of stuff do you have?" she asked, stalling until her wits could catch up with her loathing for the man sitting inches from her.

"Quite a bit. Bracelets, rings, necklaces, you name it," Hahne said smugly. "Gerard's in the place right now, if you want to see what we have."

The cop in her wanted to go inside the house, but Victoria listened to her inner fears. "Maybe some other time. Besides," she lied, "I don't have any cash left."

She saw the shadow of a frown cross Hahne's face before he recovered and retrieved his wan smile. "Doesn't cost to look," he prodded.

"Where'd you get the stuff? The guy put up a fight?" she asked, not expecting him to answer but attempting to turn the conversation in another direction.

"Plane crash. Remember the airliner that went down in the mountains near Bakersfield? December. We snipped a lot of pinkies in that one. Shrubbery nippers," Hahne smiled. "They're good for all kinds of trimming. Car wrecks. Drownings . . ."

"Suicides . . ." Victoria suggested vacantly, a specter in three dimensions before her eyes.

"Sure. Suicides. Lots of those." Hahne chuckled. "Gerard's a mortician." He started laughing harder. The merriment suddenly turned to a gurgle as Mowery reached from the backseat and with one hand grasped Hahne's neck. "Shut up, you pigfucker. We don't want any rings or bracelets."

Victoria leaned across the seat and opened the door from the inside. Mowery pushed the seat forward roughly as he continued to hold Hahne by the throat. He stepped out of the car, pulling Hahne after him. The dealer was turning purple under the glow of a distant streetlight. Mowery held him for a few seconds longer, then abruptly released him. He staggered backward off the street and onto an unfinished sidewalk. Then Mowery got back into the car with Victoria.

Victoria watched in the rearview mirror. She could not see Carlander but knew he would be nearby. She had felt a moment of exhilaration when Mowery suspended Hahne by his neck, but the dark fear, fingers of ice gripping then relaxing inside her stomach, returned. Now it was worse. The spasms caused her to pull to the side of the road and vomit.

When she got home that night Bill was still up. They greeted each other with desultory hellos. "Want a drink?" Bill asked, reaching for ice in the refrigerator.

Victoria nodded her head. "Give me a beer," she said.

"How about a gin and tonic?" he said.

"Beer's fine." Victoria sprawled into a nearby chair and clicked on the television. She clicked through several channels.

Bill regarded her for a long moment. "Why don't you have a tonic? Or maybe some bourbon and water?"

"No. Beer."

Bill reached into the refrigerator for a long-necked Budweiser, the only kind they bought now. He opened it and took a glass from a cupboard. Victoria accepted the bottle, ignoring the glass. Her eyes remained focused on the television. She came across a police show. She dropped the remote selector into her lap and tipped the beer to her lips.

Bill made himself a gin and tonic, dropping ice on the kitchen floor on the process but not bothering to pick it up. He sat heavily in a chair near his wife. For several minutes he watched while local law enforcement officers, working with Federal DEA agents, kicked in the door of an African-American family's house.

"Why don't you shut it off?" he asked.

Victoria did not respond.

Bill regarded his wife for a long moment, then leaned over her, took the remote control from her lap, and clicked off the television.

Victoria hardly glanced at him, said nothing, but took back the remote control and clicked it back on. Bill's lips compressed into a single, bloodless line. He rose, strode across the room, and pulled the television plug from the wall. "Leave the damn thing off," he said, forcing her to pay some attention to him.

Victoria stared hard at him, eyes narrowing into slits. "You motherfucker."

"What did you say? What did you call me?" His voice rose.

"I said . . ." Victoria stopped, listened, as if hearing her own voice for the first time. "I . . . Bill . . ."

When dawn came the following morning, Victoria's eyes were already open. Indeed, they had hardly closed through the night. She knew the day had arrived that Brad Gates had prophesied. It was the end for her. She hoped it was not too late.

When the telephone rang hours later she was wearing a pair of old pajamas and a housecoat. "Hello?" she said.

"Vicky," Carlander's voice said over the telephone. "Don't go to Mowery's place in the morning. Meet me at Love's. I'm bringing Ron Kreber with me and Nease'll be there. Make it about nine."

"I'm not going to work anymore," she said.

"Nine isn't my fucking idea. Kreber feeds birds or something like that at six or whenever the sun comes up. Eats breakfast, too." Carlander chuckled at his own joke. "Bill still up?" he asked.

"Yes."

"Tell him howdy. Hey, why don't you guys do a home video and we'll sell the tape to Glore?" Carlander broke into gales of laughter.

"I'm not coming in, Wayne. I won't be there." Victoria waited for Carlander's reaction, not caring much for what it would be.

She heard him sigh. "I hear you," he said. "I hear what you're saying. Well, we're finished, anyhow. I'll tell Brad. And Kreber. Good-bye, Vicky."

Victoria did not meet Carlander the next day. Or the next. Bill hardly left her bedside while she slept, woke up, slept again. After the first sixteen hours she said she was no longer tired, but he supervised a shower, helped her dry off, then gently urged her to return to bed. When she was not asleep, they talked heart to heart. Bill had witnessed the change in her character in the past seven months, changes that might have been necessary for the role she needed to play but were beginning to overtake her.

Six days later, on Friday, April 8, 1977, she met with Carlander.

He knew what she was going to say even before she said it. He wore a wan smile as she told him that it was all over, at least for her. He was nodding as she spoke, as though he approved of everything she was saying. She said that she wasn't able to go on, that the world had become warped through her eyes. Her judgment was no longer good, she thought. She told Carlander that she had almost lost her husband.

"Figured you'd say that. So Ron Kreber's got the evidence lined up. We're ready for the grand jury," he said, grinning. "Case closed."

# EPILOGUE

On Tuesday, April 12, 1977, Carlander reviewed the paperwork he had painstakingly organized throughout the investigation for Deputy District Attorney Ron Kreber to present to the grand jury. There were more than seventy cases for which Carlander would ask prosecution. Working with Nease, Sim Middleton, and Skip Mitchell, every detail was checked again: street names corresponding to legal names, all names for the right addresses, current residences checked against residence addresses taken early in the investigation, evidence log entries confirmed against proper names or John Does, physical evidence inventoried against the log. All of this was done in secret over a period of twenty-four almost nonstop hours. There was a risk, the team thought, that the indictment list could somehow leak. The sooner the indictments could be presented to the grand jury and arrests made, the less risk that fugitives could run, flee. On April 13 Carlander and his team, with Victoria and Mowery purposely excluded, went over all the evidence once again with Kreber. He commented that he had never been more impressed with such a copious, meticulous body of evidence. On Thursday, April 14, 1977, Kreber went before an Orange County grand jury and presented evidence that would cause the jury to authorize fifty-seven indictments for seventy-seven alleged felons, almost all of whom were bikers, nineteen of whom were Hell's Angels.

On Monday, April 18, twenty arrest teams composed of a hundred and twenty officers from three counties (Los Angeles, San Bernardino, and Orange) were briefed by Orange County Sheriff's Command officers. The briefing included not only where the suspects would most likely be found, but also the type of trouble arresting officers were likely to have. Most of the suspects were known to be armed or had access to weapons such as machine guns and assault rifles. Many of the suspects' women were named on the indictments as codefendants or simply accessories to crimes. A number of them were regarded as dangerous. The arrest teams dispersed through the tricounty geographical area to execute synchronized raids designed to scoop up as many perpetrators as possible simultaneously. The arrests were made that same night at 7:00 P.M., bagging sixty-nine of those indicted. Within ten days the remaining eight were found and arrested.

Carlander did not take part in any of the arrests, nor did Victoria or Mowery, who were kept well away from the Orange County Sheriff's Office, the district attorney's office, and the courthouse complex. The day before the arrests were carried out Mowery was placed in yet another motel, its location known to only four people, Sheriff Brad Gates, Carlander, Sim Middleton, and Ron Kreber.

All Hell's Angels made bail save Dago Paul, who was returned to Connecticut on a fugitive warrant for murder. He was arrested prior to the other bikers. The Hell's Angels immediately began to pay off those members whose sloppiness endangered the organization. The day after Ray Glore got out on bail, his body was found in his home with twelve bullets in it. Glore had kept at his home lists of names of virtually every member of the Hell's Angels organization not only in California but the entire nation and Europe as well. When those records fell into police agencies' hands, it made it much easier for enforcement officers across the United States to follow criminal activities.

An order was sent out by the Hell's Angels for Clifford Mowery, offering a $25,000 reward for his murder. Also included in the gang's killing wish-list were Victoria and Wayne Carlander, each with the same promised payment of $25,000 for their death. "Wanted" posters with Mowery's photograph and Victoria's physical description and Carlander's name, with rewards of $25,000 each for their deaths, were posted in biker bars throughout California. A number of bikers were known to have actively hunted for the three.

Among those not arrested in the first raids were Bugger Butch and his accomplice to murder, Little Dee. They were, however, arrested a few days later. They were arraigned and pleaded innocent.

Bruno's house was found to contain documents relating to Hell's Angels financial accounts. These records were the first to prove that the outlaw biker gang had invested large sums of money in various legitimate business enterprises, maintained cash accounts in a number of banks, even maintained a retirement fund for club members. Stock certificates were found and confiscated, and boxes full of records were pored over by police intelligence officers. It was a huge windfall of otherwise impossible-to-get information about the inside operations of a secret criminal enterprise.

The trials lasted seven months. The joint strategy of the outlaw bikers, suggested by the Hell's Angels, was for all of the accused to plead not guilty and insist upon immediate trials. They believed that the county justice system would be overwhelmed and that dismissal of cases would follow. However, numbers of judges throughout the Orange County judicial system volunteered to increase their caseloads to whatever level the trials required. Many lower-court cases and civil matters were rescheduled to night proceedings to allow judges to stack their court calendars with criminal cases brought about by Carlander's undercover investigation team. Judges worked long, continuous hours during those seven months.

It was extremely dangerous for Clifford Mowery to testify. The Orange County District Attorney's office received word that a professional hitman, a Hell's Angel by the name of Gary Stark, had arrived in town from New York expressly to locate Mowery and kill him. Stark's second target was to be Victoria, if possible. Despite this, Mowery agreed to testify in court. He was moved continuously from one secret location to another for almost a year and was brought to the courthouse every day under heavy security. Whenever he was on the stand, the courtroom would be packed with Hell's Angels who would sit, wearing their "colors," staring at him as he testified. It took incredible courage to speak in the courtrooms as he did. He never dropped his eyes, never shrank from their attempted intimidation, as he recounted drug deal after theft after arson after prostitution that he had witnessed in past months while riding with the Hell's Angels in Orange County.

All concerned wanted to keep Victoria off the witness stand at all costs in order to preserve her real identity. The media cooperated by not showing either her or Carlander's pictures and not revealing their real names. With the exception of Bugger Butch's homicide trial, in which Victoria's testimony was vital, she was kept out of the courtroom. Instead, she would wait in the trial judge's chambers in the event that something went awry in a case and her corroberation was required to obtain a conviction. That occurred in only two other cases, and her appearance was made in the judge's chamber.

Bugger Butch was convicted of murder. He is still serving a life sentence at San Quentin prison and was recently denied parole. The case was clinched when fingerprints from one of the girls with Bugger Butch and Little Dee were matched against a thumbprint taken from the bar glass.

Little Dee was arrested but released when witnesses failed to identify him with the same certainty that they had about Bugger Butch. He was released and at this writing was living in Colorado.

With the exception of Little Dee, each of the seventy-seven people were prosecuted and convicted, and every conviction resulted in a prison sentence. Gary Allen "Mad Dog" Fero died violently in San Quentin before his thirty-fifth birthday. Vic Mena died a violent death in Folsom; Whitey Parsons and Gary Robles died violently though not in prison—all before age forty.

Toni, Ray Glore's common-law wife, did ten months in jail on drug-related convictions. She traveled to San Francisco, then returned to southern California a year later. She has not been heard from by law enforcement agencies since.

Bud Nease left law enforcement on a medical disability after smashing a knee during a high-speed pursuit.

Lieutenant Sim Middleton has retired from active duty and now heads a civilian security firm.

Brad Gates continues in his fifth elected term as Sheriff of Orange County.

Sergeant Wayne Carlander is entering his twenty-seventh year with the Orange County Sheriff's Office. Wayne Carlander's son, Wayne Junior, was an All-American basketball player at the University of Southern California and for several years held that school's individual scoring honors.

Ron Kreber was recently named presiding judge for South Orange County Municipal Court in Laguna Niguel.

Mowery was leaving town. He and Carlander had breakfast at one of the restaurants they had frequented in recent months. Mowery had always wanted to see Oklahoma, he said. He would work in the oil fields, he thought, start a new life. Good climate there, and he could ride a bike almost year-round. Best of all, he didn't know anybody.

Carlander walked outside with Mowery to his motorcycle, loaded with two well-stuffed bags containing his worldly possessions. Carlander reached into his pocket and handed him a piece of paper. Mowery glanced at it, then looked to Carlander for an explanation. "It's a termination of parole. Keith Taylor came through for you." Termination of parole meant that Mowery had, in effect, served his time. All of it. No more reporting to parole officers, no more restrictions. He was free.

"Carlander," Mowery began with difficulty, "Victoria . . ."

"Yeah?"

"Tell her . . ." Mowery's voice broke. He turned momentarily away and looked into the early-morning traffic. "Tell her that I said she was . . . kind of, no, real special. Tell her that if . . ." He could not go on but looked into Carlander's eyes, pleading for understanding.

"I'll tell her," the detective said. "You take care of yourself, Cliff. And don't come back here. Hear what I'm saying? Don't come back to Orange County or southern California anywhere."

"I won't," Mowery said.

Mowery punched the electric starter on his Harley, waved at Carlander, and rode off. It was the last time Carlander ever saw him.

The State of California legislature recognized Victoria and Carlander in a special citation for their part in facilitating the largest-scale arrests ever carried out in the history of the state. Their names were purposely omitted from the public announcement of the award and ceremonies.

Victoria left law enforcement. She is a successful businesswoman now living in another state under a different name. She is still married to Bill and has three children.

Mowery did not take Carlander's advice. After working several months in the Oklahoma oil fields, he returned to southern California on his chopper. Diane Lynn Sexton called Wayne Carlander on the telephone to say that Mowery had ridden into an overpass abutment in the desert near Blythe. He was dead, she said. Police there had no explanation of how it could have happened. Accident, maybe. Even suicide. Anyway, the funeral was going to be Wednesday.

Carlander thanked her and hung up the telephone. He wondered who collected the reward.